French Accounting History

French Accounting History: New Contributions illustrates the lively research activity in the field of accounting and management history in France, thus contributing to the dissemination of French research on an international scale. Based on a collection of diverse papers by French historians in this field which have been presented at various congresses, contributing authors give an overview of French accounting, the advent of the auditing profession and management control in France. This book aims to further strengthen the development of the community and knowledge base of accounting historians, not only in France but also internationally.

This book is based on a special issue of the journal *Accounting History Review.*

Yves Levant is Professor at the University of Lille 2 and at the SKEMA Business School, France. He is a member of the research laboratory: Univ lille nord de France (LEM CNRS 8179/LSMRC). His research interests are in the field of Management Control and more particularly concerns cost calculation and its methodology. His recent works are linked to the broadcast and history of innovative management control tools as well as the interest and practices of new cost calculation methods.

Olivier de la Villarmois is Professor at the University of Lille 1, France, and a member of the LEM research team (UMR CNRS 8179). A qualified chartered accountant, he is course director of the Management Sciences Masters Degree. His research work concerns costing methods and the interactions between organisational learning and management control. His work has been published in academic and professional reviews as well as in collective works, both in France and internationally.

French Accounting History
New Contributions

Edited by
Yves Levant and Olivier de la Villarmois

Routledge
Taylor & Francis Group
LONDON AND NEW YORK

First published 2012
by Routledge
2 Park Square, Milton Park, Abingdon, Oxon, OX14 4RN

Simultaneously published in the USA and Canada
by Routledge
711 Third Avenue, New York, NY 10017

Routledge is an imprint of the Taylor & Francis Group, an informa business

First issued in paperback 2012

This book is a reproduction of *Accounting History Review*, Volume 19, Issue 2 (previously entitled *Accounting, Business & Financial History*). The Publisher requests to those authors who may be citing this book to state, also, the bibliographical details of the special issue on which the book was based.

British Library Cataloguing in Publication Data
A catalogue record for this book is available from the British Library

ISBN 13: 978-0-415-67588-8 (hbk)
ISBN 13: 978-0-415-84783-4 (pbk)

Typeset in Times New Roman
by Taylor & Francis Books

Disclaimer
The publisher would like to make readers aware that the chapters in this book are referred to as articles as they had been in the special issue. The publisher accepts responsibility for any inconsistencies that may have arisen in the course of preparing this volume for print.

Contents

Notes on contributors

Nicole Azema-Girlando teaches in the Faculty of Law, Economics and Management at LARGO (Laboratoire Angevin de Recherche en Gestion des Organisations) at the University of Angers, France.

Nicolas Berland is Professor of Management Accounting at Paris-Dauphine University, France. His research interests are focused on the institutionalisation of management and management accounting practices, particularly history of budgetary control, beyond budgeting and deinstitutionalisation of budget, New Public Management and Corporate Social Responsibility devices.

Marie Catalo is Director of MIAGE (Méthodes Informatiques Appliquées à la Gestion des Entreprises) at the University of Nantes, France.

Pierre Labardin is Assistant Professor at the Dauphine Management Research Center (DRM), Paris-Dauphine University, France. His research interests include accounting and management history, accounting words, accounting organization and accounting practices in bankruptcy.

Yannick Lemarchand is Professor of Sciences de Gestion (Management Science) at the University of Nantes, France. His research interests are accounting and management histories.

Yves Levant is Professor at the University of Lille 2 and at the SKEMA Business School, France. He is a member of the research laboratory: Univ lille nord de France (LEM CNRS 8179/LSMRC). His research interests are in the field of Management Control and more particularly concerns cost calculation and its methodology. His recent works are linked to the broadcast and history of innovative management control tools as well as the interest and practices of new cost calculation methods.

Cheryl Susan McWatters holds the Father Edgar Thivierge Chair in Business History at the Telfer School of Management, University of Ottawa, Canada. Her research interests include merchant networks and mercantilism; accounting and capitalism; profit and value creation; and economic-exchange relationships in Indigenous and slave-trading markets.

Marc Nikitin is Professor of Management Science at the University of Orleans, France. His research interests include cost accounting history, epistemology and the history of management science.

Anne Pezet is Professor of Management at Paris-Dauphine University, France. Her research interests include accounting and management history, and critical perspectives in management.

Carlos Ramirez is an Associate Professor at the Department of Accounting and Management Control of HEC School of Management, Paris, France. His research interests include the history and sociology of the accountancy and audit profession and of accounting and audit standard setting.

Henri Zimnovitch is Professor of Management Science at the University of Paris-Sud, France.

'Lady Accounting', an analogy using blood circulation to popularise an accounting view of the health of the firm

Marie Catalo[a] and Nicole Azema-Girlando[b]

[a]*LEMNA, Université de Nantes, France;* [b]*LARGO, Université d'Angers, France*

This paper examines the attempt by Deuwez in 1933 to explain accounting concepts and ideas to non specialists through the analogy of the process of blood circulation within human beings. It comprises two main sections. The first section comprises two reviews: first, of accounting ideas of the period 1900–33 and developments therein; and, second, an examination of contemporary knowledge of blood circulation and the operation of key human organs in relation thereto. In the second part of the manuscript, the analogy is examined in more depth, with some limited attempt made to consider whether or not the blood circulation system is an apposite analogy.

Introduction

Access to accounting is reputedly difficult because its vocabulary and concepts are often linked to learning about how the accounts work. This may discourage people who want to understand accounting without developing a detailed knowledge of bookkeeping. For example, people such as administrators have to understand accounting documents. In such circumstances, the issue of popularising an understanding of accounting becomes crucial. This problem is far from being new. In the booklet, *La dame comptabilité*, printed in 1933, H. Deuwez dealt with this question, using blood circulation in a female body as an analogy with accounting.

The use of analogy is common practice in the domain of social sciences (Weber 1981, 139) and in the domain of economic sciences (Ménard 1981, 139). Theoretical renewal is supported by an analogy which permits conceptual transfers. For example, according to Denis (1904, 91) and Thompson (1998, 308), Quesnay (1694–1774), who was a French doctor and king's councillor, proposed *Le tableau économique*, the first attempt to formulate a model of economic circulation, taking as his basis the model of the system of blood circulation. In the theory of evolution, as Diani (2003) shows in his PhD, there are many mutual exchanges of ideas between economics and biology. As far as accounting is concerned, the use of analogy is unusual, although not entirely unheard of. This paper analyses the analogy drawn in *La dame comptabilité* in order to demonstrate the interest, the contribution and the limits of this analogy in the specific context of teaching and of popularising accounting, in French, between 1900 and 1933.

Our perspective is restricted to accounting techniques and concepts and their use for the purpose of disseminating accounting knowledge even if we are aware that a gender-studies-focus could have been another choice for this paper.

Preconditions to analysis

The use of analogy in accounting

During the period covered by this study (1900–33), we have identified four popular generalist guides to accounting (see Table 1), the intention of which was to make the subject more accessible to the non-specialist reader. Of these four works, only two books made use of analogy: *La dame comptabilité* (Deuwez 1933) and *Les concepts fondamentaux de la comptabilité* (De Fages 1933). Both authors declared that they were writing for a specific public: De Fages for engineers and Deuwez for administrators and members of the boards of companies. Neither author searched for credibility, but rather for an efficient way – i.e. one which would be understood by their intended target readership – in which to facilitate the understanding of basic accounting ideas and concepts. Whereas De Fages based his analogy on calculation theory and fluid mechanics, Deuwez based his on the general public's knowledge of anatomy.

Deuwez's 33-page booklet, *La dame comptabilité*, was printed in 1933 by a Lagny printing house in France. Three copies of the booklet are known to have survived, one is available at the French National Library, and of the others, belonging to private collections, one was shown at an exhibition of accounting textbooks held in Lyon in 1994 (Bérard and Lemarchand 1994). It has proved impossible to find out anything about the booklet's author,[1] but on the title page his intentions are made clear: 'This small work, written for administrators and board members, aims

Table 1. Analysis of four non-specialist books.

Author and date	Targeted readership	Features
Bunau-Varilla (1924)	Traders, members of council, lawyers	Explanation of the balance sheet using the personification of the accounts approach, revisited with stock accounts
Caquas (1924)	People concerned with business	Explanation of the balance sheet and operation of the accounts by the balance sheet approach
De Fages (1933)	Engineers	Accounting explained as the science of the enumeration of the movement in values Analogy in terms of flow accounts and stock accounts
Deuwez (1933)	Administrators and board members	Accounting explained by analogy with blood circulation Analogy leading to company health: true health and manipulated health

at giving, through humour, the right ideas on the role of modern accounting and the services which can be expected from it'.

The text is divided into two parts. In this paper we limit ourselves to the first part, qualified by the author as 'the accounting'. The second part, on the '*prix de revient*'[2] will be the subject of future research. The first part of the booklet is divided into six sub-parts whose titles indicate readily the tonality of the author:

- 'Accounting as the crow flies' (*La dame comptabilité*, hereafter referred to as *Ldc*, 2–5) presents the definition of accounting, of the accounting organisation and of the various accounts, but without indicating their operating mode. The figure, 'Lady Accounting' (*Ldc*, 6, reproduced as Appendix 1), provides a visual representation of the accounting system using a complete woman's body, together with hat and accessories.
- The organs correspond to the accounts previously mentioned in the text, and they are connected to each other by blood vessels. The comments specify that blood circulates here. This creates an analogy between accounting and blood circulation which we propose to analyse subsequently in this paper.
- 'The role of the stomach and of the intestines' (*Ldc*, 7 – reproduced as Appendix 4) presents these organs as inventory accounts (warehouse and work-in-progress) and operational accounts (labour, overheads and sales). This page shows their role in the evaluation of costs (simplified version) and the determination of the net result.
- 'Lady Balance Sheet' (*Ldc*, 8 – reproduced as Appendix 2) corresponds to 'Lady Accounting' accessorised with a basket 'for contingencies' and a small cask entitled 'for profit'.
- 'The make-up of Lady Balance Sheet'. A *vademecum* for the perfect 'book cooker' (*Ldc*, 9 – reproduced as Appendix 3) underlines the operations which improve the aspect of Lady Balance Sheet before she is presented to the board members.
- 'Old Lady Accounting, former method, annual inventory' (*Ldc*, 10) depicts an alternative method of recording the inventory accounts and sales accounts.

The eye of the reader is attracted by the illustrations of a woman. Multiple interpretations as to why this choice was made are possible. One explanation would be that the words 'company', 'management' and 'accounting' are all feminine words in French and, by extension, this facilitates and/or would make it appropriate to use a woman as an analogy for how a company is viewed from an accountant's perspective. A second explanation from a gender studies perspective is that, given the historical context, women were still largely viewed by men as objects, not subjects, to be dressed, made-up, fed and doctored by men, being denied the role of actors. Therefore it seems more likely that a woman would be chosen for the analogy rather than a man. A third possible explanation is that women have a natural open blood cycle unlike men. Since the analogy refers to an open blood cycle for accounting as well, this fact may have guided the choice of the author. A fourth possible explanation reflects the fact that researchers in accounting (e.g. Gardey 1995, 415) have shown that women have been very present in bookkeeping tasks in the field of accounting since the nineteenth century. This fact may have been known by the author. A fifth possible explanation is that since the intended target readership was largely going to be made up of men, the author may have wanted to catch the reader's eye with illustrations of women. Since details relating to the author are not known to us, we cannot extend further these investigations. Nevertheless, the text itself is rich with material for our study focused on accounting.

An overview of the state of accounting knowledge c.1900–c.1933

Before analysing Deuwez's analogy in the second part of the paper, we first of all provide an overview of the state of knowledge and thinking, as it was presented in different types of books published in the French language during the period 1900–33, regarding accounting and the system of blood circulation in the human body.

The sources

In order to study the state of accounting knowledge, we examined documents contained in the Stevelinck collection available at the library of the Université de Nantes, which contains almost 1,000 references. For the period 1900 to 1933, a period sufficiently long to permit us to appreciate whether the knowledge conveyed in each studied text was standard or not, we selected handbooks[3] and books for non specialists, such as those which specialised in discussing the balance sheet. Thirty-five books, written by French or Belgian authors, were identified and examined. We chose to study French-language books[4] from both countries, not least because there appears to have existed a community of references linking the two countries. Thus, the prolific Belgian author of handbooks and texts, Daubresse (1912, 9), quotes P.J. Proudhon (French economist, 1809–65), Léon Say (politician and French economist, 1826–96) and Gabriel Faure, a prolific French author of handbooks and professional texts. Faure (1927a, 65), on the other hand, quotes Daubresse.

We have also consulted a number of secondary sources related to the theory and history of accounting (Colasse 2005; Vlaemminck undated). However, it seems to us that the handbooks and the four non-specialists books listed in Table 1 are more relevant for our research project, because they testify to the knowledge that was well diffused at the time. In addition, the study of four non-specialists books (less numerous than the handbooks)[5] reveals the particularly original character of *La dame comptabilité* compared to the handbooks. We produce here a synthesis of our observations relevant to the current study. A detailed analysis of the handbooks between 1900 and 1940 will form part of future research.

The points of interest in the 35 books[6] studied, during the period 1900–33, are as follow:

(1) the evolution of the explanation of how the accounts are operated; this testifies to the debate between two alternative approaches, namely that of the personification of accounts and the balance sheet approach;
(2) the great increase in the number of pages which focus on the balance sheet compared with a small increase in those focused on the 'profit and loss' account;[7]
(3) the diversity in the way in which people used the 'warehouse'[8] account or the 'general goods' account; this testifies to the increasing implementation of the perpetual inventory method;
(4) the evolution of the number and the types of accounts in relation to the debate on the explanation of operating the accounts;
(5) the emergence of the concept of a chart of accounts.

This diversity can be linked to the absence of accounting standardisation[9] but also to the speed at which various accounting theories were diffused, either in whole or in part. Taking into account the objective of our research, we examine only the first three points.

An overview of the explanations on the use of the accounts

Two conceptual approaches were found in the sample of books studied as an explanation for the use of accounts:

- the personification of accounts;
- the balance sheet approach.

These were the subject of debate, authors supporting one or the other explanation in a specific context. During the study period, authors sought to show that accounting was a science or a theory (Daubresse 1912; Faure 1927b, 1929).

The personification of accounts

A good explanation of the personification of accounts is given by Faure (1927a, 294): 'an account is created to know the situation of the person for whom the account is kept; one considers that only a person can have an account and then a person exists behind each account, i.e. a being having rights and obligations'. Bunau-Varilla (1924, 1) specified that:

> Accounting bases its processes on the design of a series of fictitious personalities which one calls 'accounts', each one of them acting like a delegate of the Company, charged by it with a special service. The company appears to entrust these personalities with the exclusive management of certain well defined classes of operations, which have always entries or exits of funds, and this avoids making another operation by any other means.[10]

In this case, to follow the vision of extreme personification supported by Faure (1927a), the business can be seen as funds entrusted to a succession of persons. For example, an owner entrusts funds to the general manager to run the enterprise. The general manager entrusts funds to managers of material things (equipment, warehouse and cash). These managers trade also with partners. Each transfer creates an obligation between the person and the firm or enterprise, i.e. creates debts and receivables. The account exists to keep a record of obligations which a person alone is able to have (Deschamp 1926, 156). The account is kept to give the point of view of each of these people. Briefly, the convention is: the person account which donates is credited and the account which receives is debited. The explanation is detailed in the next figure.

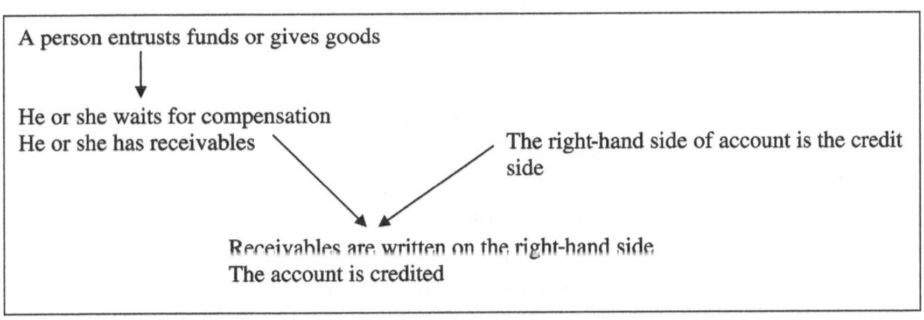

Figure 1. Example of explanation by personification.

It is the opposite reasoning for the debts when a person receives. We must correctly understand the meaning of this explanation. For example, the enterprise buys equipment. The 'equipment' account is debited to show that the 'equipment' manager is indebted up to this value to the enterprise.

But at the closing of the accounts, the balance sheet must present the point of view of the enterprise. 'The enterprise must always be thus interposed by thought as being between the account which receives and an account which gives; [as a reversible jacket, an account has two sides, one apparent and one hidden]: on the right side, we can see the credit and the debit of a person account, therefore the back of this account corresponds to the credit and the debit of the enterprise. It is essential to understand the transformation of the inventory balance into assets and liabilities of the balance sheet' (Deschamp 1926, 153). Indeed, in the balance sheet, the debit balances of the accounts appear in the assets as receivables and the credit balances of the accounts as debts in the liabilities. We see an inversion compared to the explanation of the account functioning, the debts of the company are on the right and the receivables on the left. Thus the balance sheet is not an account.

This brief restitution avoids detail, but we must notice that a few authors accept accounts of things and accounts of value instead of ones based on the management of things. Beyond this variation in the classes of account, however, it is nevertheless the same explanation of the functioning of the accounts as inherited from the eighteenth and nineteenth centuries (Lemarchand 2001). This explanation, qualified as the personification of the account, is characterised by the practice whereby 'the account which receives is debited, the account which gives is credited'.[11]

This way of doing accounting is natural for some authors, such as Faure (1927a). For others, it creates a confusion which must be cleared up (Bunau-Varilla 1924) or it deserves to be rejected: 'no fictions, no ridiculous personifications to explain the accounting principles' (Daubresse 1912, 11). From the 1920 onwards, other authors choose straightforwardly another approach: the approach of the balance sheet.

The balance sheet approach

As Faure (1927a, 294) underlined it: 'the preceding way [the personification approach] leads to the balance sheet by the synthesis of the accounts, while this method leads to the accounts by the analysis of the balance sheet'. The authors who adopted this approach begin their books with balance sheet definitions: assets, liabilities, equity. The profit is determined as the difference between final and initial equity. The assets are 'all that a company has at one moment' (Faure 1927a, 294). The assets are 'the list of the company goods with their value: means of action . . . resources . . . receivables . . . ' (Caquas 1924, 7). The liabilities are 'all that a company owes at one moment' (Faure 1927a, 294). The liabilities are 'the list of the debts of the company towards a third party' (Caquas 1924, 7).

The equity is 'the difference between assets and liabilities' (Faure 1927a, 294). 'The difference A – L (assets minus liabilities) is the equity of the company at one moment, i.e. what would remain after realisation of the receivables and extinction of the liabilities' (Caquas 1924, 7). The operations modify the values of assets and liabilities. These modifications of value are increases or decreases. In this approach, the accounts record these fluctuations which also modify the value of assets and liabilities but not necessarily in the same proportion. Consequently, some operations gave rise to a profit, i.e. modifying the equity. Depending on the authors, the explanations are more or less clear (as for the preceding method). Various algebraic approaches[12] are also proposed, e.g. Desirotte (1931) and Caquas (1924).

The explanation for the use of the accounts is based here on the balance sheet and its mathematical equation: assets − liabilities = equity. It is possible to think that this approach came from the ideas of Dumarchey, who 'presented himself readily as innovative because of the importance which he grants to the equation of the balance sheet and the classification of the kinds of balance sheets' (Michaïlesco 2005, 101). Although he wrote in French and his work, *Théorie Positive de la Comptabilité*, dates back to 1919, he is not quoted in any of the works studied, thus undermining claims that he might be the initiator of this change. Indeed, Michaïlesco (2005, 101), referencing Mattessich (2003), notes an even earlier influence in this direction: 'seeking to change the traditional teaching of accounting, Italian authors [of the second half of the nineteenth century] have already tried to propose a better comprehension of the rules of accounts often based on algebraic explanations where the balance sheet and the general ledger occupy a central position'.

In conclusion, the personification approach to accounts appears to be the only way of explaining accounting operations in 1900, the start date for our study, through until 1920 when the balance sheet approach begins to appear. After this date, these two explanations have coexisted. But the authors posted themselves as the defender of one or the other of the approaches.[13] In addition, the contribution of the qualified 'great authors' (Colasse 2005) seems to have been limited: Leautey and Guilbault,[14] for example, are quoted only for their definition of accounting in our sample. Finally, we must note that the space dedicated to the balance sheet increases during the period. The space focused on the balance sheet increased from one page to many pages or even a whole chapter. An apparent reason is the change of explanation, although the space devoted to this topic increased even where the author proposes the explanation through the personification of accounts. Besides, in the Stevelinck collection, it seems that the number of works exclusively devoted to the balance sheet increased during the period studied (this argument needs to be confirmed by future research). At the same time, the space devoted to the profit and loss account increased but remained, however, very minor in comparison with that devoted to the balance sheet. Therefore, in the following sub-section, we provide an overview of the state of knowledge about the balance sheet.

An overview of the state of knowledge of the balance sheet

Before 1940, 'the majority of companies had an accounting system based on relatively homogeneous mechanisms but the rules of asset valuation, the risk assessment methods or the presentation of the profit and loss account varied from one company to another. This diversity authorised all kinds of manipulations' (Touchelay 2005, 63). While the 35 books in our selection all include content on the balance sheet in one way or another, seven were exclusively dedicated to it: Batardon (1923), Charpentier (1921), Delaporte (1925), Faure (1926), Gersten (c.1930), Grimmiau (c.1903) and Hanon De Louvet (1939). We present below an overview based on the study of these seven books.

Presentation

The majority of the seven authors presented the balance sheet in a format familiar to the way we do today. While some recommended the presentation of asset depreciation on the assets side of the balance sheet, others suggested placing it on the liabilities side, with Faure (1914) and Batardon (1923) proposing both presentations. Charpentier (1921) recommended the inclusion of a comparison with the preceding year, and introduced the concept of consistency in the method of presentation.

Accounting principles

Historic cost principle: Batardon (1923) and Grimmiau (c.1903) deal with historic cost through the purchase price of fixed assets as it should appear in the books. Charpentier (1921, 89–90) indicates more precisely that the recording should be made at the 'prix de revient'[15] which can be reduced if necessary but never raised.

Conservatism principle: All seven authors agree on the need to depreciate fixed assets. It is necessary to underline the case of Grimmiau (c.1903), who devoted a quarter of his work to explaining the validity and the technique of amortisation. The authors also referred to the allowances which are entered in a provision account or in a reserve account.[16]

Time matching principle: This existed in the form of the recommendation to record 'expenses payable' and 'prepaid expenses' (Batardon 1923; Faure 1914) or to record 'invoices payable' and 'invoices to be paid' (Charpentier 1921, 337).

Sincerity principle: The authors of the sample were concerned about the sincerity of the balance sheet. Sincerity is often associated with accuracy. Batardon wrote: 'So the balance sheet has to be accurate and sincere' (1923, 243) and Delaporte (1925, 121) points out 'the excellence of an analysis resides in the sincerity and the accuracy of a balance sheet'. Sometimes, although the word sincerity does not appear explicitly, it is implied: 'A correct balance of the balance sheet is not enough . . . each individual item, separately considered, has to be the expression of truth' (Grimmiau c.1903, 20).

Non-offsetting principle: Charpentier (1921, 64–5) underlined that the opposite journal entries in the receivables accounts and payables accounts should not be offset against each other in a single 'net' journal entry.

Consistency principle: This was introduced by Charpentier (1921, 64) who recommended the presentation of the values of the current period using the same method as those of the prior period. (1921, 345–7).

Going concern principle: This was mentioned by Charpentier (1921, 62) in the following terms: 'the company is living', and also by Delaporte (1925, 56) who presented the balance sheet as 'the acceptance, of the continuation and the on going running ...'.

Valuation methods

Batardon (1923) questioned which type of value of inventories of finished goods must be taken into account. He proposed several possibilities: present value, sales value, salvage value. After explaining his reasons for rejecting them all, he determined that valuation should be at the 'prix de revient'. On this point, he was in agreement with the recommendation of Charpentier (1921). In the handbooks, the question of the valuation of the goods was also dealt with. The answer was the use of the 'prix de revient' instead of the old practice of valuing them at the selling price (see next sub-section below on the 'warehouse' account).

Regarding terminology

According to Grimmiau (c.1903, 23), legislation was not sufficiently precise, noting that 'it is very difficult to agree on the exact meaning of the words being used' (c.1903, 5). For example, from other sources we note that the words for 'reserve' and 'provision' do not have the same meaning. However, Batardon (1923, 102) said that the reserves 'are created for a depreciation which may not necessarily take place in the end', whereas Delaporte (1925, 92) distinguished two separate categories: 'reserves' for permanent elements and 'provisions' for temporary elements.

Regulation, irregularity and forgery

Grimmiau (c.1903, 23) would prefer that, for presentation purposes, 'balance sheet items' conform 'to a uniformity principle'. But all of the authors in our sample called for regulation to achieve some sort of fair view. Gersten (c.1930, 75–105) underlined that the balance sheet could be arranged and embellished in order to inflate income and even become a forged document. Grimmiau (c.1903, 34) dealt with the necessity of some form of control because the number of false balance sheets had increased. Regarding other principles,[17] the other authors referred to regulation.

In conclusion, we note that the terms in which the balance sheet was treated in the seven works appear familiar to us. However, there was no unified doctrine. Indeed, certain authors underlined particular concepts that others dealt with only in a limited fashion or not at all. Often, these authors presented their ideas as new but French accounting historians such as Lemarchand (1995, 7–24) have shown that this discussion about the need for principles began before 1900.

Unlike the explanation of the operating mode of accounts, their vision was not in conflict but showed a shared concern: to make the balance sheet a credible source of shareholder information.

An overview of the use of the 'warehouse' account or the 'general goods' account and, by extension, the 'manufacturing' account

The study period was marked by the question of the traditional use of the 'general goods' account as depicted in Figure 2.

At first, the 'warehouse' account or 'general goods' account is debited with the value of purchases, and is then credited with the sales at their selling price. Therefore, the balance of this account gives neither the value of remaining goods nor of profit or loss (all goods not being sold). This is why, to close the books, a correcting entry is necessary to avoid the profit or loss incorporated in the balance of this account, and its consideration is recorded in the account of 'profit and loss'. The values are calculated in two stages. The physical inventory enables us to value the goods leaving the 'warehouse' account based on the relation: inventory of prior

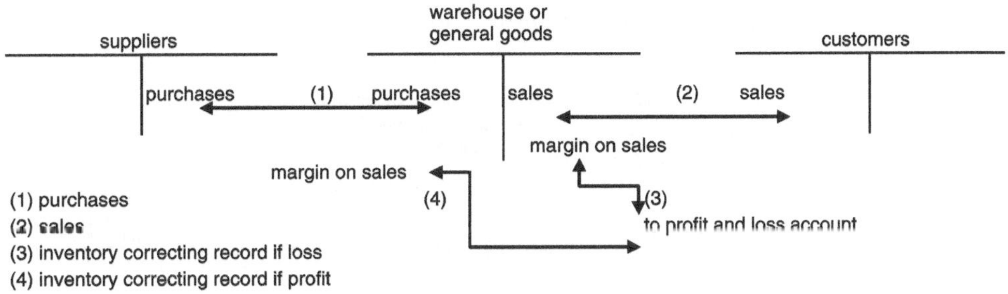

Figure 2. Simplified traditional use of general goods (or warehouse) account.

period + 'entries' − inventory of current period = exits. Then the difference between the value of sales and that of the goods remaining gives the profit or the loss.

This method was considered to have the following disadvantage: 'the balance of the account does not control the remaining goods, the physical disappearance of goods in the warehouse is not detected by the books, nobody has the assurance of the accuracy of the profit' (Desirotte 1931, 42). Alternatives existed and were presented in most handbooks. Indeed, the confusion between inventory and profit/loss worried some authors. They gradually proposed the use of an account of purchases and an account of sales, thereby dividing up the 'warehouse' account into two parts (see Figure 3). However, to close the books, the 'purchases' account must be corrected so that its balance represents the value of remaining goods. It is thus credited with the estimated value of the goods sold (obtained by calculation). For this alternative to the traditional method, the valuation can be based on the purchase price or the 'prix de revient' and the compensation is recorded in the profit and loss account at a value which is the margin on sales.

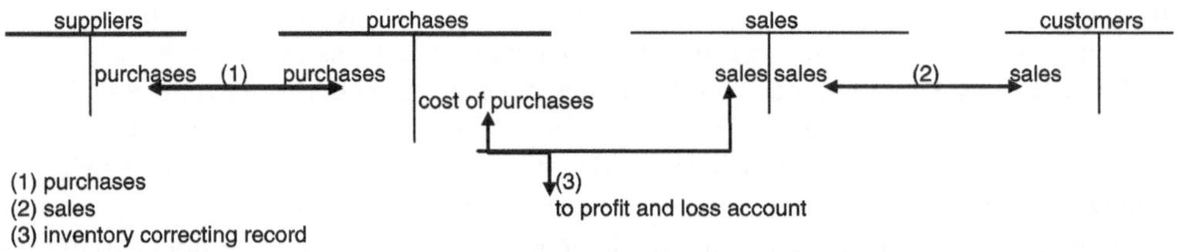

Figure 3. Improved traditional use of general goods (or warehouse) account.

For Desirotte (1931, 42), as for Daubresse (1912), the traditional method had to be replaced. Daubresse (1912) initially presented the traditional method but then proposed possible improvements. Thus, Faure (1927a) relegated the traditional method to the end of the chapter as an obsolete method, considering the improved version to now be the standard method. Some authors, however, remained unsatisfied with the traditional method, even with the improvements, wishing to know constantly the value of the inventory through use of the perpetual inventory method (see Figure 4).

This technique and its advantages were dealt with by Daubresse (1912, 58–63) and Faure (1927a), but they also highlighted the difficulty of implementing it due to the problem of determining the cost of goods sold for each sale. This is why the perpetual inventory remained an ideal for these authors. Other authors presented the perpetual inventory method as one of the possible practices (Batardon 1923) or the only practice (Caquas 1924; Desirotte 1931). For them, its implementation was not a problem. These books focus on inventory of merchandises, but what are the recommendations about inventory of finished goods?

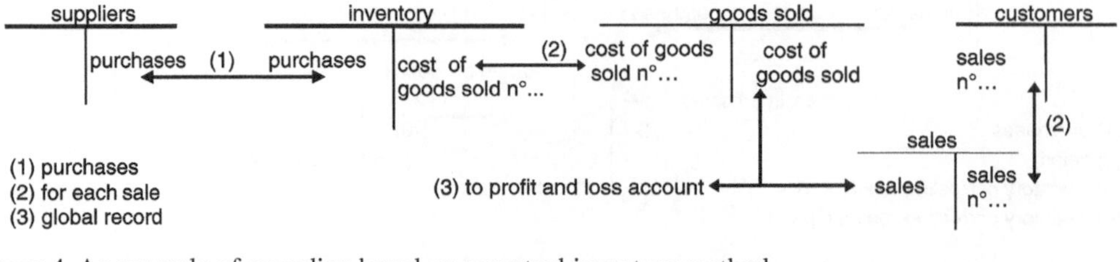

Figure 4. An example of recording based on perpetual inventory method.

The practices of an industrial company are comparable to those of a commercial enterprise: 'The trader', like the manufacturer, has a '*prix de revient*'. It is true that the manufacturer is less attentive to this, but one can only regret it. The general goods account, as the manufacturing account, must be debited with all the expenses related to the goods' (Daubresse 1912, 31). In the same way that the general goods account is debited with purchases and some expenditure, 'the debit side of the manufacturing account records all consumptions of the workshop giving thus the cost of the manufactured products. This value is credited in the manufacturing account and the compensation is the debit of the manufactured goods warehouse account when the products enter into the warehouse or of another workshop account if it is necessary' (Faure 1921, 347).

But, generally, not all products are finished ones. For Faure (1921, 348), most people make an inventory of the workshop, then they value the work-in-progress by means of more or less exact calculations. The difference between what remains and the consumption determines the cost of the finished products. Wherever possible, Faure recommended directly determining the '*prix de revient*' of the finished products by a rational method. The manufacturing account was credited with this value. Thus the manufacturing account remained debtor in respect of the sum representing the value of the work in progress.

We can conclude that the above recommendations sought to distinguish the consumption, the purchases, the sales, the profit and loss, and the value of remaining goods and products. We note that, between 1900 and 1933, little by little the perpetual inventory method was becoming the standard method.

Blood circulation and pathology and care

In this section, we attempt to evaluate what knowledge of the blood circulation system readers of *La dame comptabilité* would have possessed at the time of its publication. We do this initially by providing a summary of the timing of major scientific discoveries regarding blood and its circulation. There still remains, however, the problem of estimating the proportion of this knowledge known by groups such as administrators or members of the boards of companies. To enable us to proceed, we have hypothesised that such people had at least completed an elementary school education. Consequently, we studied elementary school handbooks to yield the minimum level of understanding. Then we studied the *Nouveau Larousse Illustré*, issued at the beginning of the twentieth century. Considering the importance of the book, seven large volumes of almost 1500 pages each, it was probably the reference book of middle-class families, i.e. those likely to have been administrators. The *Nouveau Larousse Illustré* was continually upgraded by the monthly publication *Larousse Mensuel Illustré*. The whole was published from 1907 to 1922.

The major scientific discoveries relating to blood

The major discoveries, prior to 1933, have been identified from reading the *Universalis Encyclopaedia* and *Le sang et les hommes* (Binet 2001). It was in 1623 that William Harvey, an English doctor, affirmed that the blood circulates in a closed loop, from the heart towards the organs and from the organs back to the heart. Harvey's reasoning on double circulation is still valid today: the small circulation brings blood to the lungs before its return to the heart, where, via the great circulation, the blood is sent towards all the organs before returning to the heart. Harvey specifies that the heart enables the bringing of 'nutritive rich and hot blood' to organs and to return 'poor unnutritive and cold blood'. With regard to the contents of blood, red cells were discovered around

1670 by Leuwenhoek, white cells in 1768 by Spallanzani and platelets in 1840 by Donné. We must wait for Selye in 1867 to know the role of the red cells in the transport of oxygen. Cardiac disorders were known, via listening to the rhythm of the heart (during the nineteenth century) and via the first clinical applications of the electrocardiogram (1912). It is not until 1944 that these problems could be solved through the use of cardiac surgery.

Blood-letting has been practised by physicians since antiquity. During the seventeenth and eighteenth centuries, doctors applied it without reserve, but it fell gradually into disuse, being practised only in very particular cases like those described by A. Lebigre (1984) in her book, *Et saigner et purger! Les maladies ont une histoire*. Transfusions of animal blood, which had begun in the seventeenth century, proved to be a failure, while the discovery of different blood groups in 1900 by Landsteiner initially raised very little interest. Nevertheless, as a result, in particular, of technical contributions resulting from problems arising out of the various conflicts of the twentieth century, the development of blood transfusions did occur. In 1917, Doctor Jeambreau added sodium citrate to the collected blood to prevent coagulation and to permit the storage and the transport of blood during the First World War. In parallel, the organisation of blood collection was being achieved: for example, in 1923, the first blood transfusion centre opened in Paris and, in 1929, France was the first country to have an organisation which met the needs for a blood bank.

Knowledge in the handbooks

We studied three elementary school handbooks: Brémant (1919), Lepigoché and Seltensperger (1912) and Fabre (post-1882). Each presents a chapter entitled blood circulation. All explain the small and great circulation and the various types of blood vessels. All present a cross-section illustration of the heart and indicate the role of blood as a carrier of oxygen and nutritive elements. The two most recent works also present an illustration of a human being which presents the whole of the circulation with also the small and great circulation. These books specify the contents of the blood such as the red cells (the white cells are not mentioned) and the serum, which is described as the liquid in which red cells stand. They also present information about pathologies such as anaemia, infection, apoplexy and about the rules of hygiene. Lepigoché and Seltensperger (1912, 82) note that 'The state of our health depends mainly on the number of our [red] cells. If it is too small, we are anaemic; if it is too large, we have too thick blood, as one says, and we are prone to the "coup de sang", with attacks of apoplexy'. Brémant (1919, 16) noted that: 'Because blood goes to all parts of the body, inoculation into the veins of one little drop of foreign liquid can be so dangerous but sometimes so salutary'.

In conclusion, we can assume that the intended public of *La dame comptabilité* had a basic knowledge of anatomy and that it knew about the connection between blood quality and health. This conclusion should be consolidated in future research by analysing a greater number of handbooks prior to 1912 (for instance books dating back to 1870 could be taken into account, because some of the administrators had been schoolboys before 1912).

To provide us with an idea of the knowledge available to well-off members of society, this vision of the minimal level of knowledge is supplemented by a study of the *Nouveau Larousse Illustré*.

Knowledge in the Nouveau Larousse Illustré

In the editions of this encyclopaedia, dating from 1905–6, we have found early knowledge of blood circulation and of blood identical to that conveyed by the handbooks of 1912 and 1919. However, the content is more detailed, more complete and more scientific. For example, the contents of blood are no longer composed simply of red cells and plasma but also of leucocytes (mono and polycellular, eosinophilic . . .) and of albumins, of which a portion coagulates to form fibrin. Haemoglobin, rich in iron, allows the transport of oxygen. The same precision can be found for describing blood pathologies, i.e. a very detailed, very complete and scientific approach.

In the *Larousse Mensuel Illustré*, we note two types of articles: in-depth articles (approximately one page) and topical articles. In the in-depth articles, we noted one dealing with transfusions (1914) and one dealing with blood pressure (1920). Both articles define the subject and give its detailed history. Then they present in detail the clinical procedures, the equipment, and note the difficulties. Among the topical articles, we noted one on fibrillation tests and one on transplantation tests. It appears that this encyclopaedia diffused in-depth and topical scientific knowledge. It was available in well-off households for those wishing to have answers to precise questions, but it seems unlikely that the work would have been read in its entirety – it was a reference work.

In conclusion, we can assume that the audience of administrators and board members, for whom *La dame comptabilité* was intended, would have had some basic knowledge of the connection between blood circulation and good health thanks to the growth of elementary education programmes during the second half of the nineteenth century (Faure 2002; Csergo 2002). They also potentially had at their disposal more detailed scientific knowledge.

The analogy

Without taking part in philosophical debates, we must define analogy in order to distinguish it from metaphor and comparison. We propose the definition of Coster in *L'analogie dans les sciences humaines*:

> the analogy reveals a similarity of ratios or relations which can be expressed by the next formula: $A/B = C/D$. C has a relation with D, this relation is of the same nature as the relation between A and B. The similarity does not aim to consider the terms separately, but the relation which links them respectively. Thus A and B on the one hand, C and D on the other, must be known as being connected by the same ratio. (1978, 19–20)

Coster also quotes Brown (1977, 20): 'the analogical model is based on the transfer of units (terms, features, dimensions . . .) from one domain to another: for example, the model of the human body or the model of the operation of a machine used to explain society'. This known domain is also the limit of the analogy. An analogy relevant in a given period and culture could be less relevant in another period or culture. During the nineteenth and twentieth centuries, we can observe the evolution of domains of references such as mechanics, body health, cybernetics and networks. The reason why the analogy used by Deuwez may have been chosen may never be known exactly, since we have no details on the author's personal background. At best, we can only make assumptions as to the reasons for his choice. It is important to understand that the time at which this text was written in France coincided with more than a decade of public health campaigns that emphasised this link between 'good practises' and 'good health'. The subject is shown in handbooks, in several films and advertisements (Faure 2002; Lefebvre 2002; Nourisson 2002; Zarch 2002). The good practises included eating well and washing yourself regularly. The historical context of the rise of fascism in Italy or in Germany is also rich with associations related to the health of the nation. All these elements may have impacted on Deuwez.

Consequently, the use of the model of blood circulation in order to explain the link between accounting and the health of the firm potentially constituted a good way to popularise accounting.

In the literature, the authors make distinctions between the various kinds of analogies according to the intentions (analogy of invention, analogy of evidence, analogy of representation) or the mode (analogy based on attribution, analogy based on proportionality). In our case, the author of *La dame comptabilité* does not claim to establish the conceptual bases of accounting. Rather the intention is to use the knowledge of blood circulation in order to shed light onto the less well-known domain of accounting. As we will show, this analogy is based on the similarity in circulation between the body (term A) and accounting (term C). But although this similarity is limited and weak, because it does not conform to anatomical knowledge, it quickly conveys useful information to the reader. Indeed, after having compared accounting to blood circulation, the relationship between accounting and the health of the company (D) emerges from the relationship between blood circulation and the health of an individual (B). This allows the author to underline the actions which have an impact on the true health (management) and also those which manipulate the appearance of the health (window-dressing). Thus, this exotic analogy seems relevant to the author's intention.

Blood circulation and accounting

A count of non-technical terms used in the part of *La dame comptabilité* devoted to accounting reveals the following. The large majority are connected to the lexical field of blood and of its pathologies and its treatments. Then come the references to the human body, and finally those concerning women's accessories. The first two fields are connected to the use of blood circulation as an explanatory mode. We can make assumptions that the women's accessories are used to improve the good impression given by the Lady.

At the beginning of the booklet, the author makes a short traditional presentation (prologue) of the basic knowledge elements of accounting: the kinds of accounts, the account books, single entry, double entry, etc. Deuwez showed the importance of accounting as a mechanism for recording the transfer of funds which have an impact on the company. 'Every event must be translated by the money flow from a clearly defined account to another account, named without ambiguity. . . Then, the company will be divided into compartments. . . we will consider it as a person in flesh and bone, and quite alive, we will number these organs' (*Ldc,* 2). These organs correspond to the accounts and will exchange sometimes blue blood or sometimes red blood. The flow from one account-organ to another could suggest that this explanation is of the kind 'the account which receives and the account which gives' characteristic of the personification of the accounts. But this is not the case. Indeed, the flow circulates between the account-organs within one human body which corresponds to the company and not between the account-persons which form parts of the company. This is a global vision which shows the interdependencies that are necessary for a management decision (see next section). However, the model of blood circulation is a closed flow model, whereas the conceptual model of accounting is an open model based on stocks and flows.[18] This leads the author to take liberties with anatomy and to reinvent a somewhat exotic blood circulation in order to explain accounting.

For example, the author makes reference to different kinds of blood: desiccated blood, cold run blood, new blood and old blood. This is explained by the different functions of the money-blood which are as follows (see also Table 2):

- money is an instrument of payment;
- money is a measuring instrument of the economic value;
- money is an instrument of conservation of the economic value.

Table 2. Analysis of quotations about the blood.

Quotations, *Ldc*, page 6	Analysis
Debtor and creditors – desiccated blood – which usually stays for a long time in a waiting room, awaiting the moment to join the dance, i.e. to transform itself into true blood.	Desiccated blood = instrument of conservation of the economic value => stock of receivables and stock of debts True blood = instrument of payment
In the fixed assets, the blood runs cold. There is a congestive state which decreases by depreciation of assets.	Cold run blood = instrument of conservation of the economic value => stock of fixed assets and stock of depreciation of assets
The customers are foreigners. Through the sales, they become debtors. They receive goods which contain old blood. In exchange, they give more new blood (as a principle) than the volume of old blood received.	New blood, old blood = a measuring instrument of the economic value
Suppliers are foreigners. Through the purchases, they become creditors. Sooner or later, these vampires will suck blood. On the other hand, they fill up the Lady with the veal roasts and the spinach that the Lady stores in her stomach. All occurs as if the heart directly sends blood to the store.	Will suck blood = instrument of payment. The heart sends blood to the store = measuring instrument of the economic value. Stored blood in the stomach = stock

The account-organs of the balance sheet are described as a blocked flow of blood (dried, solidified, stored blood), i.e. they correspond to stock accounts (as opposed to flow accounts). They are connected by blood vessels through which the flow of blood circulates. These vessels will disappear when Lady Accounting becomes Lady Balance Sheet. Although Deuwez specifies: 'the blood which vivifies all and bathes all the bodies, is an instrument of measure' (*Ldc*, 6), we consider that these multiple kinds of blood go far beyond the average reader's general knowledge. Indeed, the reader needs to know, *a priori*, blood circulation in terms of small and great circulation with the red blood (due to oxygen) and the blue blood (due to carbon dioxide). In addition, the text adds confusion when it associates red blood with the creditor account and blue blood with the debtor account without an explanation of this term. Consequently, at this stage of analysis, we can consider that the use of the blood circulation model to represent accounting appears badly adapted. Indeed, the same word 'blood' is used for two different concepts: the explicit concept of flow and the implicit concept of stock.

Another difference exists. The blood circulation is a naturally closed system whereas the model used in *La dame comptabilité* is open because of the exchanges with the customers, suppliers and administrators. This distortion is necessary to explain the formation of income as shown by the following quotation in Table 2 and the illustration in Appendix 2:

> the customers are foreigners. Through the sales, they become debtors. They receive goods which contain old blood. In exchange, they give more new blood (as a principle) than the volume of old blood received. The margin constitutes the profit, or more precisely, the excess to blood which is the equivalent of profits. (*Ldc*, 6)

It is useful information for administrators to understand that the profit is born from exchange with customers without making confusion between sales and profit.

There is another biological difference. 'Profit, which is the difference between new blood and old blood, becomes fat . . . because the Lady Balance-sheet will teach you that profit is fat and not blood' (see Appendix 1). This specification drives the reader to distinguish the profit-fat from the heart, treasury centre. This distinction is again underlined when the heart is described:

> [the heart] is unable alone to make either profit or loss ... When the heart is filled with blood, one says that the treasury is comfortable. It does not mean that the company has made a profit. When the heart is bloodless, it could be said that the treasury is hard up. It is a bad sign, because this could be enough to lead to cardiac arrest and death. But that does not mean inevitably that the business made a loss. This simply means that the Lady is anaemic because she has danced too much. (*Ldc*, 6)

We must underline that in this period (c.1933), the appearance of fatness was still considered to be a positive sign of health, and fat was not bad for the heart or blood circulation. In reality, of course, we now know that this is not the case, showing the historical and cultural limits of analogy as mentioned at the beginning of this section.

Regarding the inventory, in 'The role of the stomach and the intestines' (*Ldc*, 7), the work in progress is valued in the manner indicated by Faure (1921) as the standard practice (see Appendix 4). In 'Old Lady Accounting, former method, annual inventory' (*Ldc*, 10), the author Deuwez criticises the traditional method of keeping the warehouse account, but does not mention the alternative method of the perpetual inventory.

We can conclude that the presentation of accounting through blood circulation is made to the detriment of anatomical knowledge but in accordance with accounting knowledge of the time. Compared to contemporary works, this presentation gives a global view of the system and underlines the difference between profit and cash. As we specified at the beginning of this section, the interest of analogy is not in the quality of the initial similarity (the term A blood circulation compared with the term C accounting), but in the use of the ratio A/B (the relation between blood circulation and person's health) to reveal C/D (the relation between accounting health of the company). This issue is examined in the following section.

The analogy: from real health to the apparent health of the 'woman-company'

The notion of the global circulation of a vital liquid such as blood is used to transfer the teaching of the medical world to the world of business: 'a flow of blood snakes throughout an organisation. The life of a business is a phenomenon of the blood circulation' (*Ldc*, 6). Consequently, through the blood circulation and notably the pathologies and the treatments that relate to it, the events of the life of the company can be perceived by the reader (see Table 3). From the concern with health, the text then shifts to the subject of the appearance of health.

From circulation to health

References to pathology and to treatments are found on pages 6 and 8 in Lady Accounting (see Appendix 1) and Lady Balance Sheet (see Appendix 2). For example, 'we practise blood-letting known under the name of dividend. The lady hates this blood-letting, which she says weakens her'. The reader (member of a general meeting) can perceive that ill-considered distributions are dangerous for the company (*Ldc*, 6).

The heart and the blood which circulate through the 'woman company' are like cash. One negligent operation on this heart for an insufficiency of fresh money-blood puts the health of the woman-company in danger from anaemia and/or heart failure, which is possible even in the case of profits being made. It is remarkable that, very quickly, the attention of the reader is drawn to the difference between cash and profit (fat) through their localisation (the profit for the stomach and the intestine in an exchange with the exterior, and cash concerning the heart). The interest of

Table 3. Pathologies and medications.

Organs-departments	Condition of organs or pathology	Medications
Heart = cash	Never too fat, never too red	Cf. debtors problem or creditors problem
Under the heart = debtors	Prone to serious illness which is unpaid liabilities	Therefore, it will be good to vaccinate them to put the specific medication in the basket
The left arm = creditors	A voracious tribe of parasites	They must be exterminated with blood that they are devouring
Stomach = inventories	To avoid over-loading	Avoid food which is full of blood and indigestible Put in the basket a good amount of rhubarb
The right side of the trunk = fixed assets	The fixed assets paralyse the right side	Input energy by accumulation of depreciation

the comparison is the use of accounting/circulation as an explanatory model for the health of the company by the accounts/organs.

In Appendix 2, the balance sheet of the company is represented by a lady where the assets (debtors accounts) would be the torso in which the heart is compared to the cash, the stomach to the inventory, the fixed assets on the right side, when the liabilities (creditors accounts) would be the arms: on the right depreciation, on the left the creditors, and the head would be the equity. In fact, it is Lady Accounting whose blood does not circulate any more. But the organic image is not strong enough; the author uses some accessories such as the cloche hat, which covers the equity and the reserves (retained earnings) and which 'gives it a more majestic air'; the shopping basket, which is garnished 'with a good dose of rhubarb' (allowance for inventory losses) or some vaccines for the shortfall in payments; and finally a small cask containing the profit 'pure nectar'. One can think that the accounts represented in the form of accessories are in fact those which result from a voluntary decision. Dressed as such, Lady Balance Sheet can be presented to the administrators who will appreciate her health.

In the text (*Ldc*, 8), Deuwez highlighted a certain number of events or practices affecting the health of the firm:

- cash: the heart 'never too large';
- debtors: 'subject to a rather serious disease such as the shortfall in payments';
- creditors: 'a voracious tribe of parasites';
- fixed assets: which 'paralyse the right side of the chest';
- inventories: 'it is necessary to avoid overloading it [the inventory]'.

So, Deuwez stressed facts about the different items of the balance sheet, highlighting those of concern to administrators (the weak points which will affect the viability of the company). Regarding the result, the analysis remained limited (only two sentences), echoing our finding of the minimal interest shown by the authors of accounting handbooks to an analysis of the result.

From health to the appearance of health

Subsequently, Deuwez (*Ldc*, 9) bases his argument on the preceding organic and accessory representations to explain how to give the appearance of health in a sick company. This point of interest for administrators, members of general meetings and readers of the book was approached in a critical way, since the author highlighted the means of disguising elements in the balance sheet and thereby of falsifying the accounts. We find again the concerns raised by the authors of the time but illustrated in the most pessimistic and nightmarish way, as illustrated in Table 4, which recapitulates the manipulations described in the text and the illustration. The author stressed that everything can be modified except for equity and cash.

Appendix 3 illustrates all of the possible manipulations. The shopping basket is abandoned; administrative expenses and labour are injected into the fixed assets; water is reddened with wine but, even so, it is not blood, i.e. it represents a pseudo-value injected into the inventories and accounts receivable. Value is pumped out from the liabilities. Consequently, thanks to these manipulations, into the small barrel of profit we inject artificial fat.

We can note that the recommendations aim at improving the income. As the aim of Deuwez is to popularise the accounting point of view using humour, he proposed recommendations to fake the balance sheet. The comic effect is here; the reader is addressed as a faker whereas, in reality, the reader is a potential victim.

But Deweuz warns also that the authorities can intervene when there has been a lot of obvious falsification (the law of 1867, for example, punished the distribution of fictitious dividends):

> You could go much further, and you could follow all the whims of your imagination; as fertile that this could be, accounting would be able to follow some the creations easily, because it is a docile servant and full of resources but you would then arrive in another situation where the authorities of your country could try to pick a quarrel with you. Although examples abound and although newspapers are full of them, we will not follow you as far as there. (*Ldc*, 9)

The final advice given by Deuwez is to be ‘an average swindler’ in order to pass unnoticed: ‘dress the Lady well without disguising it’ (*Ldc*, 9). If we were being anachronistic, we would speak of income smoothing.

In conclusion, starting from a limited similarity between blood circulation and accounting, in which the author has avoided some explanations as to the operation of accounts, this analogy helps to increase the reader’s awareness of potential problems with the quality of the information which is produced and of the need to ask appropriate questions at the administrators’ meeting.

Analogy in the accounting domain: usual practice?

In this study, we have examined an example of the use of analogy in the accounting domain. But to what extent was it usual practice as a means of trying to diffuse accounting knowledge during the study period? For this purpose, we identified three groups of work: the books specialising in balance sheets; accounting handbooks; and popular books for a general readership.

In the books devoted to the balance sheet, we note the use of images related to clothing but only rarely to humans. For example, Liesse states (1919, 3rd edition, quoted in Hanon De Louvet 1939, 13)[19]:

> Make them speak, have them open their mouth, examine them with the magnifying glass and the microscope; like a doctor, check if the organs of the balance sheet are not atrophied or are not hypertrophied, finally do not let yourself be taken in by the phantasmagoria of the figures, because many companies whose assets are not very significant are in a better situation, are more solid and, more attractive than others for which the figures are excessive.

Table 4. Analysis of quotations about the manipulations.

Manipulated item	Manipulations	Quotations	Problem dealt with in book
Fixed assets	To increase the value	'you can inflate the value of a piece of land under the pretext that the value has tripled'	Problem of the evaluation
		'write down small repairs of buildings as new works'	Historical cost
		'enter the administrative expenses in installation account or equipment account under pretext that you moved a machine or a boiler'	
	To increase the value	'do not depreciate'	Conservatism principle
	To mask information	'for avoiding indiscreet questions, include them in a group account'	Standardised presentation
Debtors	To backdate	'Why could you not backdate some invoices?'	Matching principle
	Absence of allowance	'and for the worst accounts count for the value the account as receivable'	Conservatism principle
Inventories and work-in-progress	To increase the value	'chicanery on the quantities, also chicanery on the values'	Evaluation and sincerity
	Absence of allowance	'the damaged goods and unsold old goods will be quoted at the highest quotation possible'	Conservatism principle and evaluation
	To mask information	'the works in progress are very advantageous because they are ongoing and it is not possible on the 5 January to know what occurred on the 31 December'	Evaluation and sincerity
Various	To mask information	'you can create some complicated and obscured accounts . . . you can hide them in a group account'	Standardised presentation and sincerity
Creditors	To mask information	'you put them in a corner and you act as though unaware of some invoices'	Evaluation and sincerity

Grimmiau (c.1903, 5) presents the following quotation of a parliamentary speaker, Bara, before the adoption of the law of 1881 on false balance sheets: '"post-closing balance" and "balance sheet" are identical twin brothers; it is the same person who presents himself twice with different clothes, sometimes more and sometimes fewer clothes'. These images have an air of familiarity with the analogy of Lady Accounting, but they illustrate simply the speech of the parliamentary speaker without being used to introduce a reasoning based on the ratio A/B. This can be connected with the objective of these books. They are written for professionals or for the teaching of professionals who already have some accounting or legal knowledge.

In the handbooks, the balance sheet is presented either as a synthesis of the accounts (as in the approach of the personification of the accounts) or by its definition (the balance sheet approach). The comprehension of the balance sheet is conducted within the context of the explanatory method of the operating accounts. This seems coherent with the intention declared by the majority of the authors. They want to show accounting as a theory or as a science. The objective of this type of book could also explain the lack of analogies. Firstly the use of an analogy borrowed from another science can point to accounting's lack of resources to produce its own explanation, and thus to its lack of credibility. Secondly, since these books are aimed at future professionals, we assume that the authors did not want to divert their attention away from the core of the matter by using analogies borrowed from another discipline.

In our sample, only four books are popular generalist guides, i.e. adapting a subject to make it available to the non-specialist reader. As indicated earlier, of these four works, only two made use of analogy: *La dame comptabilité* (Deuwez 1933) and *Les concepts fondamentaux de la comptabilité* (De Fages 1933). Whereas De Fages used fluid mechanics to explain the recording of accounts and accounting, the analogy based on blood circulation used by Deuwez enabled him to avoid explaining the technique of bookkeeping. Within nine pages, he reveals:

- that accounting records flows and stocks (as opposed to just flows);
- the difference between income and cash balance;
- the retention of cash in the inventories, the debts;
- that accounting produces a view of the financial health of the firm and that this is subject to deconstruction and manipulation.

Finally, although *La dame comptabilité* is not representative of the diffusion of accounting knowledge, it is a very instructive book on accounting's didactics.

Conclusion

First, our study has examined the state of knowledge and discussions between 1900 and 1933 regarding explanations of how the accounts, the balance sheet and the inventory work. However, this contribution is only an analysis of 35 works and in one French-speaking context. It would be useful to continue with a thorough study of the various books on accounting from this period. The comparison with studies from other countries would also enable us to trace the mode of diffusion of the accounting concepts (but not their implementation).

Second, as far as accounting is concerned during the period studied, we make the assumption that analogy is reserved for the purpose of popularisation, particularly for a specific public. This use of analogy would benefit from a comparison of its use in other disciplines.

Finally, with regard to the *La dame comptabilité*, the analogy can be a good means of popularisation. Indeed, the useful concepts are made available through the means of health problems which are a shared concern for the intended public. However, it would be interesting to test this document with a public not trained in management to validate our impressions. This document also challenges us as teachers, particularly with those students who are not graduating in management.

We are aware that our analysis is based on accounting domain references. It would be useful to enrich it with research knowledge about gender or about hygiene. The document can also be studied in its historical context. Indeed, the period of the 1930s presents specific economic, political and social characteristics.

Notes

1. Details of the author, H. Deuwez, remain unknown. We will sometimes refer to the author 'he', designating not the gender but the professional category to which this person belongs.
2. For the period studied, the 'prix de revient' is the purchase price of general goods or material with some expenses added to it.
3. *Petit Robert* (a famous French dictionary) defines a handbook as follows: 'an educational book which presents essential notions of a technique in a handy form'. In our collection, those books are characterised by a large section devoted to exercises and to applications unlike other kinds of books.
4. Bulletins of professional or academic reviews were not systematically examined.
5. In the Stevelinck collection, for the period studied, we have only identified four works of this type so far.
6. Two later works are included in this group, namely Hanon de Louvet (1939) and Delaporte (1925). In the case of the first, the reason is that there is only a later version of an earlier work available in the Stevelinck collection, and for the second, the earlier version on the rational method is being restored at the present time.
7. This is the exact translation of the terms used by French authors at the time.
8. The term 'warehouse' is used as a translation of the French term 'magasin' which can also mean shop.
9. However the handbooks make reference to a conformity with the programmes for the athenaeums (Belgium) and for the education of school teachers (France). Regarding France, *Le nouveau dictionnaire de la pédagogie* (1911) shows us, under the reference 'accounting', the programmes whose contents primarily refer to the organisation of the accounting entries.
10. We could note that this personification of the accounts is associated in the handbooks with a distinction between the firm and the owner which has been described as the theory of the double personality (Degos 2005).
11. According to Lemarchand, André was the first in to use this formulation: 'Qui entrera ou recevra sera débiteur, et qui sortira ou baillera sera créditeur'.
12. The signs + and − are also used by certain authors in the person-account framework but not in the same way.
13. Faure (1927a) is a particular case because he presents the two approaches in the same handbook even though he is an ardent defender of the personification approach.
14. For more details about theses authors, (Degos 2005) and (Labardin and Nikitin 2009)
15. See note 2.
16. Throughout the period studied, the concepts of 'provision' and of 'reserve' (retained reserve) were not used or differentiated consistently in the manner in which they are distinguished in modern usage.
17. Lemarchand and Praquin (2005) point out that financial scandals continued after 1914 until halfway through 1930, when light accounting regulation intervened.
18. This explanatory model of bookkeeping (Grenier and Bonnebouche 1998) is not contemporary to the studied document, but it seems relevant to us for this analysis.
19. We could only consult only the 4th edition where this quotation no longer appears. Two of the eight chapters of this work are devoted to the symptoms of the social body corresponding to an analogy.

References

Batardon, L. 1923. *L'inventaire et le Bilan chez le commerçant seul, dans les sociétés de personnes et les sociétés par action*. Paris: Dunod.

Bérard, V., and Y. Lemarchand. 1994. *Le miroir des marchands*. Paris: Editions comptables Malesherbes.

Binet, J.-L. 2001. *Le sang et les hommes*. Paris: Gallimard.

Brémant, A. 1919. *Sciences et enseignement ménager. Cours moyen*. Paris: Librairie Hatier.

Brown, R.H. 1977. *A poetic for sociology. Toward a logic of discovery for the human science*. London and New York: Cambridge University Press.

Bunau-Varilla, P. 1924. *Le mécanisme du succès en affaires: La comptabilité telle que l'on la parle et telle qu'on devrait la parler*. Paris: G. and M. Ravisse.

Caquas, J.M. 1924. *Initiation algébrique à la comptabilité à partie double*. Paris: G. and M. Ravisse.

Charpentier, J. 1921. *Traité pratique des bilans et inventaires*. Nancy, Paris and Strasbourg: Berger-Levrault.

Colasse, B. 2005. *Les grands auteurs en Comptabilité*. Colombelles: Ems.

Coster, M.D. 1978. *L'analogie en sciences humaines*. Paris: Presses Universitaires de France.

Csergo, J. 2002. Propreté et enfance au XIXème siècle. In *Education à la santé XIXe-XXe siècle*, ed. D. Nourisson, 31–42. Rennes: ENSP.

Daubresse, L. 1912. *Organisation comptable*. Mons: Librairie Comptable.

De Fages, E. 1933. *Les concepts fondamentaux de la comptabilité*. Paris: Librairie de l'enseignement technique Léon Eyrolles.

Degos, J.-G. 2005. Eugène Léautey et Adolphe Guilbault. In *Les grands auteurs en Comptabilité*, ed. B. Colasse, 55–71. Colombelles: Ems.

Delaporte, R. 1925. *La lecture du bilan*. Paris: Syndicat des employés du commerce et de l'industrie.

Denis, H. 1904. *Histoire des systèmes économiques et socialistes. Les fondateurs*. Paris: V. Giard and E. Brière.

Deschamp, H. 1926. *Précis de comptabilité*. Paris and Lyon: Emmanuel Vitte.

Desirotte, H. 1931. *Comptabilité commerciale Application pratique et raisonnée aux entreprises à petite moyenne ou grande activité*. Brussels: Editorel.

Deuwez, H. 1933. *La dame comptabilité*. Lagny: Imp. Emmanuel Grevin.

Diani, M. 2003. Economie évolutionniste et culture d'entreprise. Unpublished doctoral thesis, Université Louis Pasteur, Strasbourg 1.

Fabre, H. post–1882. *Eléments usuels des sciences physiques et naturelles à l'usage des écoles primaires*. Paris: Delagrave.

Faure, G. 1914. *Cours de comptabilité à l'usage des écoles primaires supérieures*. Paris: Masson and Co.

Faure, G. 1921. *Cours de comptabilité à l'usage des écoles primaires supérieures*. Paris: Masson and Co.

Faure, G. 1926. *Bilans et comptes en francs-or*. Paris: Nouvelle librairie nationale.

Faure, G. 1927a. *Comptabilité générale*. Paris: Masson and Co.

Faure, G. 1927b. *Considérations sur le raisonnement comptable*. Paris: C.C.C.

Faure, G. 1929. *L'évolution de l'esprit comptable*. Paris: Société de comptabilité de France.

Faure, O. 2002. Hygiène, hygiéniste et santé publique en France XIX–XXème siècle. In *Education à la santé XIXe-XXe siècle*, ed. D. Nourisson, 13–30. Rennes: ENSP.

Gardey D. 1995. Un monde en mutation: les employés de bureau 1890–1930: féminisation, mécanisation, rationalisation. Unpublished doctoral thesis, Université Paris VII.

Gersten, C. c.1930. *Petite méthode graduée pour apprendre à lire un bilan et contrôler des écritures*. No place or publisher given.

Grenier, C., and J. Bonnebouche. 1998. *Système d'information comptable*. Paris: Foucher.

Grimmiau, P. c.1903. *L'analyse d'un bilan*. Brussels: L. Vanderlinden.

Hanon de Louvet, C. 1939. *Analyse et discussion de bilans à l'usage de la pratique et de l'enseignement*. Brussels: ECCF.

Labardin, P., and M. Nikitin. 2009. De la comptabilité à la littérature (et retour), XIVe Journées d'Histoire de la Comptabilité et du Management, Sceaux. http://jhcm.fr

Lebigre, A. 1984. Et saigner et purger. *Histoire* 74: 110–13.

Lefebvre, T. 2002. Cinéma et hygiène, les débuts d'une fructueuse collaboration. In *Education à la santé XIXe-XXe siècle*, ed. D. Nourisson, 71–81. Rennes: ENSP.

Lemarchand, Y. 1995. 1880–1924, L'échec de l'unification des bilans. *Comptabilité, Contrôle, Audit* March: 7–24.

Lemarchand, Y. 2001. 'À la conquête de la science des comptes', variations autour de quelques manuels français de tenue des livres. In *Ars mercatoria. Handbücher und Traktate für den Gebrauch des Kaufmanns, 1470–1820. T. III, Analysen 1470–1700*, ed. J. Hoock and P. Jeannin, 91–129. Paderborn: Schöningh.

Lemarchand, Y., and N. Praquin. 2005. Falsifications et manipulations comptables. La mesure du profit, un enjeu social (1856–1914). *Comptabilité, Contrôle, Audit* July: 35–60.

Lepigoché, A., and C. Seltensperger. 1912. *Le livre unique de sciences et d'agriculture*. Paris: Librairie classique Paul Delaplane.

Mattessich, R. 2003. Accounting research and researchers of the nineteenth century and the beginning of the twentieth century: An international survey of authors, ideas and publications. *Accounting, Business and Financial History* 13, no. 2: 125–70.

Ménard, C. 1981. La machine et le coeur. Essai sur les analogies dans les raisonnements économiques. In *Analogie et connaissances. De la poésie à la science*, ed. G. Gadoffre, A. Lichnerowicz and F. Perroux, 137–65. Paris: Maloine.

Michaïlesco, C. 2005. Jean Dumarchey: Une contribution à la théorie du bilan et de la valeur. In *Les grands auteurs en Comptabilité*, ed. B. Colasse, 92–110. Colombelles: Ems.

Nourrisson, D. 2002. Consommations alimentaires, publicité sanitaire. In *Education à la santé XIXe–XXe siècle,* ed. D. Nourisson, 91–101. Rennes: ENSP.

Thompson, G.F. 1998. Encountering economics and accounting: Some skirmishes and engagements. *Accounting, Organizations and Society* 23: 283–323.

Touchelay, B. 2005. A l'origine du plan comptable français des années 1930 aux années 1960, la volonté de contrôle d'un Etat dirigiste. *Comptabilité, Contrôle, Audit*, July: 61–88.

Vlaemminck, J. Undated. L'évolution historique de la comptabilité. Techniques et doctrines (Contribution à l'histoire de l'économie appliquée et du commerce). Typescript, Stevelink collection, Library of the University of Nantes.

Weber, H. 1981. L'analogie corps humain- orps social dans la pensée politique du XVIème. In *Analogie et connaissances. Aspects historique*, ed. G. Gadoffre, A. Lichnerowicz and F. Perroux, 139–48. Paris: Maloine.

Zarch, F. 2002. La caméra sanitaire. In *Education à la santé XIXe–XXe siècle,* ed. D. Nourisson, 83–101. Rennes: ENSP.

Appendix 1. Lady Accounting

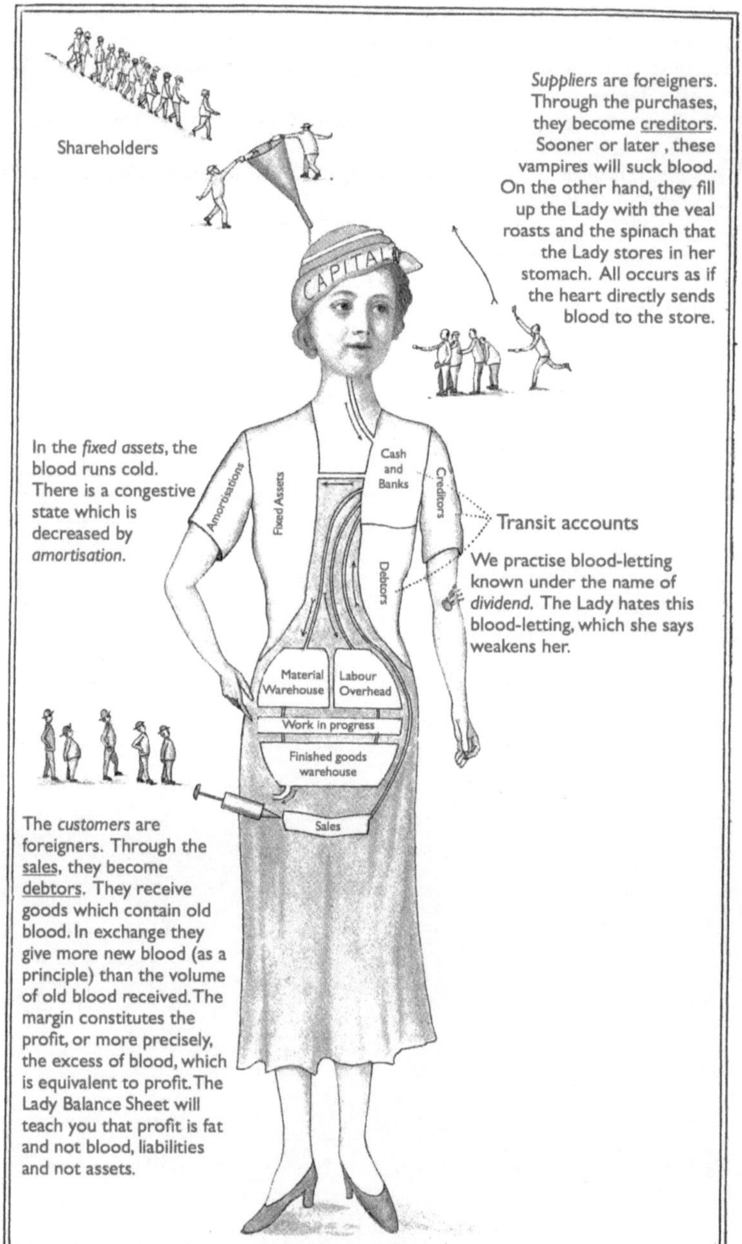

Source: Deuwez (1933) *La dame comptabilité.*

Appendix 2. Lady Balance Sheet

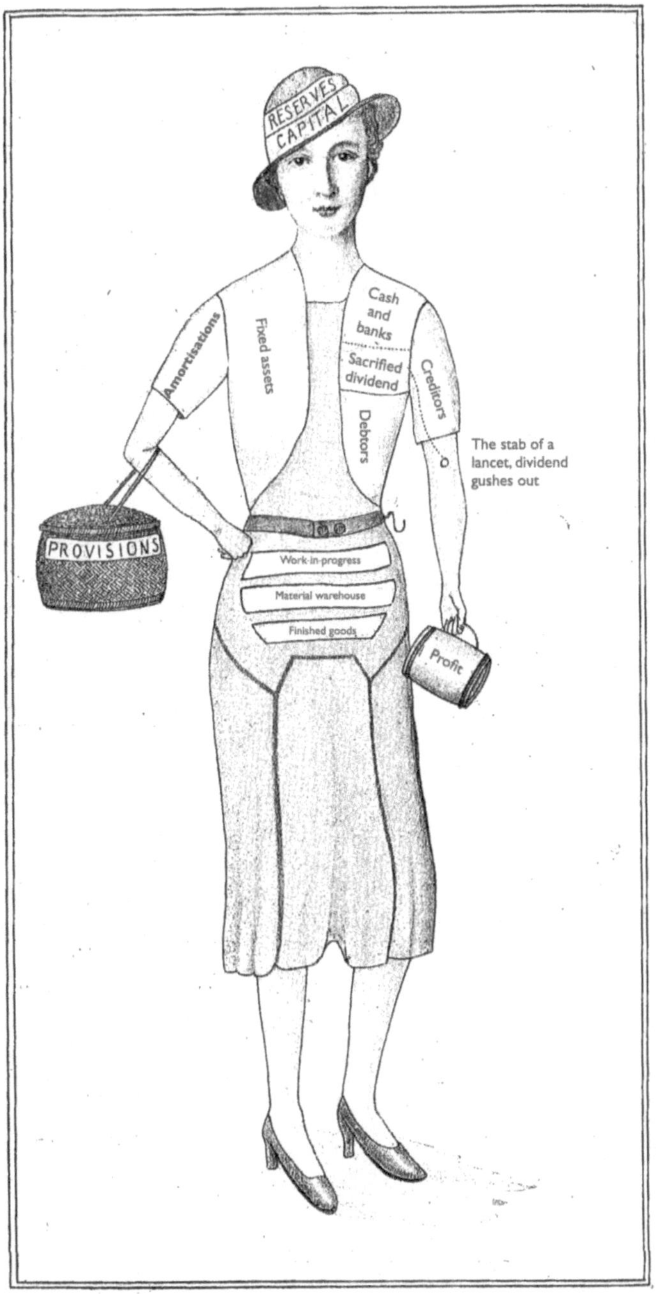

Source: Deuwez (1933) *La dame comptabilité*.

Appendix 3. The make-up of Lady Balance Sheet

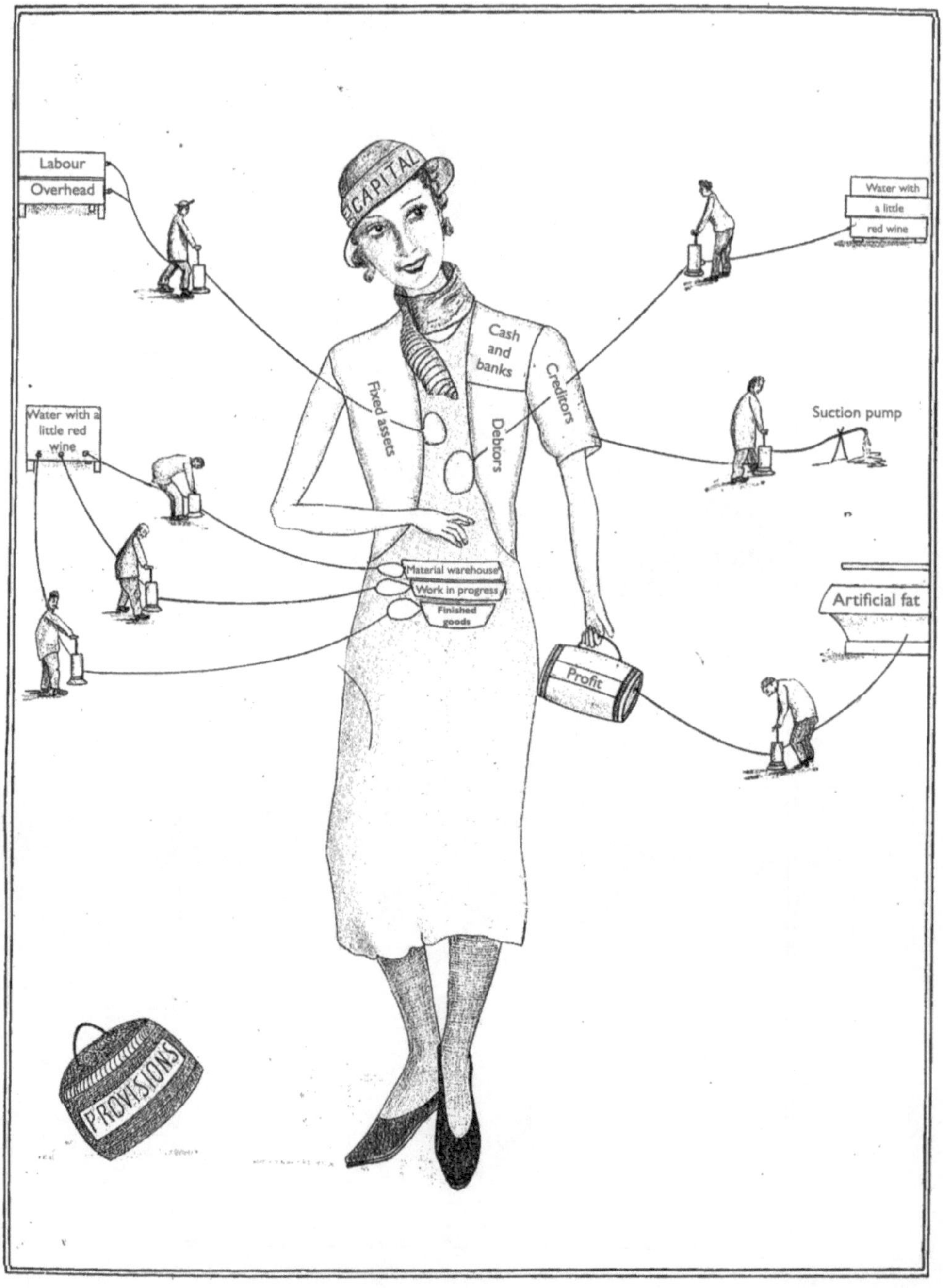

Source: Deuwez (1933) *La dame comptabilité*.

Appendix 4. Role of the stomach and the intestines

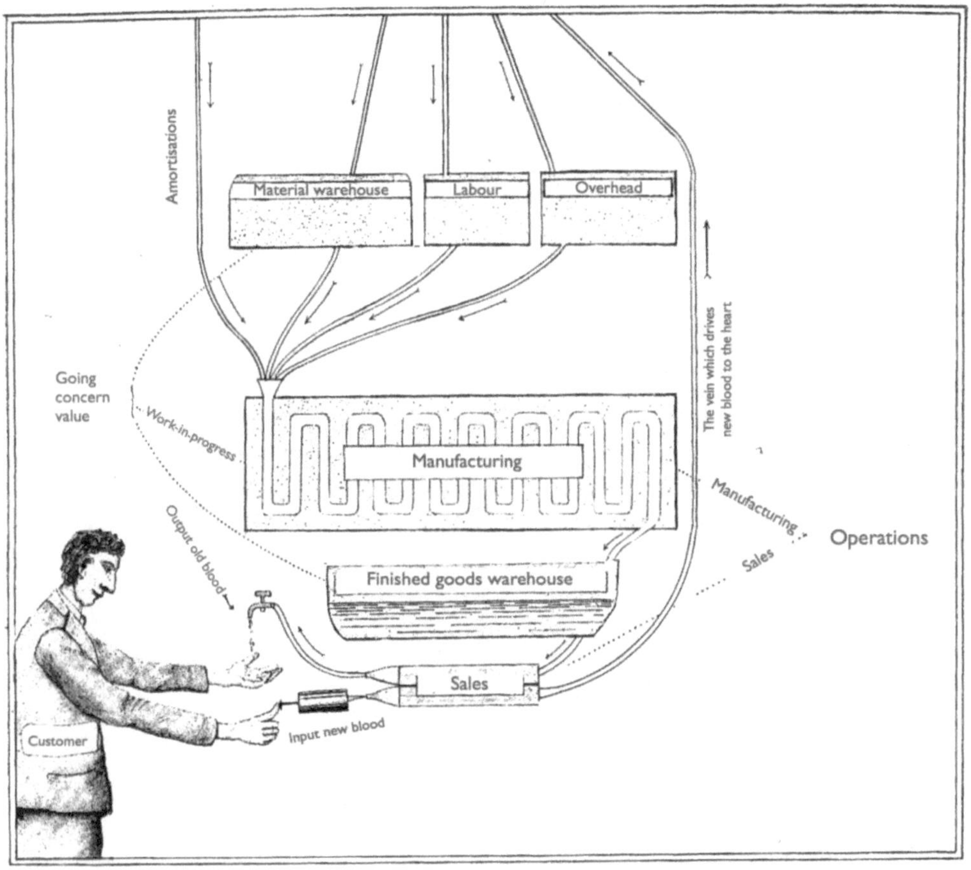

Source: Deuwez (1933) *La dame comptabilité*.

Charles Eugène Bedaux (1886–1944): 'cost killer' or Utopian Socialist?

Yves Levant[a] and Marc Nikitin[b]

[a]*Lille University of Sciences and Technologies, GREMCO LEM (UMR CNRS 8179)/Lille Graduate School of Management, Lille, France;* [b]*Laboratoire Orléanais de Gestion, Université d'Orléans, France*

Charles Eugène Bedaux is best known by social scientists for his labour organisation method. This method was a great success with companies during the interwar years, thus enabling its author to set up a multinational business consultancy. The Bedaux method was, however, violently contested by employees and their unions, who organised many strikes to protest against it. Some of those who knew Bedaux, however, claimed that his method was in reality merely one part of a larger system, a simple component working towards a broader and more generous vision of society (known in French as équivalisme). His project was inspired by the Utopian Socialists of the last century, intended to provide a solution to the widespread disorder experienced by industrial societies during the interwar period. This paper explores the credibility of this project from two perspectives: a critical examination of his biographies and investigations conducted in the places where experiments in 'equivalism' were supposedly undertaken.

Introduction

Charles Eugène Bedaux is a particularly controversial figure: a self-made man who became a business consulting engineer in the USA in 1912, and the owner of a large multinational consultancy business at the end of the 1920s. To most people, he is best known for the labour organisation method to which he gave his name. It made him his fortune, in that it was highly successful among the managers of large companies that were his clients, although it was rejected violently by the unions as a brutal method of exploiting the workers. Some of those who knew Bedaux, however, have claimed that his method was in reality merely one part of a larger system, a simple component working towards a broader and more generous vision of society. According to some of his biographers, Bedaux was thus the designer of a project for the economic and social organisation of society, otherwise known as 'equivalism', a project inspired by the Utopian Socialists of the previous century and intended to offer solutions to the widespread disorder experienced by industrial societies during the interwar period.

In this article, we will attempt to answer the following question: Was the Bedaux method a component of a vast social project ('equivalism') or was it simply a management technique for times of economic crisis, cloaked in rhetoric? We could also word the question as follows: Was Bedaux the author of a theory of human work (although he did not leave any completed formulation of this theory) or did he simply create a practical method which has stood the test of time?

To date, what we know about the life of Bedaux is mainly through six published biographies. As regards his method, there are numerous well documented academic papers on its implementation. In addition, we had at our disposal two unique sources of information, in the form of documents which we were able to consult within the framework of private archives[1] entrusted to one of us by one of Bedaux's descendants, and a survey we conducted among the workers in a paper mill ('Société des Papeteries de Roquefort'), in Roquefort des Landes, which experimented with the Bedaux method in 1941–2.[2]

After a critical examination of his biographies, we will present the main stages of his professional life. The rest of our paper will be divided into three parts. The first will recap on the Bedaux system and its social consequences as well as the context in which it was developed. We will, in particular, attempt to explain how his system was implemented in businesses in the form of particularly severe disciplinary adjustments related to the implementation of scientific management. In the second part, we will study the social project which most of the biographers of Bedaux attribute to him. His intended aim was to justly remunerate the working time and efforts made by each worker. We will not only question the ambition of such a Utopian vision, but also whether the first attempts to experiment with the method actually took place. Finally, we will conclude with some hypotheses on the motives and intentions, whether real or more probably supposed, of Bedaux, a particularly ambiguous figure.

Bedaux's biographers and his life

Of his six biographers,[3] Steven Kreis (1999) and Marie-Françoise Sassier (2005) stand somewhat apart. Firstly, Kreis (1990) is the author of a PhD thesis on the history of scientific management in Britain, and Sassier works with the Ministry of Culture in France. Three of the other biographers, however, are either journalists or consultants, while the remaining individual is Bedaux's own brother, Gaston Bedaux. Secondly, Kreis and Sassier do not tackle the question of 'equivalism'. None of those who attribute social concerns to Bedaux claim that their work has scientific value, and each of them has their own particular intentions and preoccupations. Flanner (1945), Christy (1984), Hardwick (1993) and Sassier (2005) are particularly interested in Bedaux's private life and shady relations with the Nazis. As for Gaston Bedaux (1979), he attempts to redeem his brother's reputation.

The first biography, taken in chronological order, is that by Janet Flanner (1892–1978), an American journalist and writer. She lived in Paris and, among other things, used to publish her 'Letter from Paris' in the *The New Yorker* magazine from 1925 until around 1970 (Wineapple 1989). In this regular feature she would comment on European culture and politics. On her return to the States when the Germans invaded France in 1939, she began writing about Marshal Pétain and began a biography of Bedaux, who she knew and had already interviewed before the war. She returned to France at the end of November 1944 as war correspondent for *The New Yorker*, and reworked her notes with Bedaux's former secretary. The article on Bedaux was published in three parts,[4] under the general title *Annals of collaboration*, between September and October 1945. Flanner primarily concentrated on the more sordid affairs, especially in the last ten years of Bedaux's life. She mainly describes Bedaux's activities during the occupation and his links with Nazism; she apparently had access to US Department of Justice[5] documents which recounted the interrogations to which Bedaux was subjected in his Miami jail, and upholds the standpoint of the US government that Bedaux was a traitor to his mother country and that he killed himself because he could see no other way out of his situation.[6] She implies, however, that nobody really wanted the trial of Bedaux to go ahead. Although she uses the term *equivalism* in the title of each of her three articles, Flanner does not linger on this aspect of Bedaux's ideas.[7] She simply mentions that the project was conducted from 1941–2 in Roquefort des Landes (France), and was, in her words, 'the greatest social experiment since the failure of the transcendentialists of *Boston in Brook-Farm*'.[8]

In 1979, Gaston Bedaux wrote a biography intended to redeem the moral reputation of his brother under the title *La vie ardente de C.E. Bedaux*, in which he only devotes a few lines to 'equivalism', while the rest of the book is full of details lauding the humanist and social qualities of his brother. As a child, Gaston, five years younger than Charles, had been the privileged and admiring playmate of his older brother. Later on, this graduate of the prestigious *polytechnique* school for civil servants[9] became the manager of the Paris subsidiary of the group, the International Bedaux Company, founded 25 years earlier by his sibling.

In 1984 Jim Christy, a journalist and writer born in the USA in 1945, published *The Price of Power*. Like Flanner, he puts more emphasis on the biography of Bedaux than on his system. He published a 20-page appendix containing a text written by Charles Emile Bedaux, the son of Bedaux (undated and no sources given[10]), describing the principles of 'equivalism'. In fact, it is the preface of one of the last versions of the manuscript named 'equivalism' which his son wished to publish. Christy, who has been presented as 'one of the last unpurged North American anarchistic romantics',[11] states that he has spent 11 years of his life searching for first-hand accounts about Bedaux. He was clearly fascinated by the personality of Bedaux and devotes some pages of Chapter 17 to 'equivalism'; his main sources are the documents held by the US Department of Justice and interviews conducted with people close to Bedaux: an associate (Marcel Grolleau), his brother (Gaston Bedaux), his widow and especially his son, Charles Emile, who had spent a year in captivity with his father in Algeria in 1943. Most of Charles Emile's account is taken up with memories of discussions they had at that time, and Christy appears to simply repeat the account he was given without checking its veracity. For example, he indicates that Bedaux received the Legion of Honour medal in October 1944, but this is not confirmed by the website of the Legion of Honour.[12]

In 1993 C.M. Hardwick, a consultant, published *Time Study in Treason; Charles E Bedaux Patriot or Collaborator?* He did not, of course, know Bedaux, but speaks about 'equivalism' without offering any new information or quoting any sources, which makes one think that he took his inspiration from previous biographies.

In 1999, Kreis wrote a biography of Bedaux, published in the *American National Biography,* but makes no mention of 'equivalism'. His sources relating to Bedaux's professional career are taken from the archives of Bedaux's companies, and as for his personal life, he uses Flanner's articles (Flanner 1945) and Christy's book (Christy 1984). In his thesis (1990, 326), Kreis states that Bedaux was not a theoretician. The contrast with the Taylorians was marked in that Bedaux did not belong to any professional association and 'tended to regard scientific management theory with cool detachment' (Kreis 1990, 326). On the next page he comments:

> In fact, the several thousands engineers' reports in the Bedaux archives never refer to a theory of Bedauxism nor even to Bedaux himself. We could argue that by 1930 at the very latest, Bedaux and the Bedaux system were two decidedly different realities.
>
> (Kreis 1990, 327)

Kreis concludes by noting the difference between consulting engineers, such as Taylor, Gilbreth and Emerson, and those like Bedaux who could be rightly qualified as management consultants. While the former had an engineering background and were theoreticians in principle, the latter were first and foremost salesmen.

Finally, in 2005, Marie-Françoise Sassier, who works for the Department of Culture in the Indre and Loire region, published a history of the chateau of Candé and its owners. Bedaux lived there with his second wife, Fern, from 1927 to 1942, and she continued to live there until her death in 1972.[13] In fact, almost half of the book is devoted to Bedaux, who was by far the most interesting owner. Bedaux's biography refers more to the personality of Bedaux and his wife rather than to his professional career. Equivalism is not mentioned. Sassier's sources are mainly former employees and the archives owned by the heirs of Fern Bedaux.

According to the first four of his biographers, and particularly Flanner and Christy, there are in fact two different characters: one that was only ever considered as a 'cost killer', and the other who was a misunderstood Utopian Socialist. These authors speak of an ambitious social project devised by Bedaux, who wished to apply the system that made him his fortune in business to states or regions. However, this is based on tenuous accounts, while the only academic research that exists concerns the implementation of the Bedaux method in business.[14]

If we go by the information provided by his biographers, the life of Bedaux (1886–1944) could be the subject of a movie; it was so brilliant and romantic, with a dramatic ending. But what we are mainly interested in here are his professional activities, which can be divided into three main periods: his beginnings before he went into business (1906–16); success (1916–33); and decline (1933–44).

After leaving primary school, where he displayed neither any great interest nor talent, and after having had various jobs in Paris,[15] Bedaux left for the United States in 1906, where he occupied some casual jobs and thereby discovered his talent as an organiser. Through a series of chance encounters, he moved into an area in full expansion, that of organisational consulting. Unlike consulting engineering, the job Bedaux chose to do did not need any particular technical qualifications. As the brother of a high-up civil servant, it is possible that Bedaux saw in this profession the means to climb up the social ladder and earn the recognition that his modest education did not afford him. In December 1912, he met a certain Morrini, an Italian consultant visiting the United States[16] to observe how the Harrington Emerson[17] system was being implemented in business (Fridenson 1987; Kipping 1999; Moutet 1975; Vielleville 1914). Morrini hired Bedaux to be his assistant during his visits to factories on the east coast and, when Morrini returned to Europe with engineers of the Taylor and Emerson systems, he took Bedaux with him to serve as interpreter. Bedaux then returned to France and met another consultant engineer, Louis Bernard Duez.[18] In 1914, Bedaux, Morrinni and Duez joined forces and founded the first bureau of consulting engineers in France. The same year, Bedaux returned to the States and worked for Morrini until 1916, when he set up the first Bedaux company. In 1917, the first application of his system took place and *The Bedaux Efficiency Course for Industrial Application*,[19] which was to be his only major work, appeared. He also gave some lectures on the subject. A second edition of the work was published in 1921, and was to become the reference manual for Bedaux engineers in the 1920s. Henceforth, other manuals of the same type were written in 1928, 1930 and 1933 (Kreis 1992, 172). These manuals were not, of course, widely distributed, for fear that the method would be copied by other consultants.

The method rapidly earned great success. First in the USA (where Bedaux advised Henry Ford, General Motors, DuPont, ITT, Standard Oil, etc.), then all over the world. He set up a number of subsidiaries in around 30 countries, and thus made a fortune. He enjoyed an extravagant lifestyle and travelled the world, living off the royalties paid by the subsidiaries to his holding company. From 1933, however, problems began to accumulate as the trade unions incessantly denounced his method as inhuman. The negative reactions of the workers and the consequent criticism of his method resulted in Bedaux losing control of his British and American subsidiaries in 1933. The same year, the Nazis closed his offices in Germany, arguing that the Bedaux system was in contradiction with their attitude towards workers. Business nevertheless continued, but Bedaux found himself implicated in the political turmoil of the time. Suspected by the Americans of being involved in 'enemy intelligence', he was arrested with his son in Algeria[20] and interrogated in El-Biar[21] during 1943 (see Figure 1). At the end of 1943, he was transferred to the USA, and he finally committed 'suicide' in a Miami prison on 14 February 1944.

The Bedaux system and its social consequences: reflection of an era

In this section we examine the nature of the Bedaux system for remunerating workers according to their output and its social consequences, noting that this system was part of the development of scientific management. We will also see that the latter, like the Bedaux system and the social utopia attributed to him, can not be understood independently of the social and political context of the first four decades of the twentieth century.

The Bedaux system

The Bedaux system,[22] is based on the fact that human labour has to be measured in terms of both effort and fatigue. Bedaux claimed to have discovered a scientific formula for calculating the amount of fatigue produced by a given effort and thus the necessary recovery time. From this could be determined the optimal pace of work. Bedaux thus claimed that the standard time for any activity could be expressed in 'Bedaux points' or 'B units'. The standard unit measure of energy is the work minute (rest included), and depends upon the difficulty of the work to be accomplished. He defined this unit as 'a fraction of a minute of work and a fraction of a minute of rest which together form a unit, that will vary in proportion to the nature of the effort' (Bedaux 1979, 34). It is a universal unit:

> representing the quantity of physiological energy a human being of normal constitution can deploy in one minute, taking into account the necessary rest time, when performing the actions and physiological efforts required by the industrial operations for which he has been adapted and trained, working at a pace equal to 3/4 of the normal physiological rate of exertion that a human being can withstand during the normal working day, while remaining fit to fulfil his domestic and social obligations at the end of the day.
>
> (Bedaux 1979, 34)

The optimum rate was 80 Bedaux per hour, while 60 was a norm (or rather a minimum). These ideas essentially led to a system of remuneration per unit of output. It was also a method for improving and controlling productivity. The worker incentive system was just one aspect of the method. Bedaux used the term 'functional analysis [...] all the methods for improving the general organization of a business based on the information supplied from an analysis of work using the Bedaux method' (Laloux 1950, 105). A 'trend chart' of how the business was working could thus be put in place.

According to a study conducted in Britain by the National Industrial Board (mentioned by Laloux 1950), there was on average a 50% increase in productivity in companies using the Bedaux method. It is, however, difficult to distinguish between the improvement in the productivity of the workers and the benefits of reorganisation. In financial terms, however, implementing the Bedaux system meant high operating costs. But Bedaux was not the only one to investigate the question of fatigue. In Britain, for example, many studies were undertaken by the 'Industrial Fatigue Research Board' alongside the trend for industrial psychology (Kreis 1990). For the critics of the Bedaux method, behind a technocratic process and a mask of scientific truth lay an arbitrary process, a coercive system for increasing productivity through the pace of work (Downs 2002; Montgomery 1987). That Bedaux 'discovered' the fundamental laws of fatigue, then hid behind the excuse of trade secrets so as not to justify his theories, is hardly convincing. His supposed laws were never the subject of explanations or publications by him (Kreis 1990), nor were they scientifically evaluated. Only his mysterious 'fatigue curve', determining the necessary recovery times, developed between 1911 and 1916,[23] was supposed to have been presented.[24] It is possible to imagine that it never existed. The scientific basis of the method must be treated with care: the measurements were made on elite workers, the research having been conducted on a reorganised activity, implying that older workers had been eliminated. According to Bedaux, the effort factors were independent of speed and work rate! What is more, these factors were identical for all individuals! Conceptually speaking, if rate '60B' is a scientific norm combining effort and rest and maintaining the balance of the individual, his '80B' rate implies that either the worker sacrifices some rest time, which is harmful to their well-being, or otherwise that the working methods had been improved, which should have been done before the system was put in place. We have here an internal contradiction between a pseudo-scientific norm and a system for increasing productivity (Littler 1982).

In spite of all the criticism it received, the method was widely disseminated even after the death of Bedaux. By the eve of the Second World War, Bedaux had opened offices in 22 countries and employed 400 engineers. The largest American (Kodak, Standard Oil, General Electric, etc.) and British companies (including Imperial Chemical Industries) used his method (Kreis 1990, 1992). Laloux (1950) estimates that, by 1937, 500 American, 225 British, 144 French, 49 Italian and 39 German firms had used the services of Bedaux. After the Second World War his method continued to circulate through his successors, who often used different names for their consultancy operations for commercial reasons. Later on, a new generation of methods for measuring time and remunerating according to output appeared, using more sophisticated techniques, breaking down the work tasks in the laboratory and not on the shop floor.[25] In parallel, American management methods appeared which took the 'human factor' much more into account (Boltanski 1982). The Bedaux method therefore seems to be a system for improving human output under the guise of a pseudo-scientific discourse on fatigue.

Technical and social dimensions of the criticism of the Bedaux system

The Bedaux system uses scientific language designed to show the rational nature of its measurement of effort. Bedaux engineers boast that they are neutral and that they were only the representatives of a science of organisation that was intended for the common good. But for its critics, the method conceals, behind a technocratic process and a mask of scientific truth, an arbitrary process, a coercive system for raising productivity by means of increasing the pace of work (Downs 2002, 417). Furthermore, according to Geerkens (2002, 2005), an analysis of the records of Belgian businesses having used the Bedaux system shows that the main reason for adopting it and its objectives were 'either to detect the numbers of workers in excess of the required numbers, or to impose extra efforts on workers without extra pay'.[26] Reorganisation was also used to de-skill certain positions.

According to Montgomery (1987), the Bedaux system generated overworking and fatigue wherever it was implemented. It was a complex system, particularly with regard to the effort factors. The American trade unions were hostile to the method, as were the British unions (Kreis 1990, 1992; Littler 1984). Implementation of the Bedaux system often gave rise to massive strikes, often lasting 30 to 60 days (Brown 1977; Whitston 1997). The name 'Bedaux' fell into such disrepute that the consultants of his companies were instructed to no longer use it and the terminology of the method was changed. For example the 'B' was replaced by the 'AM' or 'P' as in the USA. In 1937, according to the Congress of Industrial Organization union, it 'lived on worker's sweat', and Bedaux was 'the father of the most completely exhausting, inhuman "efficiency" system ever invented' (Flanner 1945, 22 September, 40). The American Federation of Labour added that it was 'indirect, cumbersome, and mystifying' (Flanner 1945, 22 September, 40). In Britain, in 1933, the Trades Union Congress declared that 'the workers were not receiving the whole fruits of their increased efforts' and 'the feeling that the human element is being mechanised; that pride of craftsmanship, quality of work, even health and comfort are being sacrificed to speed production' (quoted in Kreis 1990, 385). An article was also published in the *World Digest* in 1938 relating to C.E. Bedaux and his method entitled: 'Labor's Public Enemy No. 1'. In Belgium, during the strikes of 1936, while the Bedaux system was the best known and most widely used system of productivity organisation, its name bore all the rancour that had built up during the discontent over the attempts to introduce various measures by which to rationalise work. In Belgium, however, the productivist tradition of the large reformist unions and their culture of negotiation had generally enabled the Bedaux system to be introduced without any great opposition from the workers (Geerkens 2002, 121). In Italy, there was also some reticence on the part of the workers, but Mussolini imposed the involvement of both the workers' and employers' unions in putting the method in place (*Feuille d'informations corporatives* 1934, 1935; Antonelli, Boyns, and Cerbioni 2008, 57–9). In France, the method was met with hostility from the unions. The Bedaux method was disallowed by the Matignon agreements[27] but reappeared after 1938 as part of the rearmament policy.

These misgivings can be explained by the fact that the introduction of the Bedaux system meant that a minimum level of output, greater than the previous level, was required, for just about the same wages, and with constant control. For Bedaux, what used to happen before his system was put in place was not normal; previously, a Bedaux/hour output of 35 to 40 was observed. Under his system the minimum Bedaux wage corresponded to a Bedaux/hour of 60. Bedaux, however, only promised workers a wage increase of 15 to 20% if they increased their productivity (Kreis 1992). The labour force therefore hardly profited from the advantages gained by the company when they introduced the Bedaux system. The unions considered it to be a means of maximising the output of the workers to the detriment of their physical and mental health, de-skilling them and treating them like machines. They demanded that the basic wage rates for output-based wage rates should be 20 per cent higher than the previous time-based wage rates, thus claiming the full benefit afforded by the increased output.

The central aim of the Bedaux system was to share the productivity gains between the workers and the employers, yet the workers felt that the complexity of these wage-linked calculations was a means of tricking them (Brown 1977). Furthermore, for the workers and the junior management, the imposed rationalising of work implied that they would lose their autonomy and therefore part of their skills: indeed, the Bedaux system took away from the workers all control over the time they took to accomplish a task, and transferred this control to the employers (Downs 2002). When the method was introduced, apart from the many strikes, some of which were quite violent, it generated much hostility, or at best a lack of cooperation, which hampered its success.

The dissemination of scientific management in the interwar period

Control of the hours worked and measurement of the time spent on each task date back to the nineteenth century, in parallel to the increase in working hours forced on workers by employers. Labour and work, however, remained under the control of the workers, and were not yet under any pressure from the employers. It was only in the twentieth century, with the advent of scientific management, that the anticipation and normalisation of the time that was humanly necessary for accomplishing each task and the sequencing of operations between workstations in a chain appeared. There followed what Foucault (1975) called the discipline of corps in the factory, on the same lines as that used in the army. According to Simmel (1900), the objectivation of economic time as pure spatial time is a form of social domination that is as strong as it is impersonal and seems to be outside any social interaction. This scientific management was widely disseminated during the interwar period against a background of economic recession, aggravating even further the conflicts related to the just remuneration of work.

Our overview of the dissemination of scientific management will only examine the USA, Britain and France, as the other major industrial countries were less affected by the Bedaux system, and many were in the throes of a totalitarian regime with its particular type of social relations. In the USA, at the time of Taylor's death in 1915, it has been suggested that as many as 200 companies had adopted scientific management (Nelson 1992a), but a more recent survey has suggested that this is a gross over-estimate (Fleischman 2000, 605). After the death of Taylor in 1915, his followers broke up into separate groups. However, scientific management was given a boost with the decision of the United States to go to war in 1917, since the war effort implied having to cooperate with the unions and meet the demands of the workers via collective bargaining (Nelson 1984). After the war and before the slump of 1929, Taylorism continued to spread, thus enabling the restrictive effects of labour scarcity within the expanding American economy to be at least partly offset (Nelson 1992b).

According to Nelson (1992b), outside the USA, it was in France that the scientific management movement enjoyed the most success. It was the engineers that set about disseminating Taylor's ideas from 1906 (Fridenson 1987; Moutet 1978, 1984, 1985, 1992, 1997), a fact that can possibly be explained by their possession of a technique that only they knew how to use. Scientific management became a means by which engineers could assert their power within the company (Moutet 1985), particularly in relation to the sales and finance staff (Fridenson 1987), and through which to justify their corporatist claims in the struggle to limit access to the engineering profession in France.[28] There were few applications of scientific management in France before 1910. After this date, it became more widely used, for example at Panhard and Levassor, Michelin and Renault. The First World War generated a need for increased production, there being a lack of skilled workers owing to those called up for service having been replaced by women and unskilled workers. This need to increase output made the introduction of scientific management necessary. In the face of the German threat, the *union sacrée*[29] was formed (between left and right, employers and workers) and time-keeping, in which Le Chatelier[30] and Albert Thomas[31] played an important part, was introduced with little opposition.

Taylorism continued to spread in France after the First World War. The unions tried to slow the movement down, although some unionists were, however, convinced that Taylorism could be a motor for progress. They tried to reconcile their condemnation of worker exploitation with their convictions that productivism could sometimes benefit the workers, providing that they had some control over the sharing of these benefits. In parallel, the multiplication of consultancies such as those of C.B. Thompson, Planus, Wallace Clark and Bedaux (Kipping 1997, 1999; Henry 1993;

Moutet 1985) and the setting up in 1926 of CNOF, the *comité national de l'organization française* (French national committee for organisation) demonstrated the craze for rationalisation. However, this movement died down after the Great Depression. There was conflict between the engineers, eager for economic rationality and social recognition, and the employers, who criticised Taylorism for its bureaucratic, or even socialist, nature and the cost and time it took to put the method in place.

There was a comparable movement in Britain, where piece-work was widespread before the First World War. After the war, Taylorism gradually developed owing to the economic slump. To combat its effects, employers turned to bonus wage systems (Littler 1982, 1984; Boyns and Matthews 2001; Smith and Boyns 2005).

Confronted with economic recession, business leaders, especially in Europe, sought to reduce their costs without investing in mechanisation or in complex reorganisations. The Taylor system could only be efficient, however, if the organisation actually enabled the workers to increase their productivity. Fearful of increased overheads owing to the number of unproductive staff and the time needed for reorganising (Moutet 1985), employers responded to the recession, particularly in those sectors having reached a stage of maturity, by reducing wages by means of a system of timed bonus-based wages as in the Bedaux system.[32] In order to meet the demands of factory owners, some consultants took the opposite approach to that advocated by Taylor and his early disciples: 'determine the basis of the wage system, the task, before improving working conditions' (Moutet 1985, 94). All that was retained from the concept of scientific management and Taylorism was the timing of tasks and the introduction of a time- and bonus-based wage system. The Bedaux system, although it had benefited from the scientific management trend, was one of the systems most suited to meet this demand.[33] According to Danty-Lafrance (1957), this system was the successor of bonus-based wages used for many years in industry. Backed up by its 'pseudo-scientific' basis, its success was more due to the exceptional selling talents of its designer. This commercial competence meant the Bedaux system was the most widely used output-based wage system between the two world wars.

Having thus learnt something about the consultant and businessman side of Bedaux, an avid supporter of scientific management who successfully disseminated his own method, it is also the case, though of less interest to us, that he was a frivolous society animal who courted controversial relationships. According to some, there was a third dimension to this man, that of a generous Utopian wishing to put his 'science' to the common good. It is this aspect of Bedaux's character that we will now explore.

The Utopia of Bedaux: equivalism

In order to understand Bedaux's concept of Utopia, it is first of all necessary to present the political, social and economic context of the period between the wars. We must also indicate the possibility that Bedaux, the Utopian, passed down his ideas to his son, although as far as we know the latter never made any reference to them. We will then examine his Utopia and its supposed implementation in Roquefort des Landes, in the south-west of France.

The background

The interwar period was particularly marked by monetary disorders following the First World War and by the heightening of ideological and political debate following the Russian revolution. Both of these were to have a particularly strong impact on the stance taken by Bedaux.

The First World War had been very costly for all involved, and it became essential after the war to address the problems created by the large increases in liquidity that had occurred in order to pay for the war effort and to reduce the debt burden of the allied European nations, particularly towards the USA. The massive issue of money that had occurred during the war generated a monetary crisis, a gold embargo, an enforced exchange rate and controlled prices designed to reduce inflation in Europe, especially in Germany and the Eastern bloc. In spite of the latter measure, inflation was rife everywhere and even worsened after 1918. All the European currencies were devalued at the end of the war, but the situations in Germany and Russia were particularly devastating. These disorders generated deep feelings of injustice and were the inspiration for Utopian systems that allowed money to be done away with. Somewhat surprisingly, these ideas were being voiced both in Western Europe and in Soviet Russia.

We can easily understand that the attempts to find solutions to the problem of inflation, no matter how radical and lacking in credibility they may have been, were given much attention by all observers of the economic situation. In his project for economic organisation, Bedaux made a reference to the attempt to replace money with an equivalent in hours of work, as had been envisaged in the Soviet Union in 1920 and 1921.

The First World War, the early days of the Russian revolution and the Wall Street crash of 1929 gave credit to the idea that capitalism had failed: some doubted a system that had not been able to prevent war and misery, while others were convinced that it was the direct cause of these ills. These were the ideas circulating in the West, while a new model of production organisation was being developed in the Soviet Union. The search for a third way was naturally one of the preoccupations of all those who, in Europe, were exploring the question of organising economic activity and its social dimension.

Bedaux's son summed up the position of his father: 'A handful of our old industrial engineers who worked with our founder [i.e. his father] on the principles jokingly referred to Equivalism as the 'ism' to end all 'isms' – Socialism, Capitalism, Communism and defeatism' (Christy 1984, 300). It is highly unlikely that these 'old industrial engineers' would have heard about 'equivalism', but this is of little importance to us.

The debates about the just remuneration of work had begun in the nineteenth century, at the same time as the struggle to appropriate labour time with the arrival of a new type of capitalist, who could have been defined as 'someone who has the monetary means to command and appropriate the time of others on a large scale and reduce this time to an abstract evaluation, while striving to increase productivity' (Zarifian 1997, 110). Apart from Marx (1950), among those politicians who wanted to protest against this situation, we may cite the so-called 'idealist' or 'Utopian' socialist thinkers of the nineteenth century. With regard to the just remuneration of work, the ideas of Bedaux owe much to the French Utopian Socialists: Saint Simon (1760–1825), Cabet (1788–1856), Fourrier (1772–1837) and Proudhon (1802–64), to whom we can add the Englishman, Owen (1771–1858), and the German, Rodbertus (1805–75). Their aim was to build a better society. The practical impact of these ideas never got past the scale of small communities, which gave them their reputation as Utopians. We can find some of these authors' ideas in Bedaux, particularly in his wish to replace money with a work equivalent and in his rejection of mercantilism.

This issue, a major preoccupation in the nineteenth century owing to its connection with the misery of the working classes, reappeared in the 1930s with the economic depression. We find it reflected in the ideas of Bedaux in different forms: criticism of shopkeepers and other parasites, rewarding hard work and talent, valued in the same way as capital; the regulation of the economy by an elite[34] and not by capitalists; and a money-free bartering system, rendering to the workers all the fruits of their labour. What Bedaux added was a solution for measuring 'complex' work which was incorporated in the value of the goods produced.

To this picture we need to add three proposals from idealist socialists, also found in Bedaux's discourse: first of all the payment of a guaranteed minimum wage even when unemployed;[35] second, the importance of training the workers;[36] and finally, a new system of ownership rights.

All of these ideas relating to the distribution of wealth sanction the precedence of an individual's abilities over his social origins. We can perceive here the bitterness of a Saint Simon or Fourrier, a nobleman or petit bourgeois ruined by the French revolution, or that of a Proudhon or a Cabet, self-made men and the sons of craftsmen, all of whom struggled to achieve their ambitions through lack of funds, while nevertheless considering themselves among the most competent assets to the nation.[37] We can also perceive the recollections of the self-taught, fortuneless Bedaux who found it difficult to accept these handicaps.

Apart from the notes that Bedaux dictated to his secretary in 1944 as part of his defence in preparation for his trial after having been deported to the US (see above), Bedaux's ideas have only been passed down to us indirectly through the accounts of some of his workers and those who were close to him, particularly his son, Charles Emile Bedaux. Most of his biographers have taken these accounts at face value, particularly the manuscript written by Charles Emile from the notes he was supposed to have taken during the long conversations he had with his father when they were held prisoner in North Africa in 1943 (see above). One edition of the first version of this manuscript (which was regularly amended by Charles Emile Bedaux until his death) was found in his personal belongings after his suicide, which led Flanner to believe that it was his own. We adopt a more cautious approach on the authorship of the content of the manuscript (we have had the opportunity to consult an example in private archives). We suspect that Charles Emile, obsessed by this theory, adopted it without verifying if it was true and somewhat embellished it as a means of trying to boost the image of his father, who had been the subject of much criticism after the liberation. We present evidence of such a distortion of reality, at least with respect to the Roquefort experiment (see below).

According to some of his biographers, Bedaux wanted to put the theoretical basis of his management method to the purpose of reorganising society. After having presented his sources of inspiration, we will now examine his ideas on a new society and his supposed attempt at a practical implementation of them. The sources that we have used are particularly tenuous. They are mainly biographies written by authors, none of whom have a background in history (they do not give their sources) and of whom only two actually met Bedaux. These biographers mainly base their facts on accounts by those who knew him. It is therefore solely for the sake of simplicity of style that we will systematically use the term 'supposed to'.

Equivalism outlined

After the stock market crash in 1929, Bedaux apparently imagined an economy based on a unit of human energy. This was to have been the culmination of his life's work. After developing his method of measuring human work, the Bedaux point (the 'Bex') in 1916, in the early 1940s he devised a new way of organising society: 'equivalism'.

The lynch-pin of Bedaux's concept is the Bex, or the theory of the value of work revisited. His followers gave his theory the name of 'equivalism'[38] because, in Bedaux's opinion, most economic exchanges are just about value equivalences. When applied at the level of a nation, this theory envisaged a system of remuneration according to output, using as a measure the cost of any human activity in 'units of human effort'. Bedaux thought that he could thus determine the economic value controlling the cost of goods and services consumed. He referred to Adam Smith, for whom the wealth of a nation is what is produced by its workers or what is purchased from the production of other nations. According to him, it is habitually money that serves as an intermediary for work and goods, but the value of money can be determined at any time by the quantity of physical, or even intellectual, human energy it can buy. The laws of supply and demand could make the price differ from the value in terms of human effort, but this occurs rarely on a large scale or over a long period of time. In fact, when the price of a product rises, production rises, and when there is a price drop, more profitable goods are made in their place. Monopolies can also divert prices from their value in terms of human effort, but in 'equivalism' monopolies and large inherited estates would be banished.

The cost of production measured in units of human energy could therefore determine the price of consumer goods, which would be based on work. Thus, if this theory called 'equivalism' was in use, all activities producing goods and services would have an economic value equivalent to the quantity of human energy deployed. The measurement of human activity, whether mental or physical, would then become a reference value which would serve as a basis for exchange, thus eliminating commercial speculation. The unit of measurement was given the name 'Bex' with the unit symbol 'B', invariable in the plural, written with a tail like that which distinguishes a Q. According to Bedaux, the Bex is defined as 'one minute of normal human effort including a rest time. The proportion of rest time to be linked to the degree of effort required is that of a man having no specific qualification other than the normal intelligence of the human race' (as quoted in Christy 1984, 228). It is a different definition to that of the 'B' (Bedaux point), but is merely an extension of it in that the Bex measured the production of a physical or mental effort. The issue of the weaknesses of the Bedaux system regarding the subjective evaluation of what is an average normal man and mental effort for intellectual activities still remains to be tackled. According to Bedaux, this problem could be easily solved. If creative work could not be directly measured, Bedaux engineers, with their great experience in judging and estimating competence in most types of business, had developed methods for awarding incentives based on the intensity of the effort and qualification of workstations that were used successfully everywhere, and they claimed never to have found a profession to which their methods could not be applied.

Bedaux's social project was an attempt to reconcile the working class with scientific management. Not only does he borrow Taylor's ideas according to which 'prosperity is associated with improving productivity' (Taylor 1912, 10), but also proposes to calculate wages according to a just base, incorporating the theory of the value of work.

Like many Utopians, he only envisaged the long term application of his project after a long period of transition. To begin to familiarise the population with his methods, he proposed to indicate on the product both the price and equivalent units of human energy expended to make it (Christy 1984, 315). It is on the strength of this project that some considered that he wanted to establish a link between fascism and scientific management (quoted in Littler 1982, 106). According to Christy (1984, 228), Bedaux proposed his theory of 'equivalism' to the Nazi regime, but Dr Hjalmar Schacht[39] was opposed to it. Later, in 1941, he tried to develop an ideal town in Roquefort des Landes, a sort of social laboratory for his ideas.

In the main, however, we only know of Bedaux's generous ideas and hypothetical intentions to apply them from what he is supposed to have confided to his son when he was 56 years old, in prison and just about ruined financially, and to his secretary when preparing his defence. However, there has survived (private archives) a document quoting the speeches made by Bedaux's colleagues on the occasion of the Silver Foundation Anniversary of the first of Bedaux's companies.

At the meeting held in Paris on 11 October 1941, Jean Caudron, Director of the Bedaux (France) Company, spoke of the BM unit devised by Bedaux which could be used to measure all sorts of activity. It should also be pointed out that one of the chapters of Bedaux's book was entitled *Du bien être social* (*On social well-being*).

The supposed attempts at setting up a 'social laboratory' in Roquefort

An initial, perhaps over ambitious, attempt is said to have been made to implement Bedaux's Utopian system by signing an agreement with the Greek authorities to apply the Bedaux system to the whole of Greece. The Second World War supposedly prevented the plan from going ahead. It is his second attempt, this time limited to a small French town, Roquefort, in the Landes region, which appears to have been more complete both in terms of time and ideas. However, in the introduction of the manuscript by Bedaux's son (private archives), published as an appendix to Christy's work (1984, 300–19), only general remarks about 'equivalism' are made. There is no mention of the experiment in Roquefort des Landes, even though this manuscript was written in 1943, that is to say, after the experiment is supposed to have taken place. The answer to this paradox can be found in later letters (letter from Charles Emile Bedaux to Gaston Bedaux and Marcel Grolleau dated 30 November 1976; letter from Charles Emile Bedaux to Gaston Bedaux dated 7 November 1978; private archives) in which Charles Emile asked for details of the experiment of which he had heard. In chapter 17 of his book, Christy (1984, 228–9) refers to accounts given by Marcel Grolleau, who participated in the experiment, and also to the US Department of Justice archives where a copy of the notes dictated to his secretary in 1944 can be found (see above):

> The people of Roquefort embraced the experiment whole-heartedly. After several town meetings, the actual work got underway; the day it did, the severe unemployment that had kept the area depressed came to an end. As well, half the employed people joined in the new project, many of them having worked at jobs that were now unnecessary.

However, Flanner (1945, 6 October, 41) speaks of the experiment in the conditional tense, but does not go into any details about its implementation. She may have known about the experiment from people who had not participated in it but, above all, she was aware of the dictated notes (see above) and the statement of the interrogation of Bedaux during his captivity in the USA.

According to these sources, Bedaux was supposed to have envisaged a large-scale human experiment. He wanted to set up a harmonious and prosperous community which would serve as a model for post-war reconstruction in France, Europe and the world. The best way of proving his ideas was, according to him, to put them into practice in a small community[40] where all trades were represented. In 1941 he was said to have suggested to Marshal Pétain that his idea be tested in France. Bedaux claimed that the old Vichy France leader had not understood much about the system[41] but had given it an excellent assessment and gave his agreement, on condition that the population of the chosen community were also in agreement. He chose Roquefort, a small French town with a population of 2200 in the Landes department, 100 km north of Bayonne. It is important to note that this town was in the zone occupied by the Germans, just on the edge of the demarcation line. It had a 'perfect economic system', operating in a limited geographical zone made up of agriculture, craftsmen, tradesmen, sheep breeders and an intellectual elite. According to Bedaux, many painters and writers had been attracted by the beauty of the place. He had discovered this small town when the Bedaux company was setting up its system at the Société des Papeteries de Roquefort. The population were apparently in agreement. Bedaux had gone to Roquefort with engineers Marcel Grolleau, Jean Valdaron, Fernand Dujardin and Jean Caudron, the chairman of the French Bedaux company, in order to perfect his theory of 'equivalism'. They all stayed in a luxury villa placed at their disposal by the Société des Papeteries de Roquefort[42] in Lencouacq, a tiny village near to Roquefort. From March 1941 until the attack on Pearl Harbor on 7 December 1941, the period during which the experiment was conducted, this place was both the HQ for the setting up of the Bedaux system in the paper mill and a centre of reflection on 'equivalism'.[43] It was impossible for Bedaux to remain in Roquefort, being taken up as usual with other projects. However, with the exception of two trips to North Africa in the summer of 1941, Bedaux returned there regularly until he left to settle permanently in Algeria. He had no trouble with the German authorities who, when informed about the project, sent some officers to the town. When Bedaux explained his intentions, they considered that he was no danger to them. Whilst at Roquefort, he also considered a project to commercialise the use of 'Brandes' as a fuel for automobiles. 'Brandes' is a form of parasitic heather which, capable of growing to a height of 15 feet, is to be found underneath the canopy of pine trees on the sandy soil of the Landes region. According to Bedaux, this heather was capable of absorbing the oil contained in the soil, making it highly inflammable and a potential fuel source.[44]

As for the social experiment in Roquefort des Landes, it has remained quite unknown to the rest of the world and even in the town of Roquefort itself. It would be more circumspect to speak of an imagined experiment. When we visited Roquefort in the autumn of 2004, we met Georgette Laporte, a retired primary school teacher and local historian, who introduced us to five ex-employees of the paper mill who had been working there at the time of the supposed Bedaux experiment in 1941. They all remember the visit by Bedaux engineers and by Bedaux himself, as well as the introduction of the Bedaux system of remuneration[45] in the Roquefort paper mill. Located in the occupied zone, this company worked mainly for Germany. With low productivity and many workers still being kept prisoner in Germany or having been called up for *Service du Travail Obligatoire* (Compulsory Labour Service),[46] it was urgent for the Germans to improve

Figure 1. A discussion on 'equivalism'? Bedaux (on the right) and his son (on the left) with an unidentified third person (centre) during their detention in Algeria in 1943.

productivity, and the Bedaux method seemed to be a solution to this.[47] That it was effectively put in place is supported by the accounts given by ex-employees. None of them, however, remembers a social project of any sort. Only one of them, employed in the offices, heard the Bedaux engineers speak of a study on the operationalising of the measurement of qualification of the various jobs (including housework) performed in the town. This can be qualified by Charles Emile's letters to Gaston between the 12 March 1976 and 26 January 1977 (private archives) in which he thanks Gaston for the engineers' notes (especially those of Grolleau and Valdaron) concerning their studies into equivalism at Roquefort and the corrections made by Bedaux. The notes suggest merely the conducting of theoretical research, especially on the part of Grolleau, whose study focused on the domain of wood within 'equivalism'. Such a study, however, was too remote to form the basis of support for any claim relating to a social experiment. The latter was never mentioned in either the manuscript or letters of Charles Emile; Gaston Bedaux, in a letter to Charles Emile dated 19 September 1978 (private archives), asks for information concerning the notes written by Bedaux during the Roquefort experiment which were found in his archives. Despite having gone to Roquefort with his brother, he had never heard talk of this social experiment during his stay there.

Discussion: the ambiguous motives of an individual and his biographers

We may consider the Bedaux method (the one that he actually put in place in businesses) from two standpoints. It is firstly an idea, an intellectual creation by its author, and secondly an accumulation of the individual accounts of its applications. If we wish to approach his method from the first standpoint, we soon find ourselves limited to what the author says about it. It is a common fact that one can never be certain of what an author really thinks, and it is very risky to rely simply on what he says. Indeed 'any discourse, even if it claims to be scientific, is produced in the context of a project pursued by the subject' (Guerin 1998, 105). This is particularly true of those who seek to convince rather than to prove, and of consultants in particular. All the evidence concurs to make us believe that Bedaux was above all a salesman and that, in this respect, he effectively sought to convince rather than to prove. He apparently had some vague convictions, such as summed up by Flanner (1945, 6 October, 39):

> He has always had the grandiose notion – compound of humbuggery, sincerity, lack of culture, impatience with mankind's stupidity, and a profound belief in the Bedaux system – that production organized by his methods could do away with poverty; that an efficient society could come only from a revolution on the right, led by people, preferably engineers, who knew how to run things.

But these convictions never went further than simple discourse, addressed solely to those who were prepared to listen to him.

Furthermore, an author never has total control of his ideas once they begin to be disseminated and used by others. As soon as a new management technique is launched in a company, it is 'regurgitated' by those who use it to the point where it can become unrecognisable. In most cases, wide distribution of such innovations is the result of mutual interests, conflicts or compromises between different stakeholders having varying interests and varying levels of involvement in them (Calon 1989; Latour 1987). Each individual only retains (and considers) the part relating to his or her own interests. The Bedaux method may therefore be considered as simply an accumulation of individual experiences of its application, independent from the author's intentions, whether supposed or real. It has thus survived, up to the present day, as a method of organising salaried work, and has been subjected to the influences of those applying it in very different contexts. It can subsist or be reborn as the eternal management dilemma: auto-organisation versus discipline. It is thus that we can today[48] speak of a 'new form of Taylorism', 'arising from such principles as total quality, zero stocks and lean manufacturing' and found in the work organisation of supermarket checkout operators, call centre personnel or waiters in fast food restaurants.

Bedaux modelled himself on Taylor, and it is tempting to draw comparisons between the two men. Studies of Taylor's writings by different researchers (Aktouf 1990; Butler 1991; Centlivre-Petit and Journé 1996; de Montmollin 1974; Guerin 1998; Hatchuel 1995; Pouget 1998; Rouzé 1993) show that the father of the 'scientific organization of labour' was perhaps misunderstood and misread on the one hand, and that his social project was given little recognition on the other. In fact, Taylor's system of remuneration according to output created a link between the factory floor and the common good on the basis of scientific standards. According to Rouzé (1993), Taylor's works are the expression of an essentially liberal democratic project, with a strictly technocratic and managerial content. Hatchuel (1994, 1995), however, differentiates between three levels of interest with Taylor: the expert; the theoretician in *Shop Management*, published in 1903; and the doctrinarian in *The Principles of Scientific Management*, published in 1911. According to Centlivre-Petit and Journé (1996), hiding behind a series of cold and scientific statements, Taylor was actually a committed Utopian. They credit him with a project for a true Utopia, a better world, that is more efficient and more just, based on science and social harmony: 'the organization of labour can be summed up thus: science instead of empiricism, harmony instead of discord, cooperation instead of individualism, maximum output instead of reduced production, training each worker to achieve maximum output and prosperity' (Taylor 1911). This lack of knowledge of Taylor's social ideas had already been exposed in the early twentieth century by Le Chatelier (1915) and Danty Lafrance (1957), and even by Pouget (1914), a revolutionary unionist who, when speaking of French employers, declared that: 'most of them have crudely imitated his ideas: they were attracted by the advantages they hoped to reap from the study of labour time and contented themselves with imposing time-keeping in their factories'. According to Aktouf (1990, 60), 'all that management took from Taylor was what helped them to make the cake bigger, but virtually nothing that would have helped them to reduce the damage done, or share the cake more fairly, of which Taylor was fully aware'. The same applies to those engineers who used his ideas to achieve their own aims, that is, to play a role in the economic and social organisation of labour. They only kept the practical aspects without the ideology. Taylor himself was an obsessive perfectionist, to the point of being an 'obsessive neurotic often given to melancholy, bitterness and despair over the lack of understanding and scepticism with which his ideas were met' (Kakar 1970, 156). He lacked a natural ability for rhetoric according to Copley (1923), his official biographer. He was also a consultant who had to sell his ideas to company managers looking for fast results and reduced overheads (Fridenson 1987; Moutet 1975; Nelson 1984). He needed to convince, simplify, summarise, reassure and dispel objections and criticism. He had had to seek allies and bend to their demands. He said himself, before the US House of Representatives, that 'both of these books were written with a view to presenting them to the American Society of Mechanical Engineers (ASME). And the ASME is probably the most demanding organization in terms of the brevity with which writings have to be presented' (Taylor 1912, 208). It was only in 1901 that he withdrew from public life and devoted himself wholly to disseminating his works. After making his fortune, he became an indefatigable traveller both in the USA and Europe. A propagandist, he had to confront many different audiences. Chairman of ASME from 1905 to 1906, Taylor then became more ambitious and more of a doctrinarian.

Can the same be said of Bedaux? He was also a supporter of scientific management organisation. Like Taylor, he began as a worker, and the last chapter of his book (Bedaux 1917) was devoted to social welfare. He also defends the idea of a better technocratic world, where scientific management would allow each worker to be assigned to jobs in keeping with their abilities and which would enable them to improve their standard of living. With Bedaux we are also confronted with two very clear-cut opinions: the many applications of his method have damned him in the eyes of the humanists, while his biographers ascribe to him a wish to build a better world. The file of evidence against him is, however, very thick. He always showed goodwill and allegiance to company owners, that is, his clients and relations, but never showed any compassion towards the workers who he invited unrelentingly to work harder.

As regards 'equivalism', it was not a completely new idea: Bedaux simply unearthed some old romantic socialist ideas, dressing them up as a method of remuneration according to output. If he had any social projects, he only revealed them later on in his life, only to his family and to certain close friends and colleagues. He had already become a very rich man with an international reputation, a personality introduced into political circles, described by his biographers as a smooth talker and a charmer.

It therefore seems highly likely to us that the social aspect of his work was simply an alibi for Bedaux, designed to redeem him in the eyes of his close friends and family and posterity, or even to show another side to his character in view of the legal proceedings that awaited him on his transfer to the USA. In one of his statements during his interrogations in the USA in 1944 (private archives), Bedaux declared that the experiment on 'equivalism' and the extraction of heather roots in Roquefort des Landes (see above) had been two of his five main occupations between 1940 and 1943. For those who knew him, 'equivalism' could have also been a way of reinstating Bedaux, and we can understand that they were happy to believe his declarations. As for his biographers, and in particular his contemporary, Flanner, and Jim Christy, they were probably taken in by the romantic side of Bedaux. How could one fail to be impressed, if one were a journalist and not a scientist, by both the sportsman (the croisière blanche[49]) and the society status of a 'French charmer' who was also supposed to be a spy working for the Germans against the USA? For newspaper readers, and therefore for journalists, Bedaux was a personality that 'sold well'.

So what is our conclusion? Was it a sincere Utopia or a clever public relations operation on the part of Bedaux, taken at face value and romanticised by his friends and biographers? Both solutions are not incompatible where a complex person such as Bedaux is concerned, yet the second seems nevertheless more plausible. Flanner (1945, 22 September, 30) can be quoted in support of this contention:

> His genius was his promoter's faculty for making men want to believe what he said. He had a demagogic gift for convincing hard-headed businessmen that they were public benefactors, as he essentially believed he was himself. When some big millionaire Scrooge in Chicago would frankly say that he was interested only in profits, Bedaux would tell him that he, the poor millionaire, was really interested in bettering man's conditions, Illinois world. The triple miracle of making the Scrooge believe this, buy the Bedaux system, and actually start bettering something besides his bank account was an accomplishment Bedaux pulled off so often that he dazed and silenced even his most critical employees.

Acknowledgements

The authors would like to gratefully thank the *Association Francophone de Comptabilité* for the grant which was given in order to enable this paper to be translated. We are also grateful for their comments to the referees and to participants at the following conferences: 11th World Congress of Accounting Historians, Nantes, 2006; 18th Annual Accounting, Business & Financial History Conference, Cardiff Business School, 2006; and 12th journées d'Histoire de la Comptabilité et du Management, Lille, 2007.

Notes

1. Practically, the only accessible archives concerning Bedaux are those held by the US Minister of Justice. Regarding his professional career, archives located at the Business Office of INCUCON Management Consultants Ltd in West Sussex, England, have been used by Littler (1982) and Kreis (1990). Other archives – both personal and professional – can be consulted: those held by the heirs of his second wife (Fern Bedaux): his two nieces (Elizabeth Hanley and Aletha Hext Martin in England) and above all, in France, heirs of Herbert Bigelow, Fern's estate manager and confident, and the heirs of Gaston Bedaux, Bedaux's brother, living in France. However, these archives are private and extremely difficult to access due to the great age of those concerned.
2. There are many witness reports given by workers in factories using the Bedaux method (Anonymous 1936; Kreis 1992; Geerkens 2005). The interest of this particular factory is that Bedaux implemented his equivalism here (see below).
3. A film directed by George Ungar in 1995 entitled 'The Champagne Safari' is a documentary on the expedition of Bedaux in Alaska and of his life using data from the book written by Christy (1984).
4. Entitled 'Equivalism', 'Equivalism II' and 'Equivalism III' respectively.
5. In a letter addressed to his uncle Gaston Bedaux and Marcel Grolleau dated 30 November 1976 (private archives), Bedaux's son, Charles Emile, claimed to have met Janet Flanner following the publication of her articles. She confided in him that they were written on the demand of the US Justice Department, whose archives were accessed, including the manuscript by Charles Emile on equivalism. In this same letter, Charles Emile accused her of attributing the BEX to his father instead of to himself.
6. Bedaux's family holds to the belief that he committed suicide because he felt that, if he were put on trial before the end of the war, he would not be able to defend himself without endangering the lives of his wife, family and workers who had stayed behind in occupied France. He was much in love with his wife, unable to bear their separation due to his imprisonment, and committed suicide on St. Valentine's Day.
7. Less than 3% of the entire text, found on page 41 in the second article.
8. The Brook Farm experiment involved setting up a commune based on the model of the Utopian Socialist Charles Fourier (1772–1837), and lasted from 1841 to 1847. The tone of her writing gives the impression that Flanner simply recorded the enthusiastic intentions of Bedaux without really believing them herself.
9. To clearly underline the differences with his brother Gaston, Flanner (1945, 6 October, 43), qualifies the latter as follows: 'highly educated, respectable, stay-at-home, state functionary brother Gaston'.
10. The text is preceded by the following words: 'This is an introduction by Charles Emile Bedaux to the theory of Equivalism which he had been developing since the talks with his father at El Biar in 1943, and which he has explained elsewhere in book length'.
11. According to George Woodcock: http://www.abcbookworld.com
12. http://www.culture.gouv.fr/documentation/leonore/pres.htm
13. The château was also the scene, in 1937, of the marriage ceremony of the recently abdicated king of England, Edward VIII, and his twice divorced American bride.
14. See, for example, the paper delivered by Eric Geerkens at the 127th National Congress of Historical and Scientific Societies (Nancy, 16 April 2002), entitled 'The implementation of the Bedaux system in Belgian industry in the 1930s'. For applications of the system in Britain and in the USA, see also Kreis (1992) and Downs (1995). For applications in France, see Kourchid (1991, 1994).
15. According to Christy (1984) he might have become part of the troubled Paris nightlife.
16. According to Henry (1993, 38), Morrini was American, whereas Kreis (1992) says he had Italian nationality.
17. Harrington Emerson was himself a disciple of Taylor before becoming his adversary. He is, amongst other works, the author of *Efficiency as a Basis for Operation and Wages* (1909) and *The Twelve Principles of Efficiency* (1912).
18. Duez was an Arts et Métiers engineer who had set himself up as a consultant. Bedaux and Duez had been schoolmates. He later became his brother-in-law and set up the first Bedaux company in France.
19. According to Kreis (1992, 161), this is a practical manual in which we can see the influence of Taylor and Emerson.
20. C.E Bedaux was in Northern African when the Americans arrived on the 8 December 1942. He was working on a big pipeline project which would have allowed the transportation of peanut oil, which Occupied France needed desperately, from the Niger to Algeria. The Niger and Algeria were French colonies at this time and still under the power of the Vichy Government.
21. El-Biar is on the outskirts of Algiers.
22. Our description of the Bedaux method is based on first-hand accounts given by engineers who used the method (see, among others, Anonymous 1936) and the literature dealing with it, in particular Laloux (1950).
23. See Bedaux (1928, 1932).

24. According to Kreis (1990, 271), no traces of this famous curve linking effort and fatigue (and, therefore, rest) have been found, even though this curve was central to his system.
25. Such as, for example, the TMM (Time Measurement Method).
26. Quote taken from an abstract published at http://www.cths.fr/4DACTION/http://www_con_communic/882
27. Agreement between the government and the unions after the strikes of 1936. These agreements included the introduction of paid holidays (two weeks) and a working week limited to 40 hours.
28. The law of 10 July 1934 regulated the awarding of engineering diplomas.
29. The 'Union sacrée' was a consolidating movement which united the French of all beliefs (both political and religious) during the hardship of the First World War.
30. Henry Le Chatelier, *polytechnique*-educated and founder of the *Revue de la métallurgie*, was, from 1906, the unrelenting disseminator of Taylorism, and translated and published most of Taylor's writings. We may also cite Charles de Fréminville, educated at the prestigious *Ecole Centrale*, and Georges de Ram, an engineer with Renault.
31. Socialist minister for armament during the First World War.
32. For a presentation of the different systems of remuneration, see Danty-Lafrance (1957), Mottez (1966) and Shimmin (1959).
33. Smith and Boyns (2005) describe the Bedaux system as a 'bastardised' version of Taylorism, favoured in Britain because it could be easily bolted on to existing organisational structures without requiring the need for large expenditure on making changes thereto.
34. The idea proposed by Bedaux of regulating the economy through the banks, which is simply an illustration of the predominance of talent over social origin, can also be found in Saint Simon. According to the latter, the banks have to play an essential role in the economy by organising the system for sharing the means of production. They grant loans to factory owners on the grounds that they have the ability to generate a profit from them.
35. This can be found in Fourrier and in Proudhon, in the form of a right to work.
36. Owen, for example, imposed a paid training time on his workers at New Lanark during their working hours.
37. According to Christy (1984, 19) on arriving in the US in 1906, Bedaux was acquainted with the anarchist movements helping to distribute their publications. This was when he read Marx, Engels, Thorsten and Proudhon.
38. As Bedaux himself did not publish anything on this subject, we only know this term through the biography written by his brother Gaston and the manuscript of Bedaux's son (Charles Émile).
39. Ex-chairman of the *Reichsbank*, then Minister of the Economy of the Nazi government. He fell into disgrace for criticising Nazi policy towards the Jews.
40. The idea of a small community reflects a tradition with all Utopists: the phalanstery of Charles Fourier counted 1600 people and Robert Owen left in 1825 for New Harmony (Indiana, USA) with 800 people (Harrison 1969). Another experiment also deserves to be mentioned, on account of its great impact in the USA, where Fourier's ideas had been introduced in 1840: Brook Farm or 'the Port-Royal of American transcendentalism' (Desroche 1975). Ten or so families were part of this community, but insufficient farming know-how and resources, philosophical dissention and the fire of the phalanstery in March 1846 put end to this project. This experiment was likely to be known to Bedaux, whose second wife (Fern) was an American from the liberal society of the east coast.
41. 'The old marshal can repeat your words and reformulate them without having understood anything' is what Bedaux was supposed to have said (quoted in Flanner 1945, 6 October, 41).
42. Not rented from an Englishwoman as it is often said in his biographies.
43. The French Bedaux company had developed 30 factors (physical fitness, environment, education, experience, ability, talent, risk, responsibility, etc.) on the basis of which they built a scale of qualification of human activity for all types of professional people; doctors, lawyers, shopkeepers, company owners, etc. Each engineer was allotted two or three of these, and charts and graphs were produced for each factor, enabling the factor to be measured.
44. Research engineers of the National Institute of the Agronomic Research (INRA) have been unable to scientifically prove this idea of Bedaux. Although oil has been exploited at Parentis, some 80 km from Roquefort, various prospecting activities conducted in Roquefort have yielded nothing.
45. At present, over 60 years after this happened and over 20 years after the company closed down, the Bedaux system still remains a taboo subject for many. Although the system was implemented for a very short time, it generated such friction amongst the employees that the scars have still not healed.
46. Many French workers, among the most highly skilled, were forced to go to work in Germany.
47. In fact, this method, imported by 'foreigners', was in complete opposition to the paternalist management system used in paper mills and employed with a rural labour force. The system was abandoned after just a few years.
48. Dossier in the newspaper *Le Monde Initiatives*, no. 17, published in March 2003, pages 1 and 12.

49. The Croisière blanche (July–October 1934) was the fourth car rally organised by André Citroën, instigated by Bedaux following the success of the Croisière noire and the Croisière jaune. Bedaux ran with five latest model Citroën-Kégresse to cross north-west Canada from Edmonton. The expedition was a failure.

References

Aktouf, O. 1990. *Le management entre tradition et renouvellement*. Chicoutimi: Gaetan Morin.

Anonymous. 1936. *Le système Bedaux*. Nancy: Berger-Levrault.

Antonelli, V., T. Boyns, and F. Cerbioni. 2008. The development of accounting in Europe in the era of scientific management: The Italian engineering conglomerate, Ansaldo, 1918–1940. *Accounting Historians Journal* 35, no. 1: 49–81.

Bedaux, C.E. 1917. *The Bedaux efficiency course for industrial application*. Grand Rapids, MI: The Bedaux Industrial Institute.

Bedaux, C.E. 1928. *Measures labour*. New York: The International Bedaux Institute.

Bedaux, C.E. 1932. *Measures labour*. New York: The International Bedaux Institute.

Bedaux, G. 1979. *La vie ardente de Charles E Bedaux*. Unknown: The author.

Boltanski, L. 1982. *Les cadres; la formation d'un groupe social*. Paris: Les éditions de Minuit.

Boyns, T., and M. Matthews. 2001. Scientific management in Britain and comparisons with other countries to 1939. Unpublished paper presented to Management History Workshop. Open University, 27–28 March.

Brown, G. 1977. *Sabotage: A study in industrial conflict*. Nottingham, UK: Spokesman Book.

Butler, G.R. 1991. Frederic W Taylor: The father of scientific management and his philosophy revisited. *Industrial Management* 33, no. 3: 23–7.

Calon, M. 1989. *La science et ses réseaux: genèse et circulation des faits scientifiques*. Paris: La découverte.

Centlivre-Petit, D., and B. Journé. 1996. Taylor: Observateur en quête d'utopie? *Gérer et Comprendre-Annales des mines* 44, June: 85–94.

Christy, J. 1984. *The price of power*. Toronto: Doubleday.

Copley, F.B. 1923. *Frédérick W Taylor, father of scientific management*. New York: Harper and Brothers.

Danty-Lafrance, L. 1957. *Pratique de la rémunération du travail*. Paris: Les éditions d'organisation.

De Montmollin, M. 1974. *Le taylorisme à visage humain*. Paris: PUF.

Desroche, H. 1975. *La société festive; du fouriérisme écrit aux fouriérismes pratiqués*. Paris: Seuil.

Downs, L.L. 2002. *Manufacturing inequality*. Cornell University Press; French translation: *L'inégalité à la chaîne; la division sexuée du travail dans l'industrie métallurgique en France et en Angleterre*. Paris: Albin Michel.

Emerson, E. 1909. *Efficiency as a basis for operation and wages*. New York: *The Engineering Magazine*.

Emerson, E. 1912. *The twelve principles of efficiency*. New York: *The Engineering Magazine*.

Feuille d'informations corporatives. 1934. *Le système Bedaux, décisions du comité corporatif central en matière d'ordonnancement du travail*. Rome: Ministère des corporations du Royaume d'Italie, année VI, LXII (5), November.

Feuille d'informations corporatives. 1935. *Le système Bedaux, les collèges de conciliation dans le rapport de la conciliation générale du budget*. Rome: Ministère des corporations du Royaume d'Italie, année VII, LXIII (3), March.

Flanner, J. 1945. Annals of collaboration. *The New-Yorker*, 22 September: 28–47; 6 October: 32–45; 13 October: 32–48.

Fleischman, R.K. 2000. Completing the triangle: Taylorism and the paradigms. *Accounting, Auditing and Accountability Journal* 13, no. 5: 597–623.

Foucault, M. 1975. *Surveiller et punir*. Paris: Gallimard.

Fridenson, P. 1987. Un tournant taylorien de la société française (1904–1918). *Annales ESC* September–October, 5: 1031–60.

Geerkens, E. 2002. L'application du système Bedaux dans l'industrie belge des années 30. Lecture presented at the 127th congress of historical and scientific societies, Nancy.

Geerkens, E. 2005, L'application du système Bedaux dans l'industrie Belge dans les années 30. In *Le travail à l'époque contemporaine*, eds. D. Barjot, 87–101. Paris: Editions du Comité des travaux historiques et Scientifiques.

Guerin, F. 1998. *Faut-t-il brûler Taylor?* Caen: Editions Management Société.

Hardwick, C.M. 1993. *Time study in treason*. Chelmsford, UK: P. Horsnell.

Harrison, J. 1969 *Quest for the new moral world Robert Owen and the Owenties in Britain and América*. New York: Charles Scribner's Sons.

Hatchuel, A. 1994. Frédéric Taylor: Une lecture épistémologique. L'expert, le théoricien, le doctrinaire. In *L'invention de la gestion: histoire et pratiques*, ed. J.P. Bouilloud and B.P. Lécuyer, 53–64. Paris: L'Harmattan.

Hatchuel, A. 1995. A propos de la thèse de Madame Aimée Moutet: La rationalisation industrielle dans l'économie française au XIXème siècle. In *Actes du GERPISA, Ford et les autres entre les deux guerres* 16, août: 51–7.

Henry, O. 1993. *Un savoir en pratique les professionnels de l'expertise et du conseil*. Paris: thèse EHESS.

Kakar, S. 1970. *Frederick Taylor: A study in personality and innovation*. Cambridge: MIT Press.
Kipping, M. 1997. Consultancies, institutions and the diffusion of Taylorism in Britain, Germany and France, 1920s to 1950s. *Business History* 39, no. 4: 67–83.
Kipping, M. 1999. American management consulting companies in western Europe, 1920 to 1990: Products, reputation and relationships. *Business History Review* 73, no. 2: 190–220.
Kourchid, O. 1991. La réintroduction du système Bedaux aux mines du Nord-Pas-de-Calais. *Cahiers d'histoire de l'institut de recherches marxistes* 47: 17–27.
Kourchid, O. 1994. Le système Bedaux dans les mines. *Cahiers de l'Institut d'histoire sociale minière* 3: 19–23.
Kreis, S. 1990. The diffusion of an idea: A history of scientific management in Britain, 1890–1945. Unpublished PhD thesis, University of Missouri, Columbia.
Kreis, S. 1992. The diffusion of scientific management: The Bedaux company in America and Britain, 1926–1945. In *A mental révolution: Scientific management since Taylor*, ed. D. Nelson, 156–74. Columbus, OH: Ohio State University Press.
Kreis, S. 1999. Bedaux. In *American National Biography*. New York: Oxford University Press.
Laloux, P. 1950. *Le système Bedaux de calcul des salaires*. Paris: Hommes et Techniques.
Latour, B. 1987. *Science in action*. Cambridge, MA: Harvard University Press.
Le Chatelier, H. 1915. Le système Taylor, science expérimentale et psychologie ouvrière. *Revue de la Métallurgie* XII: 197–232.
Littler, C.R. 1982. *The development of the labour process in capitalist societies*. London: Heinemann.
Littler, C.R. 1984. L'essor du Taylorisme et de la rationalisation du travail dans l'industrie Anglaise. In *Le Taylorisme*, ed. M. de Montmollin and O. Pastré, 83–98. Paris: La Découverte.
Montgomery, D. 1987. *The fall of the house of labour*. Cambridge: Cambridge University Press.
Mottez, B. 1966. *Systèmes de salaries et pratique patronale*. Paris: CNRS.
Moutet, A. 1975. Les origines du système Taylor en France. Le point de vue patronal (1907–1914). *Le Mouvement Social* 93, October–December: 15–49.
Moutet, A. 1978. Patrons de progrès ou patrons de combat? La politique de rationalisation de l'industrie française au lendemain de la première guerre mondiale. *Recherches* 32/33: 449–92.
Moutet, A. 1984. La première guerre mondiale et le Taylorisme. In *Le Taylorisme*, ed. M. de Montmollin and O. Pastré, 67–82. Paris: La Découverte.
Moutet, A. 1985. Ingénieurs et rationalisation en France de la guerre à la crise (1914–1929). In *L'ingénieur dans la société française*, ed. A. Thepot, 71–108. Paris: Les éditions Ouvrières.
Moutet, A. 1992. La rationalisation industrielle dans l'économie française au XXème siècle Etude sur les rapports entre changements d'organisation technique et problèmes sociaux. Unpublished thesis, Paris X Nanterre.
Moutet, A. 1997. Les logiques de l'entreprise; la rationalisation dans l'industrie française de l'entre-deux-guerres. Unpublished thesis, Paris, EHESS.
Nelson, D. 1984 Le Taylorisme dans l'industrie américaine, 1900–1930. In *Le Taylorisme*, ed. M. de Montmollin and O. Pastré, 51–66. Paris: La Découverte.
Nelson, D. 1992a. Scientific management in retrospect. In *A Mental revolution: Scientific management since Taylor*, ed. D. Nelson, 5–39. Columbus, OH: Ohio State University Press.
Nelson, D. 1992b. Introduction. In *A Mental revolution: scientific management since Taylor*, ed. D. Nelson, 1–4. Columbus, OH: Ohio State University Press.
Pouget, E. 1914. *L'organisation du surmenage; le système Taylor*. Paris: Marcel Rivière.
Pouget, M. 1998. *Taylor et le Taylorisme*. Paris: PUF.
Rouzé, J.P. 1993. Frédérick W Taylor, inventeur de la démocratie moderne? *Gérer et Comprendre-Annales des Mines* 30, mars: 97–105.
Sassier, M.F. 2005. *Candé entre rêves et réalité*. Joué les Tours: La Cimaire.
Shimmin, S. 1959. *Payment by results*. London: Staples Press.
Simmel, G. 1900. *La philosophie de l'argent*. Paris: PUF.
Smith, I., and T. Boyns. 2005. Scientific management and the pursuit of control in Britain to 1960. *Accounting, Business & Financial History* 15, no. 2: 187–216.
Taylor, F.W. 1911. *The principle of scientific management*. French translation: *La direction scientifique des enterprises*. Paris: Dunod (1957).
Taylor, F.W. 1912. *Taylor's testimony before the special house committee*. French translation, in *La direction scientifique des enterprises*. Paris: Dunod (1957).
Vielleville, A. 1914. Le système Taylor. Unpublished thesis, Université de Paris.
Whitston, K. 1997. Worker resistance and Taylorism in Britain. *International Review of Social History* 42, no. 1: 1–24.
Wineapple, B. 1989. *Genet; a biography of Janet Flanner*. Lincoln, NE: University of Nebraska Press.
Zarifian, P. 1997. *Eloge de la civilité*. Paris: L'Harmattan.

The history of the French *tableau de bord* (1885–1975): evidence from the archives

Anne Pezet

Université Paris Dauphine, DRM, France

The history of the *tableau de bord* in France has never really been written. This paper sets out to draw up a history using the archives of three large industrial companies – Lafarge, Pechiney and Saint-Gobain – as source material. This paper seeks to revisit the myth of the French *tableau de bord* as presented in a great many comparative management studies (typically, *Tableau de bord* vs. *Balanced ScoreCard*). This myth rests on more or less implicit assumptions regarding, for instance, the central role played by engineers in the emergence of *tableaux de bord*, the single and unified way in which this instrument is used in companies from top to bottom and, of course, its French specificity.

Introduction

The French-style *tableau de bord* is often compared or contrasted with what is commonly considered to be its American equivalent, the *Balanced ScoreCard* (BSC) (Bessire and Baker 2005; Bourguignonn, Malleret, and Nørreklit 2004; Epstein and Manzoni 1997; Gray and Pesqueux 1993). These comparisons use technical, strategic, cultural or ideological criteria. However, they are founded on a 'history' of the *tableau de bord* that has never been carried out in accordance with the methods of historical research. The sole exception appears to be Malo (1995), who sought to retrace the history of the *tableau de bord* using studies from the past (notably, Satet and Voraz 1946) and using 'leads' that appeared in historical research papers not pertaining to *tableaux de bord*. Consequently, comparative studies – generally the fruit of collaboration between French and foreign researchers (contributing research on BSC) – are based on a history of *tableaux de bord* that remains largely mythical. In this regard, Lebas (1996) outlined a history ('a little history') highlighting the major roles played by the State and engineers in the emergence of management accounting and *tableaux de bord* in France. Unfortunately, this little history, interesting in itself, lacks references to primary sources. Even though it may be likely, intuitively speaking, that the State and engineers did play a role in this case, the elements of proof are still required. This paper's purposes are, therefore, twofold: first, to compare the myth of the history of the *tableau de bord* with the reality observed in the archives; and second, to rethink the *tableau de bord* along the lines of a more theoretical perspective.

A fundamental issue for this research is the question of what, conceptually, constitutes a *tableau de bord*. Trying to unveil this, and the use made of a *tableau de bord*, raises the potential problem of anachronism. In this article, we have aimed to find the first appearances of what would be subsequently identified as the French *tableau de bord*. This quest through the archives arouses an ambiguity: if we are to discover *tableaux de bord* before they were conceptualised, we need to have an *a priori* definition. Only then can we both trace the device through the archives and conduct a reflection about its meanings.

These observations beg the question of what, in a practical sense, constitutes a *tableau de bord*. A survey of the main French management accounting textbooks tends to provide a broad definition: combining the normative and the cognitive approaches, we can define the French *tableaux de bord* as a system of indicators that aim at monitoring and conducting economic operations and individual behaviours in a way that is compatible with the business strategy. The *tableau de bord* is generally considered as a supplement to financial and accounting measures. It has to gather, in the same device (paper sheet, log or, today, electronic spreadsheet) quantitative and qualitative data as well as financial data. This comprehensive definition will help us to assess the historical development of the *tableau de bord* compared with what theorists think it should be.

However, rethinking the *tableau de bord* along the lines of a more theoretical perspective is a major purpose of our study. The history of the *tableau de bord* in France retraces the steps of industrial leaders in their quest to find a device enabling them to see and to observe companies that had moved out of sight, physically speaking. The *tableau de bord* is a device that associates 'representing' and 'intervening', to use the terms suggested by Hacking (1983). The *tableau de bord* is firstly a means of representing a reality common to any large company in which operational activities move away from the centre and become less visible. The *tableau de bord* is also a means of intervening because, if 'the theories force themselves to say how the world is, the experimentation and technology that stem from them change the world. We represent and we intervene' (Hacking 1983, 31). The *tableau de bord* combines seeing with doing. It provides the senior manager with an insight into what he can no longer physically see due to distance; and it also provides the means of intervening through the decision-making that it engenders.

The archival research revealed in this paper shows that the *tableau de bord* arose out of the issue of seeing and doing. In the context of the 1920s and 1930s, the *tableau de bord* seemed to be the answer to the changes in progress. Strong growth and a powerful movement towards concentration at the macroeconomic level converged with the emergence of certain schools of thought such as the technocracy and *planisme* movements (Kuisel 1984) at the macro-social level. At the meso level – the level of the corporation – the period was favourable to holdings and alliances, to the creation of subsidiaries in large companies and to the weakening of centralisation (Levy-Leboyer 1980). At the micro level – the level of the manager – these phenomena raised new questions: how to control (command) these increasingly large and dispersed entities? A new mode of representing was sought, which would also change the ways of intervening.

Yet, it was at the end of the nineteenth century that leaders began to gather information through the *rapport hebdomadaire*, a 'weekly report', or through a *journal de marche*, or 'logbook'. Essentially, this information was presented in the form of a narrative. From the 1920s and 1930s onwards, the *tableau de bord*, before it was named as such, appears from our contemporary viewpoint as the device that senior managers had sought after. They proclaimed their need for information, for 'statistics' on sales and production. Alas, although everything seemed to suggest that the *tableau de bord* would finally emerge in its canonical form, the boards of the three companies studied adopted budgetary control! To borrow terms from Giddens (1990), it seems that, in the end, a 'modern global expert knowledge system', i.e. budgetary control, had gained the upper hand over the 'local process knowledge' that would have been the *tableau de bord*. The senior manager's *tableau de bord* would not take 'definitive' shape until the 1950s. This is not to mention the rapid changes which it underwent at that time towards more financial data, significantly altering the model that is presented in today's literature; in practice, the conventional 'definitive' shape of the new device seems to have lasted but a short moment in time.

This history of the practices of the three companies examined highlights in particular the fundamental ambiguity on which the myth of the 'French' *tableau de bord* has been built. Are we talking about the *tableau de bord* used by operational managers or about the *tableau de bord* used by the board of directors? What representing/intervening tandem are we dealing with? The 'little history' of *tableaux de bord* refers to the model of the engineer based on the operational data/operational decision-making tandem. It portrays engineers as the source of *tableaux de bord* which they designed to convey operational information for decision-making of the same type. Yet, archival research produces more mitigated findings. The role of the engineer was perhaps less central than it first appears and the representing/intervening tandem in particular seems to rely on a blend of financial data and management by numbers. In this respect, the archives reveal the fundamental ambiguity of *tableaux de bord*: does the single, unified *tableau de bord* used at all levels of the corporate hierarchy really exist? And, as a corollary, this begs the question: is the *tableau de bord* specifically French?

The following paper sets out to show that the history of the French-style *tableau de bord*, broken down into four stages, is less linear than it first appears. From this history, we draw out discussion points relating to the concept of the *tableau de bord* and point to new paths for interpreting the representing/intervening tandem. To this end, the paper is structured as follows. Firstly, we describe our methodological approach and indicate the nature, and limitations, of the archival material to be used. We then discuss the concept of the *tableau de bord* around three critical issues: the role of engineers in its early design; its uniqueness as a device in the organisation; and its French specificity. In conclusion, we will try to outline what is the purpose of *tableaux de bord*.

Methodology and sources

In order to confront the general idea of a *tableau de bord* and the reality of practices, our study is based on an examination of the archives of three large companies: Lafarge, Pechiney and Saint-Gobain. Since *tableaux de bord* have generally been seen to have been implemented in large industrial firms, the selection of these three companies will enable us to shed new light on the history and emergence of *tableaux de bord* in France. It will enable us to place in perspective the largely mythical view that has previously existed regarding the development of the *tableau de bord*. Lafarge, Pechiney (taken over by the Canadian firm Alcan in 2003) and Saint-Gobain are multinational industrial companies of French origin. Their particularity is that they have all been in existence for over one hundred years. Today, Lafarge operates mainly in the sectors of cement, plaster and aggregates; Pechiney, in the aluminium sector; and Saint-Gobain, in the sectors of glass, insulation and building materials. In the past, Pechiney and Saint-Gobain also operated in the chemicals sector.

Our choice of companies obviously provides a limitation to the study, as does the nature and scope of their archives. Indeed, the archival sources studied vary in size and are uneven in value. The Saint-Gobain archives were the most fertile in terms of both quantity and quality. The Lafarge archives were low in quantity but high in quality (e.g. Marcel Demonque's *tableau de bord*). The

Pechiney archives have been studied previously and have generated many research works that have been useful for the purposes of this article. Nevertheless, the choice of companies to study is not without significance: one of the strongest assumptions underlying previous research cited above is that engineers played a central role in designing the first *tableaux de bord.* Each of three companies examined exhibited a strong technical culture over the study period, and this will therefore allow us to test this assumption.

The methodological approach adopted here is based on the critical approach to history. This requires studying the archives (primary sources) within a four-dimension protocol: utilising cross-checking procedures, both internal (within the archives) and external (with secondary sources); choosing a chronological sequence and building a storyline; referring to local sources; and layering the story obtained with quotations taken from the archives.

A turbulent history

Four stages mark the emergence of *tableaux de bord* in the three companies studied. The first, at the turn of the twentieth century, was characterised by the appearance of written reports, i.e. use of the narrative form to convey information from the periphery to the centre. The second stage, during the interwar period, was marked by the increasingly commonplace use of 'statistics' for sales, production, etc. This stage foreshadowed the emergence of *tableaux de bord* but, in the end, it was budgetary control that would be adopted. The third stage in the 1950s and 1960s marked the true emergence of *tableaux de bord.* However, in the final stage, we observe the *tableau de bord*'s rapid slide towards a reporting device of a financial nature.

Narrating the running of factories: written reports

Lafarge set up *conseils de fabrications,* or 'manufacturing committees', from 1885 onwards. They brought together the company's senior management and operational managers/engineers. The purpose of the *conseils de fabrications* was to address essentially technical questions and to find solutions for a number of production problems that Lafarge was experiencing at that time. Each meeting was the subject of a report, hand-written in the early meetings and subsequently typed. These reports were then bound into volumes. From that point onwards, the information gathered took a narrative form; incidents, problems and solutions were related in the form of a story.

At Saint-Gobain, a reference to *rapports hebdomadaires*, or 'weekly reports', figures in a 1916 memorandum relating to a period beginning in 1880. In 1912, new recruits from the *Inspection des finances,* top-tier civil servants specialising in public finance, set up financial reports. Finally, in 1920, a memorandum from general management entitled *journal de marche*, or 'log-book', reiterated senior management's expectations (Saint-Gobain Archives, CSG Hist 00077/26, Memorandum of 6 October 1920 from head office to factories):

> We would remind you of our memorandum 38-F of 29th June 1916. Several plants possess books that are kept up-to-date and are likely to provide accurate and interesting data: this should be the case for all our sites. Please specify where your site is with regard to this issue and, if our prescriptions have not yet been followed, to move forward rapidly to make up for lost time.

However informative they may have been, from the perspective of the theoretical definition these reports did not constitute *tableaux de bord.* The portion set aside for story telling remained significant and the data that appeared in them were not systematically organised.

Over time, the written reports would incorporate increasing amounts of data in the form of figures. After the First World War, boards proclaimed their need for 'statistics' relating to sales, production and personnel. However, in the end, this demand for figures would lead to the adoption not of *tableaux de bord* but of budgetary control.

Statistics, **tableaux de bord** *or . . . budgets?*

The interwar period saw the development of schools of thought in management among French industrialists (Berland 1999; Kuisel 1984). A book published by Robert Satet in 1936 illustrates well the style of the literature that proliferated in this era. He argued in particular for the adoption of 'appropriate documentation', i.e. 'statistics of which a judicious selection is necessary to reach the goal that has been set out' (Satet 1936, 85). To give an example, Satet (1936, 85) presented the case of a textiles company:

> In the company in question, three types of statistics are kept depending on whether they methodically bring together in the following domains facts that lend themselves to numerical assessment:
> 1. Commercial and economic statistics;
> 2. Industrial statistics;
> 3. Financial statistics.

Table 1 shows what kinds of statistics should be implemented in practice in each of these three categories. Satet attributed to each of them a goal, a frequency and, where appropriate, observations.

Table 1. The statistics recommended by Satet (extract).

Type	Goal	Frequency	Observations
Commercial statistics			
1. The actual price of wool and combed wool	Orientation for purchasing raw materials	Monthly or daily (combed wool)	It also serves in interpreting variances between results and forecasts
Industrial statistics			
6. Workshop production rates	Observation of production rates in order to regulate the pace	Daily	
7. Contractors' production costs (on average and per item)	Comparison of the real cost of production with that of contractors	Monthly	In some cases it may be advantageous to turn to contractors that are cheaper; likewise in cases of seasonal backlogs of orders to respect delivery deadlines
Financial statistics			
13. Statement of price reductions granted to clients for second-choice goods	Wastage in sales which must be accounted for in the general operational budget	Monthly	Also serves to monitor defects in the departments concerned

Source: Satet (1936, 87).

Although we can see the first outlines of a *tableau de bord* in this example, it still remains the case that Satet's book pertained to budgetary control (1936, 85):

> One can hardly conceive of budgetary forecasts being developed without the support of appropriate documentation, drawn from observations of phenomena proper to the company and from those of a more general nature that relate, for instance, to markets for materials purchased and manufactured by the company.

Satet therefore assumed strong complementarities between statistics and budgeting, making the former the prerequisite for the latter to exist. This complementarity between the two devices would certainly contribute to the ambiguity that was to characterise the history of the *tableau de bord* (see below).

Indeed, statistics did appear in our three companies during the interwar years. At Lafarge, figures had been incorporated into written reports from 1905 onwards and the table format came to be used. By the end of the 1920s, these data, dispersed until then, became more consistent, in particular information on technical and commercial matters (namely, customer complaints). At Pechiney (at that time, called Alais, Froges et Camargue or AFC), commercial statistics were kept from the 1920s onwards. Another domain given to statistics was personnel management.

The development of statistics was often in response to external demands from various sources: commercial expectations, professional bodies (such as the *Union des industries métallurgiques et minières* or the *Union des industries chimiques*), public authorities (notably during the war), and even national and international bodies (for instance, from the INSEE, the French Statistics and Economics Institute, or the OECD). Tabulating (statistics) machines[1] contributed to the rise of statistics from the 1930s onwards. Cailluet (1995) points out that, at the end of the Second World War, 11 statistics machines were in common use at AFC. In addition to accounting, they handled sales statistics (AFC and Aluminium français) per region, per agent, per client and per product (40% of total machine activity), and provided various statistics on the personnel. A restructuring programme carried out by the White consultancy in 1947, which would mark the onset of budgetary control, revealed the true position of statistics in the company's management system. At that time, the head of the financial department shared his concerns with the managing director, Raoul de Vitry:

> Neither of these reorganisers [. . .] seems to have very precise notions of accounting strictly speaking, of which bookkeeping is a mandatory feature and which they tend to confuse with simple statistical indicators that we may envisage deleting.
>
> (Memorandum of 24 January 1948, quoted in Cailluet [1995, 81])

The author of the memorandum makes a clear distinction between accounting (financial in this case) and statistics.[2] We later observe that this distinction has not always been respected.

Yet, it was at Saint-Gobain in particular that the slide from demanding 'statistics' – a requirement clearly formulated by senior management and backed by consultant engineers – towards adopting budgetary control would be observed. The work of Lacoin, a consultant engineer, between 1934 and 1936, included among other things a study of the documentation needed by the board. 'Statistics' were mentioned; Lacoin recommending the implementation of a 'method of documentation' for each sales agent to include the following information:

> – Sales results – current and comparisons with those of previous years – for each and all of the main products [. . .];

- Remuneration and expenses of the agency included in the turnover and in the means of action: mileage, business trips, advertising, etc.;
- The main clients ranked by volume of sales and notably clients won or lost over recent years, with the reasons for their loss;

  [...]
- Delays or quality defects that gave rise to customer complaints, actions taken;
- Sales with critically weak profit margins and the local competitive environment;
- The share of St Gobain sales in relation to total sales in the agent's zone – Potential sales in light of rival products [...]

(Memorandum of 19 June 1934, Saint-Gobain Archives, CSG 000420/18)

Lacoin also underscored the importance of commercial information for positioning the company in relation to competitors: 'how do Saint-Gobain's means of action behave in relation to those of its main competitors, with respect to both its geographical distribution and the tooling of its factories, and to its commercial organisation [...]?' (Executive committee report, 1934, Saint-Gobain Archives, CSG 000420/18). Finally, the report emphasised the need to 'choose several important issues by studying them in depth' (Memorandum of 22 October 1936, Saint-Gobain Archives, CSG 000420/18). The tone of this text makes us think unquestioningly of *tableaux de bord*, since it stresses the relationships between various means of action and outcomes. Furthermore, it supplements financial data in a way that anticipates the systemic reasoning of the BSC. However, we should note that its subject matter was exclusively commercial.

More broadly, the context of the 1930s brought with it dissatisfaction with 'the absence of command' by the board of directors, with difficulties in getting information to flow upwards in light of the increasing dispersion of activities. A memorandum circulated on 13 September 1933 (Saint-Gobain Archives, CSG 000417/171) describes the 'tentacle-like developments [...] in the most diverse countries and in the widest variety of domains' of the company. The numerous memoranda of that period issued by either the consultant engineer Lacoin or by the company's general management reveal a growing need for information. A large number of requests conveyed by the general management to factories demanded that information be communicated: monthly deliveries per product/market; inquiries into wages and employees; accident reports, etc. (Chemical Products – General Management Memoranda – 1936–38; Saint-Gobain Archives, CSG Hist 00077/26). Also mentioned were demands emanating from various government departments (the Mines and Factory Inspectorates) to which senior management sought to respond in a centralised way. Printed forms to be filled in were sent out, but there was still no question of a formalised *tableau de bord*. In 1936, the memorandum of 23 June from the Department of Control and Economic Analysis recommended 'the continuous observation of the subsidiaries' (quoted in Nikitin 1989, 23). On 15 February 1938, the board requested that management teams gather from the subsidiaries, for the General Secretariat, 'the main indications of a technical and commercial nature, as well as the balance sheet and the financial results of the company' (Saint-Gobain Archives, CSG Hist 00077/26). It also referred to a quarterly frequency that was adopted in 1936. Finally, the 'reorganisation of the accounting departments' carried out by the former Financial Inspector Caillet led to an inventory being drawn up:

> But analysis, statistics, financial studies, the analysed results, in a word 'the accounting', was only mediocre... Its sole aim remained the maintenance of cash flow. It attended to the most urgent things first [...] RESULTS, ANALYSES, and STATISTICS concerned no one.
>
> We want accounting to become once again the company's compass [...] a precious auxiliary.[3]
>
> (Saint-Gobain Archives, CSG Hist 00077/29, Memorandum of 30 November 1938)

These repeated requests corresponded, quite probably fortuitously,[4] with workshop practices. A series of reports can be found in the Saint-Gobain archives, dating from 1937 to 1953, issued by the *Glaceries* (the old term used for glass-making factories) and pertaining to shifts in production costs (monthly, per product, per type of expenditure, per manufacturing stage) as well as to technical information (production levels, yields, energy overheads, etc.). These reports were printed on large A3-sized pages and were completed with written analyses in the form of small reports.

In 1938, a memorandum circulated by the same sector of activity stated:

> the usefulness of a comparison between the figures provided by the different factories is self-evident. This comparison is currently very imperfect because any single figure is not interpreted in exactly the same way by all the sites. The aim of the present memorandum is to specify the definitions of the items that appear in the technical reports and the production costs.
>
> (Saint-Gobain Archives, CSG Hist 00006/06, Memorandum *Halle à verre mince* – 'Instructions on drawing up technical reports and production costs' – 10 January 1938)

This memorandum recommended writing bi-weekly and monthly technical reports containing manufacturing data and including an executive summary (the 'salient facts'), information on manpower (employees, time worked, wages, etc.), as well as information on production costs. This memorandum also presented models of tables. It specified that 'the figures used in the bi-weekly report must be as accurate as possible without necessarily being accounting figures. Figures presented in the monthly report will be, in contrast, "accounting" figures'. Here, we should note the board's goal of having at its fingertips information that went beyond accounting and financial accounting.[5]

The demand for information was therefore recurrent in a context perceived as complex due to geographical dispersion and diversification in the activities of a group in full mutation. However, the ambiguity inherent in this quest for information was strong. Thus, a memorandum from Lacoin, although emphasising the need to 'choose several important issues by studying them in depth', drew up the following list:

> 1. An in-depth periodical examination of financial results, and, from there, the examination of the situations to which they pertain:
>   - Annual profits per product and margins compared with the working capital tied up in the main products.
>   - Factory results, production costs, margins, utilisation of capacity. These results will be compared with observations relating to scopes of action and potential factory closures.
>   - Sales results per region and per customer type – Shifts in the clientele and shifts in competition – The Board is not receiving precise information on this subject, whereas it is already possible to compile some interesting data and it would be very easy to complete this information. Shifts over several years in sales prices and production costs, and items that make up production costs. For fertilizers, comparisons with prices per region and per product from previous years, after each campaign and at the end of the year.
>
>   [...]
> 2. Examination of the means of action with a view to improving them and mainly:
>
>   [...]
>
>   [The list notably includes: payrolls, budgets, research programmes and new product launches, the organisation of departments, etc.]
>
> (Saint-Gobain Archives, CSG 000417/171, Memorandum 22 October 1936)

We can clearly see in this formulation the blurring of lines between data gathering of a budgetary nature and the basic elements for building a *tableau de bord*.

Yet, even though Lacoin specified that to these data 'should be added a control of the quality of work: customer complaints, delays in deliveries to customers, unpaid bills', what was proposed related more to budgetary control than to *tableaux de bord*, and it was indeed the former device that would be adopted rather than the *tableau de bord*.

The Héranger mission, named after another consultant engineer working for Saint-Gobain from 1941 to 1948, would result in the implementation of structures (general management organisation, the plan, and the position of financial deputy) and methods (budgeting and industrial accounting).[6] At that time, all the initiatives seemed to lead to budgets and management accounting and, despite the claim for something less financial, the *tableau de bord* was slow to materialise.

However, the need for another instrument still made itself felt. Héranger therefore put in place a system of monthly reports and inventory reports (factories, sales, etc.). In a memorandum to the Chairman in March 1945, he noted that 'in a small business, the boss sees his colleagues and his workers every day [. . .] and to manage his business he can content himself with his personal perspicacity and a minimum number of documents' (Saint-Gobain Archives, CSG 01651/10, Memorandum from Charles Héranger to the CEO, March 1945). As the business develops and tasks are delegated, however, the memo went on, the boss needs 'a small number of periodical reports, in the light of which he makes his decisions'. Competition and economic instability, the memo stated, reinforces the need 'to assess more frequently the company's situation using reports with figures designed as true instruments of management and decision-making'. Here we again find the major ambiguity of this period leading in the end to the implementation of budgetary management. Moving from direct and exhaustive information for the head of the company to information that is selected, intermediated and put into figures is not straightforward. Budgetary control, however, did not respond fully to needs; a series of memoranda dating from 1945 again referred to problems regarding information. In a memorandum of 9 August 1948, the Héranger mission stressed the need 'to study and perfect the accounting and statistical documents necessary for running senior management and the departments' (Saint-Gobain Archives, CSG 01651/10, Memorandum from Charles Héranger to the CEO).

In parallel, two other phenomena militated in favour of the adoption of the *tableau de bord*. The first was tied to requests from the State administration and from its various committees in the form of selective information or more in-depth enquiries. This was particularly true during the Second World War. The second phenomenon related to overseas trips made by the members of the board and, in particular, to the discovery of the American model. Following a six-week trip in 1946 to Ford, Blue Ridge Glass, Corning, etc., Caillet contrasted 'our diverse manufactures, our geographical dispersion' to the centralisation of American companies: 'each company has the luxury of sales statistics', and 'very advanced studies'. He enthused about the 'speed in producing accounting and statistical documents', the excellence of the personnel and the use of mechanical data processing (Saint-Gobain Archives, CSG 01651/10, The Caillet Report 'Administrative and Accounting Organisation in the USA' – 31 January 1947)

And finally, the **tableaux de bord**

In the 1950s, we find examples of both directors' *tableaux de bord* in completed form and a theorisation of the device.

In the middle of the 1950s, the *tableau de bord* underwent its first formalisation. The CRC (*Centre de recherches et d'études des chefs d'entreprise*), at Jouy en Josas, near Paris, frequented by directors of large companies including Saint-Gobain, Lafarge and Pechiney, published a handout entitled *'Industrial Accounting – Tableau de bord'* containing a section on the 'Techniques of the TABLEAU DE BORD in the service of corporate management'. It goes on to describe:

> The term suggests a car driver, train driver or pilot . . . who has displayed before his eyes a number of dials providing indications that help him to drive or fly [. . .]
> Each flight in a plane corresponds to a financial year in progress during which the role of the company boss is:
> – To develop his means in terms of materials and men;
> – To turn any unfortunate trends around rapidly, events that will not fail to occur due to the difficulties encountered en route.
> To be a good pilot who flies well and reacts quickly, the company boss must be an 'aware' and 'informed' pilot, like the captain on a flight deck. Of course, if the weather is clear and the wind favourable, the pilot barely needs to look at his dashboard. But when the bad weather comes, he must be able to fly without sight.
> (Saint-Gobain Archives, CSG Hist 00005/1)

The company boss's *tableau de bord* must therefore include: 'level gauges' (inventories, cash flow, customers, suppliers); 'totalisers' (expenditure, purchases, production levels, sales, per type, per workshop, etc.); 'ratio calculators' (production costs per unit, turnover/inventory-type ratios or indirect hours/total hours-type ratios); 'variance calculators' (comparisons between years, with forecasting, etc.; indices of a turnover N/turnover N-1 type; of a relative variance type [(real cost – forecast cost)/forecast cost]); and finally, 'indicators relating to the external environment', and notably 'items for professional or regional comparisons pertaining principally to product markets, and the labour market'. Furthermore, we find the importance of form (Saint-Gobain Archives, CSG Hist 00005/1):

> In addition to these five categories of dials that provide him with data expressed in numbers written into tables, it will be useful to the company boss to express certain indications in the form of numbers drawn on diagrams. These diagrams will transcribe all or part of the numbers written on the tables. To be drawn on the diagrams will be numbers that express facts that need particular monitoring.

This document from the CRC is interesting for another reason: it addresses the 'practical processes for implementing the dials of a *tableau de bord*'. The *tableau de bord* should possess five features to ensure 'rapid reactions':

- Displaying a limited number of indications: 'choosing between all the possible information'.
- Developing secondary *tableaux de bord*: the *tableau de bord* must be 'split' between the agents.
- Choosing the frequency of calculation depending on the type of indication.
- Ensuring the instantaneousness of the indications and the speed of the information.
- Other practical considerations.

On this last point, several methods were mentioned: duplicating selected indications on wall charts, on rotating boards, in 'a small notebook that the company director carries with him at all times'; filing without duplicating reports provided by the departments. Practical aspects were particularly elaborated:

> A practical filing process [. . .] consists in using sheets superimposed and ordered in such a way that only one column, or one row, is ever visible. This process also allows the main *tableau de bord* and the secondary *tableaux de bord* to be input simultaneously. Filing these sheets in a ring binder enables the company boss to have at his disposal a discrete *tableau de bord* (a wall chart is not discrete) that can be easily transported from the office and used in places away from the telephone to allow purposeful thinking.
> [. . .] It is essential that diagrams be placed next to the families of numbers from which they result to facilitate viewing.
> For moving from one year to the next, transparent diagrams, on frosted cellulose film (KODATRACE), can provide good service.
> (Saint-Gobain Archives, CSG Hist 00005/1)

The document finishes with an appendix containing the *tableau de bord* of a foundry with numerous diagrams, but it clearly warns, 'It is an example and not a model. Each managing director must have a *tableau de bord* adapted to his temperament. This is the first condition for its effectiveness'. In contrast, the bibliography illustrates the novelty of the instrument since it was taken from a book on *Ratios* published by the *Société Expertise comptable fiduciaire de France* (1961).

In 1959, the Cegos Institute published a 'Report of an enquiry into the orientation of works in section 3 (general management)'. It presented the results of a questionnaire of 72 managing directors relating to priority subjects for the programme of study and exchange of section 3. The subject of the *tableau de bord* is in third place in the chapter 'The boss's personal organisation', behind the topics of information and of the managing directors' documentation. Taking all the categories as a whole, it was the *tableau de bord* that was most frequently cited.

It was also in 1959 that the first edition of a work by Lauzel and Cibert appeared, *Des ratios au tableau de bord.*[7] This work, containing a fourth section dedicated to the *tableau de bord*, nonetheless remained heavily influenced by the ratio-based approach of a financial type. Only the sixth section, based on the case study of the Papeteries Schwindenhammer, presents a *tableau de bord*, undoubtedly anchored in budgeting but composed of indicators of all types.

With regard to companies, the *tableaux de bord* also began to appear during this period. At Saint-Gobain, the first genuine *tableau de bord* belonged to M. Grandgeorge, the managing director. This '*tableau de bord of the Glaceries*' spanned the period 1952–58. It contained three files, each entitled '*tableau de bord*':

- *Tableau de bord* no. 1: commercial management;
- *Tableau de bord* no. 2: technical management and financial management;
- *Tableau de bord* no. 3: wages, social contributions and purchasing power.

(Saint-Gobain Archives, CSG 01650/224)

In reality, it consisted of a collection of slightly disparate documents corresponding to different periods. Certain annual indicators went back as far as 1912, in all likelihood on the basis of reconstituted data; others were monthly (1954–55) or half-yearly, etc. Two notable features are worth highlighting, however: the first is that these *tableaux de bord* contained numerous coloured tables and diagrams; second, the data were essentially non-financial – the financial section of *Tableau de bord* no. 2 does not appear in the file.[8]

In 1955, a memorandum from general management (chemical products) addressed to Grandgeorge (Saint-Gobain Archives, CSG Hist 00074/14, Memorandum 'Tableau de bord of chemical products' – 2 September 1955) was intended to be a 'first attempt to gather together tables and diagrams relating to the activities in chemical products as seen from the standpoint of the company's general management'. Once again, it consisted of a collection of existing documents, either annual (production, sales) or monthly (here it refers to a notebook containing data on invoicing, inventories, deliveries and results). The author of the memorandum is fairly critical: he remarks on badly designed diagrams that are barely readable, but 'the main hole that still needs to be filled is the total absence of items for forecasting'. More broadly (Saint-Gobain Archives, CSG Hist 00074/14):

> To conclude on this first trial, in order to succeed in gathering really useful and easily readable documents – without imposing an excessive material workload on the different managements responsible – it would seem desirable to lay out for them a doctrine and a uniform and fairly rigid framework for presenting statistics.
>
> According to our information, such a method is in force at SHELL which is applying it in each of its operational plants throughout the world.

At Pechiney, the *tableau de bord* was first mentioned around the same time. In 1954, Jean Benoit, returning from the 10th International Congress on Scientific Management, noted in a report (Pechiney archives, 00-10-10021, Memorandum of February 1954) that, 'the method of managing by exception appears indispensable to the managing director'. Yet, in addition to 'standard cost accounting' and budgetary control, he mentioned 'qualitative methods of a self-reporting type that are beginning to emerge' and 'the interest of selective rather than complete reports'. To be considered as 'a particularly powerful means of assessment' are the 'systematic analysis of customer claims [. . .] the reasons for their leaving and complaints from the company's agents'. A link may be drawn here between commercial statistics and statistics relating to personnel (see above).

In 1955, Raoul de Vitry, Deputy Chairman and Managing Director of Pechiney, addressed a conference on the subject of 'the tableau de bord of a captain of industry'.[9] He specified:

> These terms, perhaps a little evocative, represent the set of measures that the company's Board of Directors, supported by accounting, is driven to adopt today to ensure the best possible conditions for: its information, the making of its decisions, and the monitoring of their execution. [. . .] By 'accounting', we mean all the periodical documents with figures: accounting statements, balance sheets, production costs, statistics, budgets, ratios, etc.'
>
> (Pechiney Archives, 001-7-130994)

After drawing up an American-style 'background' from the pre-1914 'treasurer' to the 'controller', Raoul de Vitry noted that the trend was moving towards more interpretation, assessment and analysis. He praised budgetary control highly, but highlighted its complementarity with the *tableau de bord:*[10]

> Which, under these conditions, appears rather more like a kind of radar and includes the following main elements that I will succinctly reiterate:
>
> 1. The choice of the key metrics of which we seek to follow the variations: production and turnover, results, investments, statistics, cash flow, employees, wages, no more than a few ratios with the denominator of gross operating margin or approved items from a year of reference appropriately chosen;
> 2. Monthly and cumulated forecasts corresponding to the previous key metrics;
> 3. Comparison through a convenient material process of real performance and forecasts;
> 4. Rapid communication to all levels of the hierarchy of the previous documents for the parts that concern them as well as interpretation of any variances, should they arise.
>
> (Pechiney Archives, 001-7-130994)

Raoul de Vitry saw in the *tableau de bord* the ideal instrument for the 'method by exception':

> the ideal would be that managers at all levels no longer have to take care of their tableau de bord – no longer set the values that condition the calibration of weighing devices – but that they are sure that there exists in the company, carefully hidden under the bonnet, a mechanism that is accurate, sensitive and error-free, that does not flash numerous lights in their eyes to signal minor anomalies but instead, selects them for each level of the hierarchy, in such a way that each manager need only take into account anomalies that are relatively uncommon and worthy of attention, and which require his attention.
>
> (Pechiney Archives, 001-7-130994)

The director's *tableau de bord* thus enables him to save time for long-term reflection. More broadly, Raoul de Vitry advocated standardisation within the aluminium sector: 'Otherwise, how can we conceive that too great a dispersion of companies and the means of production may resist internal rivalry and powerful and dynamic external competition?' (Pechiney Archives, 001-7-130994). Finally, in the conclusion to his report, Raoul de Vitry suggested that (Pechiney Archives, 001-7-130994):

> The 'machine for governing companies', a kind of ultimate term for the development of a super *tableau de bord*, may seem to come from the world of dreams and in a time span that I dare not specify, but it does not seem beyond reason.

In addition to these essentially theoretical developments, the *tableau de bord* underwent practical applications at Pechiney. The restructuring carried out by the White Consultancy in 1947 conferred a new responsibility on the Department of Industrial Organisation – building *tableaux de bord*. Cailluet (1995) points out that the Group's Chairman and Managing Director, Pierre Jouven, had at his disposal a *tableau de bord* at the beginning of the 1950s. It contained eight chapters (Cailluet 1995, 87–8):

- management accounts;
- overheads;
- production costs;
- payroll/employees/lodgings;
- productivity premiums;
- output;
- inventories;
- energy overheads.

The chapter on production did include a series of technical indicators, but Cailluet (1995) observes strong parallels between the *tableau de bord* and budgetary control.

At Lafarge, the *tableau de bord* belonging to Marcel Demonque, Chairman and Managing Director from 1959 to 1974, was presented in the form of a file. Five file-dividers split it into separate sections: deliveries; results; investments; the situation; and personnel. The information was very diverse and included both financial and non-financial data. It was composed of numerous tables and hand-painted diagrams which were directly readable. We choose two illustrations as examples: first, a diagram comparing the delivery to customers, factory by factory (see Figure 1); and second, a diagram showing details about personnel unionisation per factory and category (see Figure 2). These illustrations highlight the diversity of data collected and the importance of its 'staging' in a simple, readable form.

Nevertheless, it seems that Lafarge was behind in realising this tool's potential. In 1968, Marcel Demonque remarked that, 'it has become indispensable to define methods for managing our businesses [. . .] with the large number of our entities, geographical spread and the diversity of our business sectors' (cited in Public Histoire 1991, 45). The Group began an overhaul that was carried out by the consultancy firm McKinsey between 1965 and 1969. The new organisation aimed to be decentralised and to rely on rolling planning, budgetary control and management by objectives.

In 1973, during a seminar chaired by the Deputy Chairman, Olivier Lecerf, criticism of the budget, viewed as too cumbersome, opened the way to 'less sophisticated methods' aimed at creating 'a genuine central industrial power' to face the autonomy of the branches (Lafarge Archives, B 2-1). However, nothing specific was proposed. In 1974, a memorandum entitled 'Department of planning and budgeting' planned to reform the 'logbook'. The memorandum's

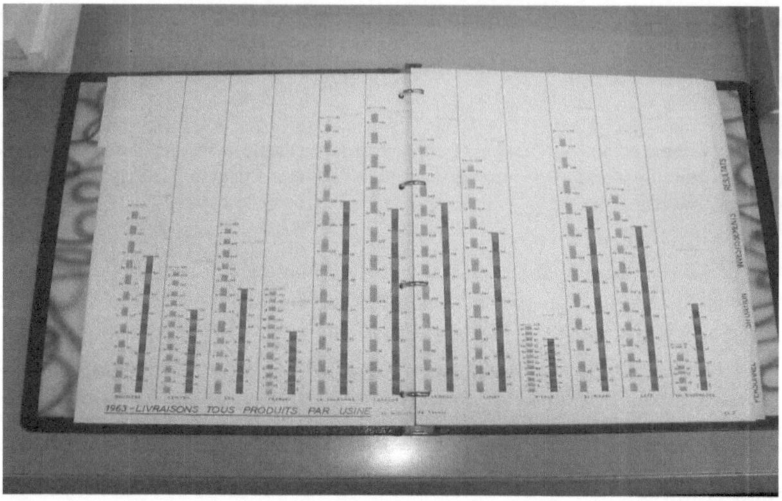

Figure 1. *Tableau de bord* of the Managing Director of Lafarge in 1963: deliveries of all products per factory.
Source: Lafarge Archives.

author specified, 'I have set myself the absolute priority of ensuring that tableaux de bord are produced in the state in which general management wishes to have them' with 'considerably shortened time lapses for providing information' (Lafarge Archives, B 2-2). The logbook had, however, a rather financial look about it, since it contained mostly profit margins. A similar trend can also be found at Saint-Gobain.

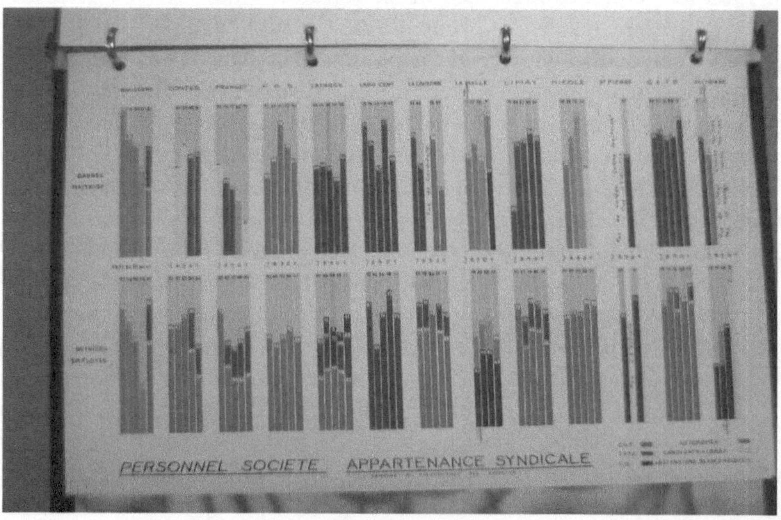

Figure 2. *Tableau de bord* of the Managing Director of Lafarge in 1963: details of the unionisation of the personnel.
Source: Lafarge Archives.

From the tableau de bord *to reporting?*

At Saint-Gobain, a study in 1959 by Paul Francin, General Manager of the Financial Department, suggested the adoption of four documents:

> 1) A *tableau de bord* for the financial department;
> 2) Financial metrics from the divisions' *tableaux de bord*;
> 3) Ratios to be used to assess an entity's situation;
> 4) An appendix: four summary tables.
>
> (Saint-Gobain Archives, CSG 01650/224, Memorandum on Setting up the Tableau de bord – Study of Ratios – 5 February 1959)

This was a specifically financial instrument that nonetheless presented some of the features of a *tableau de bord* with, in particular, objectives, definitions, norms (for instance, a ratio should be >1, according to activity type) and clearly defined frequencies for the various indicators (monthly, quarterly, annually). Its format (financial tables – profit and loss – but also ratios and diagrams), the long-term goals set (future prospects – for cash flow), and comparisons (real/forecast, real n/real n–1, Saint-Gobain/other companies operating in the same industry) also gave this instrument the look and feel of a *tableau de bord*. A reminder of the need for more than financial accounting data using ratios (the gross operating margin in particular, per product family with a turnover greater than 10%, for instance) and the selective nature of the information presented also contributed to this impression.

It was designed to complement budgeting and cost calculations:

> Given the use of the budgetary control method, it will be suitable for divisions to provide in their monthly *tableaux de bord* a brief overview of the scale and the cause of the observed budgetary variances [. . .] Furthermore, given that the budgeting method used for production costs will be a fixed budget, divisions should indicate [. . .] an order of the scale of variance in the future:
> 1) of the gross operating margin;
> 2) of percentages of general expenses.
>
> (Saint-Gobain Archives, CSG 01650/224, Memorandum on Setting up the Tableau de bord – Study of Ratios – 5 February 1959)

This undeniably makes it a financial instrument.

In the 1960s, budgeting began to disappoint as it became 'viewed more as a system for recording than as an instrument for managing'. A research project into budgetary management was conducted in 1963 by the *Institut du contrôle de gestion* (ICG) in several of the company's entities (Saint-Gobain Archives, SGV Hist 00020/04, Organisation of the Forecasting and Control Function in the Company – Investigation at the Company Saint-Gobain – November 1964). The section entitled 'Presenting Summarised Information: the tableau de bord', provided a definition:

> The tableau de bord is a summary document that brings together in a coordinated and concise manner the important outputs of the factories, divisions and the company as a whole – sales, expenditure and results – with the goal of enabling us to refer to the past, to find statistical data items and to steer the board's decision-making in line with shared objectives: in it, one will find the construction of data items, their shifts and trends, then a succession of sound information for setting future budgets and for medium-term studies.
>
> (Saint-Gobain Archives, SGV Hist 00020/04)

This definition is disappointing if compared with the theoretical definition given earlier in this paper. However, the *tableau de bord* relating to hollow glassware production that appears in the report is indeed a *tableau de bord*; that is, it contains a variety of data, especially a large number of non-financial data items. Its customised nature is recognised: 'there exist several types of *tableaux de bord* developed according to the personality of each director' (Saint-Gobain Archives, SGV Hist 00020/04, ICG memorandum).

Yet, by the end of the 1960s, the monthly *tableau de bord* for the glazing branch of the firm contained exclusively financial sections: sales, gross operating margins (with monthly variances in relation to budget targets); results of industrial operations as well as a commentary. A process whereby this tool became routinely used emerged from the restructuring of 1969. The administrative director, alongside other missions, 'operates the tableau de bord for the general management of the glass-making factories and proposes the summary formats that are most appropriate in this regard' (Saint-Gobain Archives, CSG Hist 00008/020, Job description). The management controller is responsible for 'determining, in agreement with the responsible directors, the nature of the information, both internal and external, that is worth putting into the *tableaux de bord* for the various levels of the hierarchy', and also for 'running the *tableaux de bord* of the general management and of the general director of the glass-making industries' (Saint-Gobain Archives, CSG Hist 00008/020, Job description). The administrative and financial management team was subsequently responsible for the *tableau de bord* and reporting became the norm.[11]

The history of *tableaux de bord* at Lafarge, Pechiney, and Saint-Gobain thus enables us to question assumptions underlying most research on this subject until today and, more fundamentally, to ask the question of what, in practice, is a *tableau de bord*. Indeed, the definition given earlier of a system of indicators that aim at monitoring and conducting economic operations and individual behaviours in a way that is compatible with the business strategy, does not exhaust the issue of what a *tableau de bord* really is and means. It has helped us to find, methodologically, historical traces of the emergence of the device. But it does not address, other than in a descriptive manner, the question of what is a *tableau de bord* and what it means in practice for the different individuals and groups that implemented it. The next section examines this question.

Discussion surrounding the concept of the *tableau de bord*

The history outlined above, although rather cursory, raises a number of questions relating to the 'official' history of *tableaux de bord*. Two of these questions will be discussed here: firstly, the question relating to the origins (engineers?) and the scope (a single and unified *tableau de bord*?); and secondly, the specifically French nature of the device. These questions lead on to another: in the end, what is the purpose of the *tableau de bord*?

Engineers at the birth of a single, unified tableau de bord*?*

The history portrayed by the research cited in the introduction to this paper is based on two strong, if not explicit, assumptions – the assumption of the central role played by engineers and the assumption of a single, unified *tableau de bord* used by all, right through from the workshops to general management.[12] Yet, one of the salient features of the empirical research presented above is the unobtrusiveness, not to say absence, of engineers. In this history, we find directors, sales representatives, accountants, State bodies, professional bodies, etc. Yet, engineers, in their operational role, are curiously absent. Admittedly, directors may be trained engineers – and indeed, it is often the case – but here, they are acting as directors and not as operational managers or technicians.

In the genealogy of the *tableau de bord*, the reports studied at Lafarge and Saint-Gobain that were written at the end of the nineteenth century (see above) came from the factories. These reports addressed technical issues, by and large, and were in all likelihood drawn up by engineers. At Saint-Gobain, however, it was the arrival of *Inspecteurs des finances* that was followed by a need for financial reports. From its origins, therefore, an ambiguity existed between operational information spontaneously developed in the workshops and financial information requested by the hierarchy. Lauzel and Cibert (1962, 133) raised this very issue: 'We should not be thinking of a single *tableau de bord*, but of as many *tableaux de bord* as there are distinct and complex responsibilities within the company'. However, the remainder of the text subsequently focused on information 'in the sense of moving top–down as well as bottom–up through the hierarchy' (Lauzel and Cibert 1962, 134). They still appear to have a single, unified *tableau de bord* in mind, from which the information to be disclosed at each level is selected.

In contrast, Satet's recommendation to use statistics was balanced, advocating the use of commercial, industrial and financial statistics. It also foreshadowed relatively well, aside for the learning and growth perspective, what would later become the BSC. Indeed, business process, customer and financial perspectives were present. At Lafarge, the first statistics to appear in manufacturing reports were both technical and commercial. At Pechiney, they were commercial, accounting and personnel-related. At Saint-Gobain, commercial statistics also took a central position. And although they related mostly to technical details, in the important 1936 memorandum on 'Continuous observation of the subsidiaries', these data were framed by commercial and financial statistics. We do observe at Saint-Gobain the existence of reports containing figures issued by the factories (the *Glaceries*), but it is likely that this spontaneous information was first and foremost designed for local purposes. When the board discovered the existence of this information, it was obviously tempted to request that it be sent upwards. But its own requirements went far beyond the technical information used for running the workshops, and it was for this reason that Saint-Gobain implemented budgetary control.

Finally, the role of engineers in the emergence of *tableaux de bord* is real if we consider the local *tableaux de bord* used in the factories and the workshops. Directors themselves sought to implement a 'balanced' *tableau de bord* but struggled to find the appropriate form. This appeared to have been achieved in the 1950s when the boards of Lafarge, Pechiney, and Saint-Gobain did have a *tableau de bord* at their disposal that was worthy of the name 'French' *tableau de bord* given to it in the literature. These were 'balanced' *tableaux de bord* in which technical indicators rubbed shoulders with commercial, personnel-related and financial indicators. What characterised them was that they best suited directors who knew their companies' activities intimately. For, as Hacking (1983, 245) states:

> To be sure, he [the non specialist] would be unable to make the difference between a speck of dust and the salivary gland of the fruit fly until he has undertaken to dissect a fruit fly under a low magnifying microscope. This is the first lesson: to learn to see through a microscope, it is not enough to watch; you must do it.

Beyond the role of the engineer, what is notable in this history is the role of directors who acted as if they were 'dissecting' activity. Regardless of whether they rose from the technical, commercial or other ranks, they were practitioners. Though it may be true that these directors were trained engineers, it was more their in-depth knowledge of the company's activity which was at the origins of the emergence of *tableaux de bord*, and this knowledge was not solely technical.

Furthermore, other sectors were involved: the State and its agencies; professional bodies such as trade associations through the demands they made on industrialists; competitors in the sense of their expectations; and even foreign companies through the examples they provided. The role of engineers consequently appears to have been somewhat diluted.

However, this observation needs to be put into perspective, since information used in production workshops did exist. This phenomenon is barely visible in the archives, and this constitutes a genuine methodological bias. Documentary archives tend to strongly favour sources that originate from the general management. Yet, even though our observation of the engineers' discretion should possibly be downplayed, it still remains the case that they do not appear to have been the main actors behind the emergence of *tableaux de bord* in France.

This first finding leads on to a second: the diversity of actors involved in the process of the emergence of *tableaux de bord* and, in particular, the central role of general management, also calls into question the single and unified nature of *tableaux de bord.* Indeed, it is clear that workshop *tableaux de bord* did not merge with directors' *tableaux de bord*, which, furthermore, were acquiring a distinctly financial look by the end of the period studied. The questions that emerge at this stage and that have significant ramifications on contemporary issues are fundamental in nature: what is a *tableau de bord*? Is it a totalising device that enables different levels of the hierarchy, by means of a system of consolidated indicators, to see what they can no longer see because of the factors of multiplication and distance? Or is it a local steering tool? Or are these two purposes compatible? To answer these questions, other empirical studies, and not only historical research, will be required.[13] At this stage, however, historical research suggests that the single and unified nature of the *tableau de bord* is not self-evident.

Having nuanced these first two assumptions (namely, the role of the engineer and the single and unified nature of the *tableau de bord*), we can now turn to the question of the specifically French nature of the *tableau de bord.*

A French specificity?

This is an important question. Several facts tend to contradict the thesis of a specifically French *tableau de bord* as opposed to a totally finance-based Anglo-Saxon approach to management.

Doubt was first aroused by explicit references to foreign sources in the archives studied. Although it is true that, in the work of Satet, the presence of 'statistics' only relates to the French example presented by the author and not to the American example presented as a contrast, it still remains the case that Caillet at Saint-Gobain noted the existence of the 'luxury of sales statistics' on returning from a trip to the United States in 1946. He visited, among others, the companies of Ford, Blue Ridge Glass and Corning. Also at Saint-Gobain, Grandgeorge, seeking to unify the system of *tableaux de bord* in 1955, referred to 'a method in force at SHELL that it applies to each of its operations throughout the world' (Saint-Gobain Archives, CSG Hist 00074/14 Memorandum from the chemical division). At Pechiney, Benoit seemed to discover 'qualitative methods of a self-reporting type' during the tenth International Congress on Scientific Management (Pechiney Archives, 00-10-10021). Furthermore, the shift in *tableaux de bord* towards a more classic system of financial reporting by the end of this period would mean that the specificity of the French model is weakened.

From the American standpoint,[14] Yates (1989) has shown that American management practices display strong similarities with French cases. She reveals the 'upward reporting' that is part of the techniques of 'systematic management' that appeared in the United States in the nineteenth century. A similar chronological sequence can be seen in the two countries. The technique of report writing appears in the nineteenth century:

> When sales agents located in different cities supplemented their quarterly financial accounts with frequent letters about events and competition, they were reporting. [. . .] And in the few companies in which ownership and management were separated, managers reported to owners or their representatives. In general, these reports were not particularly distinctive in form: they were simply extended (but not necessarily well-organized) letters, sometimes accompanied by financial accounts in traditional double-column form. In the late nineteenth and early twentieth centuries, the form of business reports evolved significantly to fulfil the greater demands placed on them as firms grew and as the philosophy of systematic management gained in popularity.
>
> (Yates 1989, 77–8)

The example of the American railroads is enlightening: in the 1830s and 1840s, reports were mostly financial, but operational data did still appear (on the number of miles of railroad, for instance). There was an emphasis on increasingly formalising and standardising the reports in the form of tables in particular. Their most appreciated features were readability and the ability to compare activity from one month to the next. Use of the telegraph made things easier: 'The telegraph and the tabular forms worked together to speed the flow of data without imposing excessive time burdens on senders or recipients' (Yates 1989, 78–9).

Yates observes the strong development of reports in all American companies at that time. They took different forms. Tables, whether hand-written or typed (following technical improvements in typewriters facilitating typing at the turn of the century), enabled reporters to move from description to comparison (tables with columns). The use of forms or sheets facilitated the work of 'inputting data': one just simply had to fill in the blanks. In the examples of tables and forms provided by Yates, numerous non-financial operational data can be found: 'Tables and forms made it feasible and reasonably efficient to collect, analyze, and transmit up the hierarchy the vast amounts of data needed for systematic control' (Yates 1989, 85).

The practice was theorised, in a very concrete way, however, in specialist works:

> The matter contained on the form should be arranged with reference to its sequence; the sequence of entry or computation and the sequence of matter to be transcribed from another form. On any sheet the spaces should be such that the entries are made first in the extreme left side spaces progressing across the right in order that the hand will not cover information already written down. Information to be summarized or transcribed should be placed on the right side so that the sheets may be handled with the left hand.
>
> (Quoted in Yates 1989, 81–3)

Diagrams made their appearance at the beginning of the twentieth century in response to the surfeit of tables and data at boardroom level. In his work of 1909, Carl Parsons presented diagrams as modern methods of management for anyone seeking to assess his activity at a glance. Other works on diagrammatical techniques for companies were published (Willard C. Brinton in 1914, for instance). Engineers, in particular members of the American Society of Mechanical Engineers, such as Towne, and obviously Gantt, promoted the graphical form from the 1880s onwards:

> In many cases, the graphic method requires less space than is required for words [. . .] The great advantage is that with graphic methods facts are presented so that the reader may make deductions of his own, while when words are used the reader must usually accept the ready-made conclusions handed to him.
>
> (Willard C. Brinton, quoted in Yates 1989, 85)

In the light of this American history, it is worth noting that the first edition of Satet and Voraz's work entitled *Les graphiques, moyen de direction des entreprises* only appeared in 1946.[15] The work was fairly technical, but provided numerous examples drawn from company case studies, and seems to have been the first in which the parallel with an airplane's dashboard appeared, though Satet and Voraz did not adopt the expression '*tableaux du bord*', preferring 'boardroom charts'. Finally, the work referred to professional journals (*Mon Bureau*, in particular) and to the plentiful German-language literature.

In addition to the fact that the specifically French nature of *tableaux de bord* is called into question by these various elements taken from French and American history, one remaining issue emerges: given the empirical import of this investigation, it would seem useful to take another look at what the *tableau de bord* represents in companies.

Conclusions: what is the purpose of *tableaux de bord*?[16]

The history of the *tableau de bord*, although rather cursory here, brings to light two major findings. The first pertains to the *tableau de bord*'s 'why' or, in other words, what is their purpose beyond the suitable answers along the lines of rationality/efficiency/control? Using the works of Hacking, we show that the *tableau de bord* is a mode of representation that covers a number of choices. The second finding relates to the *tableau de bord*'s 'how': in what way does the form of the device help managers? To borrow the expression used by Goody (1977, 58–60), *tableaux de bord* rely on the use of *'technologies of the intellect'* that are capable of developing certain skills in those who use them. *Tableaux de bord*, by means of 'cognitive artefacts' (Norman 1991), enable us not only to see what cannot be seen by the naked eye, but also confers on managers new competencies with which they intervene in management situations. There is indeed both representing and intervening at play here.

Tableaux de bord, and their proto-historical form, the written report, emerged when the boards of companies lost direct contact with their businesses. Size and geographical dispersion automatically distanced directors from sales representatives, producers, personnel, etc. If they wished to remain informed, they had to invent a device enabling them, if not to see the state of their business, at least to represent it for themselves. Any mode of representation, however, requires making choices. The type of *tableau de bord* (balanced, financial, commercial, technical, personnel-related, etc.), the way of processing the data presented (transformation into figures, into monetary units, modes of calculation, etc.) and the scale of magnification (level of detail, frequency, level of consolidation, etc.) must all be chosen. These choices are of a kind that will alter the situations observed. It is at this point that we move from representing to intervening.

Goody (1977, 1986) and Norman (1991) have shown how 'technologies of the intellect' or 'cognitive artefacts' such as lists, tables or diagrams modify the skills of those who use them. According to Goody (1977), the written form produces three major consequences. The first is that putting into writing allows interpretation and manipulation. However, the text[17] is also a reference because, 'literacy encouraged, at the very same time, criticism and commentary on the one hand and the orthodoxy of the book on the other' (Goody 1977, 37). The text therefore opens up opportunities to translate its meaning, even to betray its meaning, but also appears as the indispensable reference. The second consequence is that writing, and in particular the modes of communication used (texts, but also tables, lists and forms), produces effects on individuals' cognitive capacities. Goody (1977, 36) thus analyses the 'role of changes in the mode of communication in the development of cognitive structures and processes, and in developments in the growth of human knowledge and in the growth of man's capacities to store and augment that knowledge'. The cognitive artefacts act as amplifiers of aptitudes and competences for those who employ them. Finally, the third consequence of the choice of the textual form is that 'the growth of bureaucracy clearly depends to a considerable degree upon the ability to control "secondary group" relationships by means of written communications' (Goody 1977, 15) as already shown by

Max Weber. In other words, above and beyond the individual aptitudes that they produce, written forms of communication, the 'technologies of the intellect' (Goody 1977, 244), support modes of organising powers and the modes of control that are associated.

Tableaux de bord consist of cognitive artefacts. As a result, they allow a certain amount of manipulation, they dictate new behaviours/competences in users, and they are also auxiliaries of power. First of all, graphical and tabular forms do indeed open up both the possibility of building them in such a way as to highlight certain phenomena rather than others, and the possibility of interpreting them in potentially different ways. Secondly, *tableaux de bord* modify the competences of users. Yates (1989) notes in works dedicated to tables and diagrams at the beginning of the twentieth century the propensity of the authors to identify the skills developed by these cognitive artefacts: speed-reading; over-viewing (at a glance); comparison; interpretation; projection; forecasting; persuasion; manipulation; and so on. And finally, *tableaux de bord* strengthen the power of the board of directors who see, without physically being there, what operational managers are doing in the field.

Acknowledgements

The research on which this paper is based has been carried out within the framework of a project financed by the *Agence Nationale de la Recherche* (ANR) entitled 'Management: Private Practices, Public Issues'. For their help in allowing me to access to the archives, I wish to thank M. Boutiron and Mme. Malherbe (Lafarge), Melle. Carbonell and M. Grinberg (Institut pour l'histoire de l'aluminium), and M. Hamon, Mahoudeau and M. Robinet (Saint-Gobain).

Notes

1. The '*machines à statistiques*' (tabulating machines) were the antecedent of computing machines. They were invented by Hermann Hollerith at the end of the nineteenth century.
2. From a theoretical point of view, Gino Zappa was arguing from the 1920s onwards that cost accounting (which he referred to as 'statistics') should be kept separate from financial accounting. Indeed, he thought that financial accounting was incapable of capturing the reality of processes within the organisation, anticipating the later work of Kaplan and Norton (Zan 1994).
3. The distinction between accounting and other methods is not clear here. Accounting was perceived as an innovative method in contrast to merely managing cash flow. We may assume that, here, we are dealing with industrial accounting.
4. Indeed, it seems highly unlikely that data conveyed by the *Glaceries* met the requirements of general management. It seems that such data pre-dated these requests.
5. Here, the distinction with financial accounting is clear.
6. For a history of budgetary control, see Berland (1999).
7. We have only been able at this point to consult the second edition dated 1962.
8. It is unclear whether this is because they were never generated or that they simply have not survived.
9. Unfortunately, we do not know which kind of audience he addressed.
10. The ambiguities between *tableaux de bord* and budgetary control are, however, far from being clarified in this report.
11. This is how the system isstill used in Saint-Gobain today, the SIF (*Système d'informations financières*), emerged.
12. Furthermore, it was this model that has been widely theorised (see, for instance, the OVAR method – '*Objectifs, Variables d'Action, Responsables*' – developed by a French research group).
13. The examples of current *tableaux de bord* that are available to us, through the works of Masters students in particular, show that they are mainly financial reporting tools. Implementation of methods described as 'ways' (the Areva way, the Danone way, the Lafarge way, etc.) perhaps illustrates what a 'genuine' French-style *tableau de bord* would be. The company's social responsibility would appear to be the source of these initiatives (see the work of Moquet, thesis in progress at the University of Paris Dauphine).
14. Trevor Boyns has also collected some data about the case of UK industry: 'Forecasting demand: a means to more effective management' (unpublished manuscript, presented to the Association of Business Historians Conference, University of Reading, June 2002).
15. As of writing, we have only consulted the sixth edition dating from 1946.

16. In this section, it is directors' *tableaux de bord* that we have chosen as our focus.
17. Here, we use the term 'text' in its broadest sense to include 'technologies of the intellect' such as lists, tables, diagrams, forms, etc.

References

Primary sources

Lafarge – Archive collections available at the head office in Paris

B1-1 to B1-4: Management and manufacturing board meetings
B2-1 to B2-4: Management committees
B3-1 to B3-5: M. Demonque's correspondence
C1-8.1: Economics/profitability
C1-9: HR/management
C1-13.1 to C1-13.3: Statistics
C3-4 to C3-5: Strategy/planning
R4-10: Lafarge Canada (McKinsey Consultants)

Pechiney – Archive collections available at the IHA (Institut pour l'histoire de l'Amuminium), Gennevilliers.

001-7-30994: General management
00-10-10021: General management

Saint-Gobain – Archive collections available at the Centre d'Archives at Blois

CSG Hist 00074/1: General management of glass-making factories / *tableau de bord*
CSG Hist 00074/14: General management of chemical products / *tableau de bord*
CSG Hist 00005/1: CRC / Industrial accounting
CSG Hist 00077/009 to 025: Central administration / Department of control and economic studies (1872–1941)
CSG Hist 00077/026 to 028: General management of chemical products / Memoranda
CSG Hist 00077/029: Restructuring of accounting departments
CSG Hist 00004/283 to 4: IOIC
CSG Hist 00004/727: The Cegos Institute
CSG Hist 00006/06
CSG Hist 00008/020: 1969 restructuring
CSG 000417/171
CSG 000417/57 and following: Board and committee meetings
CSG 000420/171: The Saint-Gobain organisation (1932–58)
CSG 000420/18
CSG 01650/224: Financial department / *tableau de bord*
CSG 01651/10: Héranger Consultants
SGV Hist 00001/00055, 00067, 00317: General management of glass-making factories
SGV Hist 00020/04 to 05: Budgetary control, BAG

Secondary sources

Berland, N. 1999. L'histoire du contrôle budgétaire en France. Les fonctions du contrôle budgétaire, influences de l'idéologie, de l'environnement et du management stratégique. Unpublished PhD thesis, University of Paris Dauphine.

Bessire, D., and C.R. Baker. 2005. The French *Tableau de bord* and the American balanced scorecard: A critical analysis. *Critical Perspectives on Accounting* 16: 645–64.

Bourguignon, A., V. Malleret, and H. Nørreklit. 2004. The American balanced scorecard versus the French tableau de bord: The ideological dimension. *Management Accounting Research* 15: 107–34.

Cailluet, L. 1995. Stratégies, structures d'organisation et pratiques de gestion de Pechiney des années 1880 à 1971. Unpublished PhD thesis, University of Lyon II.

Epstein, M., and J.F. Manzoni. 1998. Implementing corporate strategy: From tableaux de bord to Balanced Scorecards. *European Management Journal* 16, no. 2: 190–203.

Giddens, A. 1990. *The consequences of modernity*. Cambridge, UK: Polity Press.

Goody, J. 1977. *The domestication of the savage mind*. Cambridge: Cambridge University Press. Translation used in the original paper: *La raison graphique. La domestication de la pensée sauvage*. Paris: Les Editions de Minuit, 1979.

Goody, J. 1986. *The logic of writing and the organization of society*. Cambridge: Cambridge University Press. Translation used in the original paper: *La logique de l'écriture. Aux origines des sociétés humaines*. Paris: Armand Colin.

Gray, J., and Y. Pesqueux. 1993. Evolutions actuelles des systèmes de tableaux de bord. Comparaison des pratiques de quelques multinationales américaines et françaises. *Revue française de comptabilité* 242: 61–70.

Hacking, I. 1983. *Representing and intervening. An introductory topic in the philosophy of natural science*. Cambridge: Cambridge University Press.

Kuisel, R. 1984. *Le capitalisme et l'Etat en France*. Paris: Gallimard.

Lauzel, P., and A. Cibert. 1962. *Des ratios au tableau de bord*. 2nd ed. Paris: Editions de l'entreprise moderne.

Lebas, M. 1996. Management accounting practice in France. In *Management accounting: European perspectives*, ed. A. Bhimani, 74–99. Oxford: Oxford University Press.

Levy-Leboyer, M. 1980. The large corporation in France. In *Managerial hierarchies. comparative perspectives on the rise of modern industrial enterprise*, ed. A.D. Chandler and H. Daems, 117–60. Harvard: Harvard University Press.

Malo, J.L. 1995. Les tableaux de bord comme signes d'une gestion et d'une comptabilité à la française. In *Mélanges en l'honneur du professeur Claude Perochon*, 357–76. Paris: Foucher.

Nikitin, M. 1989. *La naissance de la comptabilité industrielle en France*. Unpublished PhD thesis, University of Paris Dauphine.

Norman, D.A. 1991. Cognitive artifacts. In *Designing interaction – psychology at the human-computer interface*, ed. J.M. Carroll. Cambridge: Cambridge University Press. Translation used in the original paper: Les artefacts cognitifs. *Raisons Pratiques* 4 (1993): 15–34.

Public Histoire. 1991. *L'identité d'un groupe. Lafarge-Coppée 1947–1989*. Paris: Lafarge-Coppée.

Satet, R. 1936. *Le contrôle budgétaire, prévisions commerciales, industrielles et comptables, pour la direction rationnelle des affaires*. Paris: Dunod.

Satet, R., and C. Voraz. 1946. *Les graphiques, moyen de direction des entreprises*. 6th ed. Tourcoing: Editions Georges Frère.

Yates, J. 1989. *Control through communication. The rise of system in American management*. Baltimore, MD: The Johns Hopkins University Press.

Zan L. 1994. Toward a history of accounting histories. Perspectives from the Italian tradition. *The European Accounting Review* 3, no. 2: 255–307.

Accounting and the words to tell it: an historical perspective

Pierre Labardin and Marc Nikitin

Université d'Orléans, France

In the French language, the word *comptabilité* (accounting) first appeared in the middle of the eighteenth century. It was used in the Royal finances and its first meaning was that of accountability. Until the middle of the nineteenth century, or thereabouts, the uses of the word evolved gradually but in a somewhat confused manner. Once its meaning had become stabilised, the growing use of the word by an increasing population and the development of accounting activities created a need for adjectives to be added. Commercial, industrial and agricultural accounting, general and auxiliary accounting appeared, as well as the use of *comptabilité* to designate the accounting department. In this paper, we examine the evolution of words in the context of the development of accounting, seeking some help from amongst linguists.

Introduction

Is the word *accounting* bound to disappear? Some of the international standard setters may think so, as they have recently replaced the expression IAS (International Accounting Standards) by the more convenient IFRS (International Financial Reporting Standards). The semantic shift is not necessarily innocent, as the evolution of words just states the evolution of things: financial markets have recently taken over international accounting harmonisation, and they just need financial reporting, not accounting. We can find several other examples of the evolution of words: in the last decade or so, the French language has moved from use of the term *comptabilité générale* (general accounting) to that of *comptabilité financière* (financial accounting) as a means of coping with the ever-growing impact of Anglo-American terms in the French accounting vocabulary. Such evolution reveals the pervading Anglomania (Americanomania?) among French accounting academics, as a result of the inevitable evolution of the power struggle within the international accounting harmonisation process.

In every period, words and expressions appear and disappear. Moreover, the apparent stability of a word (the signifier) often hides a changing meaning (the signified).[1] In this paper it is our intention to clarify the genesis of the French word *comptabilité* (accounting) and its different uses,[2] from its first appearance in the eighteenth century[3] through to the present. This issue is of interest from four perspectives: epistemology; theory; practice; and methodology. From an epistemological point of view, it may be suggested that we need to question the scientific nature of our findings, so far as they are grounded in words whose meaning has fluctuated over time. From a theoretical point of view, our work could form the starting point for comparative historical research, a fruitful way of providing accounting research with an international scope. From the practical point of view, it may help teachers to enhance their explanations and practitioners to better understand the words they use every day. Finally, from a methodological point of view, it is worth showing that historical research must include the study of the evolution of words.

For our research, we have utilised various sources. First, for each period studied, we examined dictionaries. However, such a source has to be complemented by a reading of texts written by accounting authors. Thus, we systematically collected the definitions of the term *comptabilité* provided in every book which contained this word in its title.[4] To do this, we used the bibliography by Reymondin (1909), as well as the *Catalogue Collectif de France* at the French National Library[5] in Paris. In addition, we read the prefaces of many historical works, in which the author (or a friend of his) indicated the author's intentions and provides a definition of the words that he uses. Moreover, we started our work with the study of another expression (*tenue des livres* = bookkeeping), which is the ancestor of the word *comptabilité*.

To deal with our subject, we examined the evolution of words in parallel with that of the development of accounting. It seemed quite obvious to us that the evolution of words is strongly connected with the evolution of practices and doctrines. Nevertheless, we will try to show that the evolution of the uses of the term *comptabilité* may be split into two successive movements. In the first, we observed a great instability of meaning; users of this term were not numerous but their number was growing rapidly and some of these new users were tempted to propose their own definitions, which they hoped would have a significant influence on a nascent discipline.[6] This first period may be considered to be one of clarification, as the different uses[7] of the term *comptabilité* progressively came together and the use as 'accountability' gradually vanished. In the second phase, after 1850, the stabilised meaning of the term *comptabilité* and the growing number of users and practitioners entailed a need for new expressions built thereon, with the addition of an adjective, e.g. auxiliary, general, industrial, commercial, agricultural, etc.[8]

In trying to assess this evolution, we met with some difficulties:

1. In such a field of knowledge, it is quite difficult to present formal evidence,[9] since it is impossible to find people from each period who write that 'such word was utilised by such category of persons for such and such reasons'.
2. It is as also difficult to sort out, among the dozens of definitions and 'new' expressions, those which were of common use among accountants.
3. The two periods that we have mentioned over-lapped. For the practitioners, the second period had begun even though, for the public, the first had not yet come to an end. The common sense of words, as observed in dictionaries, is not always the same as the one generally accepted by practitioners; most of time, the former follows the latter with some delay. Therefore, there exists, at the same time, several groups who develop, or understand, different uses of the same word.

As we intend to understand the changing uses of a word, it is necessary to refer to the research of linguists. The latter usually insist on the necessity for a language to change: only an abstract language, a language which would not be spoken and is only contained in dictionaries, could stay unchanged. Therefore, this paper is not concerned with an exceptional event, but about the specific circumstances which led to the emergence of a new word (and/or gave a new meaning to an existing word), whose causes are due to the social and economic context of a particular time.

In order to account for the changing uses of words, linguists usually consider two points of view, which both oppose and complement each other: synchrony and diachrony. The former insists on the fact that, at a given date, all speakers must be able to understand one another, and hence need to attribute the same meaning (or so) to a word. In order to work, a language should therefore not change.[10] The latter, on the other hand, insists on the fact that it is the historical context which gives its meaning to words. An ever changing context implies changes in language.[11]

We will first examine the appearance of the word *comptabilité* (accounting) and the evolution of its uses, trying to evaluate the role of the generalisation of double entry at the beginning of the nineteenth century; we will then see how, in the second half of the nineteenth century, the division of labour among accountants entailed the use of several adjectives attached to the term *comptabilité*.

From bookkeeping to accounting

Tenir les livres, teneur de livres, tenue des livres: to keep the books, bookkeeper, bookkeeping

In order to describe their subject matter, accounting authors[12] used different terms. However, the great variety of titles reveals the use of some recurring expressions: from 1550 (Mennher de Kempten) to the end of the eighteenth century,[13] the most common expression is *tenir les livres* (to keep the books). Quite naturally, those who master that technique and wish to capitalise on their talent are called *teneurs de livres* (bookkeepers). These people belonged, in the seventeenth and eighteenth centuries, to the guild of the *Maîtres écrivains* (Master writers) and it is not surprising that most of the best known accounting authors belonged to that guild. In his book published in 1678, Claude Irson introduces himself as *juré, teneur de livres* (member of the guild of bookkeepers) and Mathieu de la Porte, another member of the guild, published in 1685 a *Guide des négocians et teneurs de livres* (*Guide for Merchants and Bookkeepers*).

The term *tenue des livres* (bookkeeping), on the other hand, only appears in the second half of the eighteenth century, but then only in a small number of cases.[14] During the second half of the eighteenth century, if we only consider the titles of books, both *tenue des livres* and *tenir les livres* coexisted alongside one another. From 1800 onwards, however, *tenue des livres* (bookkeeping) spread in almost every book published on the subject matter, only finally disappearing after the Second World War.[15]

Surprisingly, single entry bookkeeping is seldom mentioned in the titles of books published from the sixteenth to the eighteenth century books. Almost all praise the virtues of double entry. On the other hand, single entry gains more interest from authors in the first two decades of the nineteenth century, and some of these books only deal with single entry bookkeeping. On the one hand, this may be a side effect of the publication, in English, of E.T. Jones' book on the subject of double entry by single in 1796 and, on the other hand, it may be due to the low level of accounting education among the population. In a period of great industrial expansion, many small entrepreneurs could not afford a bookkeeper and were obliged to keep their books themselves. Such individuals wanted to find the simplest way to do it. That passion would be short-lived but, all through the nineteenth century, books on bookkeeping and accounting dealing with both single *and* double entry would be in a large majority.

However, the prestige of *tenue des livres* (bookkeeping) faded during the nineteenth century. In the early decades of the century, several authors did not hesitate to qualify *tenue des livres* (bookkeeping) as a science, thereby enhancing the social status of the bookkeeper. However, during the nineteenth century, and especially after 1860, there was a development in commercial and technical education, in keeping, on the one hand, with the 1865 law on technical secondary education and, on the other, with the creation of business schools after 1869. Bookkeepers therefore became more numerous and their skill became commonplace, so that their wages and social status steadily declined. The bookkeeper was exclusively a technician, unlike the accountant, who enjoyed the former status of 'a person in charge'.

Developments in France can be compared with those observed in Britain: the expression 'bookkeeping', for example, appeared in Britain at the end of the seventeenth century in the title of books, and became commonplace in the eighteenth century (Parker 1994, 115). According to Parker, the term was 'imported' from the Flemish word *boekhouden*, present in book titles since the end of the sixteenth century. A connection is also possible with the German words *buchhalten* and *Buchhaltung*, also used in book titles from the sixteenth century.

Comptabilité: 'accountability' and 'means to account', then a mere 'recording technique'

The first attested occurrence of the word *comptabilité*, according to our research, dates back to 1750[16] and concerns the Royal finances. The word is included in a document dated November 1750 (see appendix), the title of which, '*Les fermiers des Aydes, Circulaire de la Ferme générale proposant un mode uniforme de comptabilité*', was added later.[17] According to the text, the meaning of *comptabilité* may either be 'accountability' or 'set of accounts'.

The first definition of *comptabilité* appears in 1753 in the Encyclopaedia by Diderot and D'Alembert (see appendix), but in a relatively confused manner, revealing an inconsistent use.[18] We have to wait until the 1798 edition of the dictionary of the French Academy (see appendix) to obtain a quite plain and clear definition: 'obligation to account, situation of a person in charge (in an administration)'. The meaning is slightly different from that contained in the 1750 text, although neither antagonistic to nor incompatible with it. The distance between these two definitions probably delineates the complete spectrum of all meanings that could be attributed to the term in the second half of the eighteenth century.

We then observe varied senses of the word, although close to each other, which is quite normal for a new word with a limited use. On the one hand, *comptabilité* means responsibility, i.e. being equivalent, as with *comptable*, to someone who is accountable and, on the other hand, it is a means to account or it may even be a set of accounts. Let us remember that, before 1800, the term only concerned the Royal Finances (or the Public Finances after the Revolution).

Both meanings (the *obligation* to account or the *means* to account) may coexist: the *comptabilité* of a 'Receiver' or a 'Farmer General' will either be the expression of his accountability or the apparatus created in order to account to the King. One can consider that such an apparatus includes three elements: a set of accounts properly selected; a recording technique which allows one to obtain reliable and relevant information; and the organisation of the work of bookkeepers. The choice of these three elements enables the person in charge to really exert his responsibility.

The meaning indicated by the dictionary of the French Academy progressively faded, and Dupiney de Vorepierre (1876) would note, late in the nineteenth century, that *comptabilité* has two meanings, one of them, 'obligation to account', being seldom used.

It is with the second meaning of *comptabilité* ('means to account') that the expression *comptabilité publique* (public sector accounting) appears in 1800 in a book by Reys du Sully. Edmond

Degrange used it in 1807, in a book dedicated to receivers general, and the law-makers gave it acceptance in 1817, when the Monarch intended to show his will to render accounts to the Nation (Nikitin 2001).

The word *comptabilité*, considered as the means to account, was introduced in a book on commercial accounting: Pierre Boucher (1800) used the word with that meaning, in the expression *Comptabilité rurale et maritime* (rural and maritime accountability), expanding the use of the word to areas other than the public finances. Other authors, such as Degrange in 1801, soon used the term *comptabilité commerciale* (commercial accounting) and an anonymous essay on *comptabilité commerciale* was published in 1805. Lorrimier (1808) and Legret (1811) also used the term; the merchant's *comptabilité* is here the apparatus he sets up in order to render accounts to himself.

In the private sector, *comptabilité* did not mean any responsibility towards someone else, and it became quite natural to mix up *tenue des livres* and *comptabilité*. We then observe some hesitation, as some people considered the two terms to be equivalent, while others considered *comptabilité* as something superior to *tenue des livres*.

Rodriguès (1810), for example, considers the two terms as equivalent: 'Bookkeeping, or accounting, is a method used by merchants to write all their business in books'. When there is no division of labour between the owner of the firm who wants to be aware of his situation, and a bookkeeper, the confusion of the two terms is tempting. This is the case for the merchant that Rodriguès considers as an example. The preface of Chabaud (1836)[19] also illustrates the confusion between the two terms, placed here on an equal footing: the author first speaks of '*comptabilité* considered as a science, from the triple point of view of its cause, its nature and its end. Yet *tenue des livres* gathers all these principles'. Five paragraphs later, one can read: 'Like all good sciences, *tenue des livres* only relies on one principle' (quoted in Reymondin 1909, 39).

We then end up in confusion between the two terms, mainly in dictionaries if not among practitioners, so that *comptabilité* will take the meaning of *tenue des livres*, i.e. a mere technique for keeping the books.

However, early in the nineteenth century, some authors proposed a distinction. J.S. Quiney (1817) explained: 'Accounting is the science of accounts. Bookkeeping is the art of recording all operations' (quoted in Reymondin 1909, 179). L. Mézières (1849, 1) explicitly claimed: 'Accounting can be considered as a science, of which bookkeeping is the practical application'. On the other hand, the 1856 Larousse dictionary indicated that accounting and bookkeeping were synonymous. We see here the gap which exists between the language of specialists and that of the public at large. It will take time (until the 1930s) before a hierarchy appears in a dictionary. In 1906, the illustrated Larousse dictionary proposes quite similar definitions: 'The art of keeping the accounts in order'[20] for *comptabilité*, and 'the art to run a merchant's accounting' for *tenue des livres*.

In the title of one of his books, Coffy (1833) also insisted on the difference between the two terms: 'A synoptic chart of the general principles of double entry bookkeeping or experimental method through which the practical and theoretical study of accounting is explained for every pupil'. In 1834, the same author tries to explain the social and political importance of learning *comptabilité* (in the sense of accountability): 'Accountability is part of economics, and its growing importance under the constitutional regime should have made it a part of public instruction for everyone' (quoted in Reymondin 1909, 43). The importance of accountability relies, according to Coffy, in the educational role it may play in a democratic regime. That idea is confirmed by someone named Costay, in charge of examining Coffy's book after the latter submitted it to the Academy of Sciences. The Costay report, quoted by Reymondin (1909, 44), was delivered on 14 April 1834: 'Accounting methods have a great social importance; they deal with the preservation and the improvement of the wealth of persons as well as the administration of public fortune'.

During the nineteenth century, *comptabilité* progressively supplanted *tenue des livres*. We will see later the role played by the division of labour; one may also adduce the more positive social connotation of being a *comptable* (someone responsible) rather than a bookkeeper (a mere technician). In the eighteenth century, the bookkeeper enjoyed some prestige and related earnings, but that was only due to his skill, as he did not have the responsibility of an administration, unlike someone accountable.

In Great Britain, the term *accounting* appears very late in the titles of books. However, we can find its ancestors (*accompting* and *accountantship*) much earlier, e.g. North (1714)[21] and Gordon (1765).[22] An important book by Robert Hamilton (1788) does not mention the term *accounting*, but uses only *bookkeeping*. It is not before the middle of the nineteenth century that accounting (1861) or accountancy (1854) appears in the title of books (Parker 1994). This happened in concomitance with the creation of institutes of chartered accountants, and one may suppose that the new profession was anxious to create a new word in order to promote its distinctive skill. As in France, however, accountability had been used in relation to public sector finances since the eighteenth century.

After 1850, different categories of accounting

The number of accountants in France is thought to have grown significantly during the second half of the nineteenth century, but limitations of the available data make it difficult to be precise. Employment records do not make it possible to distinguish accountants from other employees, a butcher's shop assistant being classed as an employee in exactly the same way as an accountant (Gardey 2001, 41). Gardey (2001, 43) has suggested that the number of employees in France rose from 800,000 in 1866 to over 3 million in 1936. If it is assumed that accountants grew at a similar rate, then there must have been between two and four times as many of them in 1936 as there had been 70 years earlier.

Such changes in the number of accountants can be cross-checked with details known for specific businesses. Thus, when a banker went bankrupt in Bourges in 1828, his debts were over six million francs and he had 994 creditors. However, according to the bankruptcy report, he had no bookkeeper.[23] Similar facts may be observed in industry: rules at the Forges d'Allevard[24] and d'Audincourt[25] confirm that less than 1% of the workforce was employed to keep the accounts at the beginning of the nineteenth century. At Saint-Gobain, a large firm producing glass and chemical products, prior to 1867, less than 1% of the payroll were accountants,[26] but by 1912, with the company exhibiting a growing global workforce, they represented 2.5%.

The increase in the number of accountants may also be inferred from the fast growing number of accounting books published after 1860 (Reymondin 1909) and, above all, the increase in the number of editions of those books. Finally we may notice, from the 1870s onwards, the dramatic upsurge in the creation of business schools, noting that accounting was the main topic taught in such institutions (Maffre 1985, 135).

There are at least two reasons for this increase. First, the concentration of firms entailed an increase in their size (Woronoff 1998, 416), and big firms taking on most employees. A second reason, resulting from the previous one, relates to the bureaucratisation of firms, as the consequence of a need for internal coordination. At Saint-Gobain, the workforce doubled between 1867 and 1912, but the number of accountants increased fivefold during the same period. The phenomenon seems quite general, and all the examples we have found in the archives suggest the same phenomenon: in 1931, at the *Mines du Boulonnais* (coal mines), accountants represented 3.5% of the workforce;[27] in the tanneries near Tours, they were 3%.[28] Finally, as further evidence of the increase in the number of accountants, we could mention the creation, mainly after 1880, of numerous associations dedicated to the defence of their professional interest (Pinceloup 1993, 47–8).

As more and more accountants were employed, a division of labour developed: some of them were concerned with recording sales, while others only with recording purchases. This division of labour had at least three consequences: first, a hierarchy was set up among accounting employees; second, the division of labour entailed a division of space and the creation of an accounting department, also named *comptabilité*; and third, a specialisation of accounting skills.

Division of labour and the creation of a hierarchy among the accountants

The first consequence of the development of large industrial firms, especially railroad companies and banks, was on the organisation of accounting: in such firms, the various plants had to centralise their activities and their accounting system at their head office, most often in Paris. Accountants working in the plants recorded information and passed it on to the head office for it to be cross-checked and centralised. This type of organisation allowed an important internal turnover among accountants (see Omnès 1998; Bonin 2006).

The division of labour between accounting undertaken at the head office ('general' or 'central' accounting) and that at the various plants ('auxiliary' accounting) only begins to appear in the second half of the nineteenth century. As an exception, we did find use of the expression '*comptabilité générale*' at Saint-Gobain in a 'Plan raisonné de comptabilité pour la manufacture royale des glaces',[29] probably dated 1761.[30] *Comptabilité générale* actually meant the accounts held at the Parisian head office, as opposed to those held in the Chauny and Saint-Gobain plants. One may see here the influence of the public sector accounting vocabulary, as Saint-Gobain held its accounts by charge and discharge (*en finance*), i.e. according to the model used in the Royal Finances. Degrange (1801, 13), also makes an early use of the expression *comptabilité générale* with the same meaning.[31] However, at that time, he is the only author who uses the expression. In both cases (at Saint-Gobain and in Degrange's book), those first uses of the expression are closely linked to public sector accounting.[32] But even here, use of the expression seems quite rare: the law dictionary by Ferrière (1769) fails to mention either *comptabilité* or *comptabilité générale.*

Later, around 1850, *comptabilité générale* and *comptabilité auxiliaire* became commonly used in firms. Helfenbein (1845), chief bookkeeper at the St-Etienne to Lyon Railroad Company, used *comptabilité générale* in his book (see appendix). Bahier (1850) clearly differentiates between *comptabilité générale* and *comptabilité auxiliaire*. Many others followed, and the new meaning of comptabilité générale soon spread throughout textbooks and firms: Guilbault (1865), Barré (1877) and Barillot (1887) proposed the same distinction (see appendix) while at the Crédit Lyonnais, the expression is found in the internal correspondence.[33] Léautey and Guilbault (1889), the most important accounting authors of the late nineteenth century, also introduced the distinction, but initially preferred *livres analytiques* rather than *comptabilité auxiliaire* and *livres synthétiques* rather than *comptabilité générale*.

Even if we do not rule out the influence of public finances in the origin of the term *comptabilité générale*, another explanation may be put forward: *comptabilité générale* and *comptabilité auxiliaire* may be derived from *comptes généraux* and *comptes particuliers*,[34] a distinction used widely from the seventeenth century onwards by, amongst others, very prestigious authors of their time, such as de la Porte (1685), Imhoof (1786), Degrange (1801), Dupuy (1823) and Barlet (1861) (see appendix). It may happen that the division of labour between the head and auxiliary offices was related to that between real and capital accounts on the one hand and nominal accounts on the other. The former were often held at the head office, whereas the latter could easily be held in every plant.

In the mid-1860s, Beauchery also differentiates between *comptes généraux* and *comptes particuliers* (1865, 15):

> How can we legitimate the use of the expression *comptes généraux*?
> 1. The general information they contain.
> 2. The impersonality which characterises them.
>
> How can we legitimate the use of the expression *comptes particuliers*?
> 1. The particular information they contain.
> 2. The fact that they represent the relations with a person.

In this case, Beauchery intermixes two ideas: on the one hand he differentiates between general accounting (the one that gives global information) and auxiliary accounting (the one that gives specific information, on a plant, on suppliers, on cash at hand, etc.); on the other hand, he differentiates the general accounts (accounts of the owner) from the nominal accounts (debts).

Division of labour and division of space

The rise in the number of accountants had several consequences on the organisation of their tasks in every plant. One of these is related to the emergence, in every plant of every big firm, of a specific area assigned to the accounting activities: the accounting department. In the eighteenth century, such an area did not exist, or at least was not organised: in Niort, shopkeepers did not have any specific area in which to keep their accounts (Martin 1977, 48). Similarly, merchants and bookkeepers worked in the same room in Marseille (Carrière 1973, 21) and, in Bordeaux, commercial correspondence, accounting and consignments were conducted in the same room and everyone could carry out these tasks (Butel 1974, 164). Information relating to large firms of these times is generally lacking, but it is known that the eighteenth century *Compagnie des Indes* had a special area dedicated to its accounting activities (Haudrère 2005, 155). The situation of the Royal administration may provide some indications of the customs of the time. Coquery (2000, 48) states that, during the *Ancien Régime*, many employees of government departments worked at home. They were assigned a room, but they did not use it. Absenteeism was a real concern at the *Bureau de la comptabilité* during the Revolution (Herrmann-Mascard 1989, 304). For all these reasons, it seems difficult to speak of 'accounting departments' in the eighteenth century, even if we perceive the beginnings of such a development.

In the nineteenth century, the 'functionalisation' of space developed in most French firms (Foucault 1993).[35] From then on, every place must have a precise function, and accounting was no exception. Our research confirms this phenomenon: at the end of the nineteenth century, organisational plans for some firms show a place dedicated to accounting activities, a place which is clearly separated from that assigned to hand workers or to the managerial hierarchy.[36] In this way, the word *comptabilité* competed with the word *bureau* to refer to that place. However, *bureau* was used in a broader sense, as a means of designating the whole administrative services.

The new use of the word *comptabilité* as a description of the accounting department may be dated from the 1860s. At Saint-Gobain, the first occurrence of *comptabilité* to designate the accounting department dates back to 1859 in Aachen.[37] In 1862, Heudicourt introduced himself as a *chef de comptabilité*, i.e. chief of the accounting department, while three years later Guilbault (1865) does the same. In the bibliography of Reymondin, we can find other authors using the same title from the 1860s onwards.[38] In 1865, the dictionary by La Châtre is the first one to indicate the use of *comptabilité* to describe an area, albeit in an elliptical way.[39] However, neither Dupiney de Vorepierre (1876) nor the dictionary of the French Academy adopt this usage.

Division of labour and specialisation

Up to the beginning of the nineteenth century, all activities related to buying and selling goods was considered as being commercial.[40] However, from the 1800s onwards, a distinction is progressively made between commercial, agricultural and industrial[41] activities. The accounting vocabulary developed alongside this evolution and new types of accounting appeared in handbooks: agricultural accounting (farmers' accounting), industrial accounting (industrialists' accounting). These expressions only meant the application of accounting rules (mainly double entry bookkeeping) to a specific type of firm, and were not specific types of accounting. An influential author of the early nineteenth century, Edmond Degrange (father), divided his handbooks into several volumes, each one dedicated to a specific activity,[42] in order to prove the universality of double entry bookkeeping. The definitions of industrial, agricultural and commercial accounting are quite similar in Cazaux (1824), Godard (1827), Royer (1840), Joubert (1847), Bahier (1850), Lefour (1853), Hubert (1856), Coulon (1857), Matharan (1859) (see appendix) and even in Reymondin (1909).

In the early 1860s, as the number and size of industrial firms grew, a distinction was made among the accounts: those held in the factory, which mainly record movements inside the firm, formed part of what came to be called industrial accounting, while those accounts held at head office, which mainly recorded the relations of the firm with other firms, formed part of what were called commercial accounting.[43] Barlet (1861) and Heudicourt (1862) clearly distinguished two distinct accounting activities within the same firm (see appendix). Barlet characterised industrial accounting as the addition of the production accounts and the commercial accounts.[44] Heudicourt does not provide definitions for industrial accounting and financial accounting,[45] but presents the former as a means to explain the latter.[46] Both Barlet and Heudicourt were close to the practices of their times, and probably relate, in their distinction between the two ways to account, the changing nature of the organisation of firms. At the turn of the century, Andoyer (1896), Bournisien (1909) and Edom (1911) confirm this distinction (see appendix).

The distinction between commercial and industrial activities after 1800 on the one hand, and the distinction between commercial and industrial accounting after 1860 on the other hand, entailed a specialisation among accountants, in keeping with the increase in their number. Some specialised in industrial accounting while others specialised in commercial (or general, or financial) accounting. The distinction progressively gained in importance. For example, at the Dourges coal mines in 1902, the industrial accounts were held near to the pits, while the commercial accounts were held in the offices, a few miles away.[47] The same organisation existed both at the SEIT[48] and at Saint-Gobain.[49] Other confirmations of this arrangement may be found in Zimnovitch (1997).

Conclusion

At the end of our study, we would like to put some 'concluding hypotheses'.[50] Among new words and expressions, linguists distinguish innovations from adoptions. Only the latter are real new words or expressions. Many accounting authors have proposed new words with a view to enhance their own fame and prestige. For example, Joubert (1847, 1) proposed *agrométrie* (agrometrics) instead of 'agricultural accounting', in the title of his book; Gomberg (1912) proposed *économologique* to replace 'accounting' (as a science); while Léautey and Guilbault (1889, 25) use the term *comptable d'origine*, which was rarely mentioned again, etc. For all that, the accountants do not necessarily adopt all these new words or new uses of existing words. Therefore, one can wonder why, among the great many innovations in the accounting vocabulary, only a few were adopted and spread. According to Coseriu (1958, 10),[51] the selection is deliberate and at first gets rid of all the alterations with no functional value:

> one may say that an adoption always corresponds to an expressive necessity, which can be cultural, social, aesthetic[52] or functional. The one who hears (or reads) would adopt what he does not know because he finds here aesthetic satisfaction, social convenience or functional use. Adoption is therefore an act of culture, taste or practical intelligence.

Such thinking from a linguist is confirmed in the case we are dealing with: contrary to their adoption, the creation of new words is generally not due to influential authors. Let us remember those innovators who rapidly sunk into oblivion: Helfenbein (1845), first to use *comptabilité générale*, or de Cazaux (1824), first to use *comptabilité industrielle*. On the other hand, influential authors do seem to have played a decisive role in the dissemination and the final adoption of a word. On adoption, Coseriu (1958, 10) states:

> the one who listens (reads) ... always compares his knowledge to that of the one who speaks (writes) and is willing to accept his linguistic means if he accepts his cultural superiority or if he himself doubts the excellence of his own knowledge.

The choice of new words or new uses of an existing word therefore does not seem to be an accident; on the contrary, this choice seems to be the result of some process of natural selection. Because of their authority, influential authors 'naturally' play a decisive role in the adoption of words and uses.

A second point of discussion is related to the concomitance of two phenomena: double entry bookkeeping became commonly used in firms at the same moment (the first half of the nineteenth century) when the use of the word *comptabilité* stabilised. An explanation of that concomitance may be found in the assimilation of 'accounting' to 'double entry accounting'. Many authors insist on the fact that a complete system of accounting can only be held by double entry. In the first congress of the French accountants in December 1880,[53] amongst the small number of motions passed unanimously was one which stipulated that single entry bookkeeping had to be rejected and that the double entry method was the only one that should be taught. Another explanation may be suggested from the perspective of linguistics: so long as double entry and the diffusion of related knowledge were in progress, every expression seems relevant, and it is no surprise to find the coexistence of several meanings for the same word. The stabilisation of the uses of *comptabilité* was probably the consequence of the stabilisation of the technique.

Acknowledgements

The authors are grateful to Trevor Boyns (Cardiff Business School), Lisa Evans (University of Edinburgh), Julien Franco, Giuseppe Galassi (Universita' degli Studi di Parma), Esteban Hernandez-Esteve (Universidad de Madrid), Yannick Lemarchand (Université de Nantes), Robert Parker (University of Exeter) and Vyacheslav Sokolov (PriceWaterhouseCoopers Audit – Moscow) for their comments and suggestions.

Notes

1. This distinction is attributable to de Saussure (1915).
2. From the linguists we learn that a word does not have 'meanings', but only 'uses', but this distinction does not have much importance here.
3. Trésor de la Langue Française indicates a first occurrence of the word in 1579 (drawing from a journal published in 1937: *Français moderne,* p. 37). We checked in the book supposed to contain the word and only found *compatibilité* (compatibility) and not *comptabilité.*
4. For those definitions, please see appendix.
5. Bibliothèque François Mitterrand, ou Bibliothèque Nationale de France (BNF) – http://www.bnf.fr
6. In the first half of the nineteenth century, several authors claimed to be the very first to deal with such or such accounting problem; they therefore propose to ground their founding process on new definitions for accounting words.
7. In the second half of the century, the most common use was that of 'a recording technique' and we could find, more rarely, 'set of accounts'.
8. *Comptabilité auxiliaire, générale, industrielle, commerciale, agricole*, etc.
9. Coseriu 1958, chap. III, paragrap 3.2.3.
10. A paradox which is expressed as follows by Bally (1950, 18): 'Languages are always changing but can only work if they do not'. Incidentally, one could notice that it is the same for accounting rules.
11. On the complex relations between synchrony and diachrony of languages, see Coseriu (1958).
12. We consider that an accounting author is someone who wrote a published book on accounting or bookkeeping.
13. The bibliography by Reymondin (1909) is the most exhaustive document concerning accounting books published in the French language between 1543 and 1908. It includes hundreds of references.
14. Reymondin (1909, 142) mentions a book on *tenue des livres* (bookkeeping) published by Bushall in 1764. We could not find this book. Two other references mention *tenue des livres* (bookkeeping) in their title: Gentil (1777) and Degrange (1795). The 1795 (first) edition of the book by Degrange is also untraceable in any French library.
15. In addition to the bibliography by Reymondin (1909), we have consulted the Catalogue Collectif de France (http://www.bnf.fr), including all references from the BNF and from all municipal and academic libraries.
16. We initially thought that there were previous occurrences but, after a check, it was found that earlier supposed uses reflected incorrect attributions, resulting from a confusion between the words *comptabilité* and *compatibilité* (compatibility).
17. But it is not known when.
18. 'Comptabilité is a new word, only used in the chambers of accounts: it means a particular nature of receipts and expenses of which we have to account; for example, the Royal Treasury, the Marine, the Fortifications are all different *comptabilités*' (p. 792).
19. Chabaud was a professor in a college in Marseille.
20. A second use of the word is also given here, i.e. 'the part of an administration which is in charge of the accounts' (see below).
21. The sixth and last part of the book is entitled 'A short and easy VOCABULARY of Certain Words that in the Language of Accompting take a Particular Meaning'. However, *accompting* is not present in the glossary. North uses *accompting* on several occasions in the introduction, for example in a title 'I. *The Excellency of Accompting by* Debtor *and* Creditor'. A little bit further on (p.2), North mentions a synonym: 'But the Art of Regular Accompting, or Bookkeeping'.
22. 'Part I. The ELEMENTS of MERCANTILE ACCOUNTANTSHIP'. (p. 13). The term is only used once.
23. Archives of Cher. 34 U 68
24. Archives of Isère. 94 J 337. Internal rules, dates from 1831–4.
25. Archives of Doubs. 28J. Internal rules, dates from 1824.
26. Archives of St-Gobain. 1L1.
27. CAMT à Roubaix, Cartex fonds. 1994045 0005.
28. Archives of Indre-et-Loire. 48 J 272.
29. Archives Saint-Gobain. C 44. 'Accounting chart for the Royal Manufacture'.
30. Handwriting added, right at the top of the document.
31. *'Non, il n'est pas vrai qu'un teneur de livres, pour se former une idée de la comptabilité générale d'une régie, d'une administration, d'un ministère et même de la comptabilité générale et centrale de l'Etat, doive acquérir par un long noviciat ou exercice actif, les connaissances routinières des praticiens . . .'*.
32. Degrange mentions examples drawn from public sector accounting. Moreover, he was among the first to publish a book on public sector accounting in 1807, showing his interest and skill in that field of knowledge.

33. File révision de la comptabilité (1875–6).062 AH 011. Archives of Crédit Lyonnais.
34. The *comptes particuliers* are the equivalent of 'nominal accounts', and *comptes généraux* the other accounts. This distinction draws on the idea that the *comptes généraux* make it possible to account for oneself.
35. According to Foucault, the functionalisation of space is part of a general reorganisation of space: the closure between an 'inside' and an 'outside', the chequering which implies that everyone is placed in a specific area and the link between the place occupied and the hierarchical position.
36. Archives of Saint-Gobain. Hist C-3/3-2 and Plan 07 30 à 07 42.
37. Archives of Saint-Gobain. 1L1 Bis.
38. An illustration of the fact that the title had come into common use was the formation of an association of salaried accountants in 1930 (*Compagnie des Chefs de Comptabilité*).
39. '*Employé à la comptabilité, chef de comptabilité*'.
40. Even today, the law sees every industrial activity as an 'act of commerce'.
41. The word *industrie* changed its meaning at that time. Up to that period, it was a synonym for *activity*, or just *business*, in its primary use (the fact to be busy).
42. Receivers general (1807), industrialists (1824), Stockbrokers (1825).
43. In 1817, Jean-Baptiste Payen (mistakenly surnamed Anselme in several books or articles) made such a distinction, but this proposal was not followed by other authors.
44. 'Industrial accounting is a two stage activity: the first one embraces all operations relating to production until the achievement of the product; the second one, the commercial operations, relate to sales. The producer then becomes a merchant, and joins his commercial accounting to his special accounting'.
45. Surprisingly for the period, he uses the term *comptabilité financière*.
46. Industrial accounting is grounded in rules which allow one to follow the transformation of raw material, plain or complex, rare or numerous as they could be, from the time they enter the firm till they are delivered to the public.
47. Centre d'Archives du Monde du Travail, Roubaix. Cartex fonds. 1994056 0039.
48. Archives of Altadis. Factory of Toulouse (1936). J7. 100 J 112.
49. Archives of Saint-Gobain. Factories of Tours (1934) and Nantes (1933). Plan 20.
50. According to the expression of Fernand Braudel (1979, 143).
51. Chapter III, paragraph 4.3.3.
52. We recently met a colleague, a former Professor of accounting, who introduced himself as a 'Professor of financial accounting'; we asked him the reason for this new appellation, and after a few seconds, he confessed: 'Because it is more sexy'.
53. See Reymondin (1909, 290).

References

Académie Françoise. 1798. *Dictionnaire de l'Académie Françoise, Tome premier A–K*. Paris: Smits and Co.

Andoyer, M.J. 1896. *Traité théorique et pratique de comptabilité commerciale*. Paris: Belin Frères.

Bahier, J.-L. 1850. *Manuel de comptabilité agricole à l'usage des fermes-écoles et des écoles primaires*. Saint-Brieuc: Imprimerie-librairie de L. Prud'homme.

Bally, Ch. 1950. *Linguistique générale et linguistique française*. Paris: Ernest Leroux.

Barillot, A. 1887. *Cours de comptabilité*. Paris: Charles Delagrave.

Barlet, C.H. 1861. *Tenue des livres appliquée à la comptabilité des mines de houille, des hauts-fourneaux et des usines à fer*. Paris: Librairies Lethielleux et Lacroix.

Barré, J. 1877. *Cours complet de comptabilité*. Paris: Librairie de G. Masson.

Beauchery, A. 1865. *Comptabilité centralisatrice*. Lille: Perdreau.

Bonin, H. 2006. *Histoire de la Société Générale (1864–1890) Naissance d'une banque*. Geneva: Droz.

Boucher, Pierre. 1800(an VIII). *La science des négocians et teneurs de livres par feu de la Porte*. Bordeaux: Pellier Lawalle.

Braudel, F. 1979. *Civilisation matérielle, économie et capitalisme XVe–XVIIIe siècle*. Paris: Le livre de Poche.

Butel, P. 1974. *Les négociants bordelais l'Europe et les îles au XVIIIe siècle*. Paris: Aubier.

Carrière, C. 1973. *Négociants marseillais au XVIIIe siècle*. Marseille: Institut historique de Provence.

Cazaux (de), L.-F.-G. 1824. *De la comptabilité dans une entreprise industrielle et spécialement dans une exploitation rurale*. Toulouse: J-M. Douladoure.

Collectif. 1906. *Petit Larousse illustré 1906*. Paris: Larousse.

Coquery, N. 2000. *L'espace du pouvoir*. Paris: Seli Arslan.

Coseriu, E. 1958. *Synchronie, diachronie et histoire*. www.revue-texto.net.

Coulon, H. 1857. *Méthode générale de comptabilité et de correspondance commerciale*. Paris.

Degrange, E. père. 1801. *La tenue des livres rendue facile ou nouvelle méthode d'enseignement*. Paris: Libraire Hocquart.

Diderot, D., and J. D'Alembert. 1753. *Encyclopédie ou Dictionnaire raisonné des sciences, des arts et des métiers*, tome III. http://gallica.bnf.fr/.

Dupiney de Vorepierre, J.-F.-M. 1876. *Dictionnaire français illustré et encyclopédie universelle pouvant tenir lieu de tous les vocabulaires et de toutes les encyclopédies*. Paris: Michel Lévy Frères.

Dupuy, J.-B. 1823. *La Tenue des livres, ou Cours théorique et pratique de comptabilité commerciale à parties doubles, à l'usage des commerçans*. Lyon and Paris: Perisse Frères and Mequignon Junior.

Ferrière, C.-J. 1769. *Dictionnaire de droit et de pratique*. Paris. http://gallica.bnf.fr/.

Foucault, M. 1993. *Surveiller et Punir*. Paris: Gallimard.

Gardey, D. 2001. *La dactylographe et l'expéditionnaire. Histoire des employés de bureau (1890–1930)*. Paris: Belin.

Gentil. 1777. *Instruction sur la tenue des livres en parties doubles et les changes étrangers*. Paris.

Godard, P.-A. 1827. *Traité général et sommaire de comptabilité commerciale*. Paris: Librairie du Commerce.

Gomberg, L. 1912. *L'économologique (science comptable) et son histoire*. Geneva: Société Générale d'Imprimerie.

Gordon, W. 1765. *The Universal Accountant*. London: reprinted by Garland, 1986, New York.

Guilbault, A. 1865. *Traité de comptabilité et d'administration industrielle*. Paris.

Hamilton, A. 1788. *An Introduction to Merchandise*. Aberdeen: reprinted by Garland, 1982, London and New York.

Haudrère, P. 2005. *La Compagnie française des Indes au XVIIIe siècle*. Paris: les Indes Savantes.

Helfenbein, P.L. 1845. *De la comptabilité des compagnies de chemin de fer*. Lyon: Léon Boitel.

Herrmann-Mascard, N. 1989. La discipline du travail dans une administration révolutionnaire. Le bureau de comptabilité (6 novembre 1791–12 décembre 1795). In *Histoire du droit social, mélanges en hommage à Jean Imbert*, ed. J.-L. Harouel, 301–10. Paris: PUF.

Heudicourt, F.-S. 1862. *Etudes sur la comptabilité industrielle*. Paris: Imprimerie De Cosse and J. Dumaine.

Hubert, F. 1856. *Cours de comptabilité commerciale*. Angoulême: Lefraise.

Imhoof, J.-J. 1786. *L'art de tenir les livres en parties doubles, ou la Science de faire écriture de toutes les négociations de banque et de commerce*. Geneva and Paris: Libraire Barde, Manget and Buisson.

Irson, C. 1678. *Méthode pour bien dresser toutes sortes de comptes à partie doubles, par débit et crédit, et par recette, dépense et reprise*. Paris: Librairie Cusson.

Joubert, P.-Ch. 1847. *Agenda de comptabilité agricole, ou Registre comptable*. Paris: Cousin.

La Châtre, M. 1865. *Nouveau dictionnaire universel*. Paris: Dock de la librairie.

La Porte (de), M. 1685. *Le guide des négocians et teneurs de livres*. Bordeaux: Charles Osmont.

Léautey, E., and A. Guilbault. 1889. *La science des comptes mise à la portée de tous*. Paris: Librairie comptable and administrative.

Lefour, M. 1853. *Arithmétique agricole suivie de la comptabilité agricole*. Paris: Librairie agricole de la maison rustique.

Legret, G.-P. 1811. *Rudiment de la comptabilité commerciale*. Paris: Libraires Belin Fils and Le Prieur.

Les fermiers des Aydes (date unknown). *Circulaire de la Ferme générale proposant un mode uniforme de comptabilité*. Cote BNF FP-7297.

Lorrimier, D.-F. 1808. *Essai sur les comptes sociaux ou en participation*. Paris: Libraires Brasseur et Latour.

Maffre, P. 1985. La comptabilité dans les écoles supérieures de commerce au XIXe siècle. *Revue historique* 559: 133–56.

Martin, J.-C. 1977. Commerce et commerçants de Niort et des Deux-Sèvres au XVIIIe et XIXe siècles d'après les dossiers de faillite. Unpublished PhD dissertation, EHESS.

Matharan, P. 1859. *Réflexions critiques et morales sur la comptabilité commerciale*. Bordeaux.

Mennher de Kempten, V. 1550. *Practique brifve pour cyfrer et tenir liuvres de compte touchant le principal train de marchandise*. Antwerp: Mathias.

Mézières, L. 1849. *Comptabilité agricole*. Paris: Mathias.

Nikitin, M. 2001. The birth of a modern public sector accounting system, in France and Britain and the influence of Count Mollien. *Accounting History* 6, no. 1: 75–101.

North, R. 1714. *The Gentleman Accomptant*. London: reprinted by Garland, 1986, London and New York.

Omnès, C. 1998. La gestion du personnel au Crédit Lyonnais (1863–1939). Unpublished PhD dissertation, University of Paris X.

Parker, R.H. 1994. Reckoning, merchants accounts, bookkeeping, accounting or accountancy? The evidence of the long titles of books on accounting in English, 1543–1914. In *External Financial Reporting*, ed. B. Carsberg, and S. Dev, 109–22. London: Prentice Hall.

Payen, A. 1817. *Essai sur la tenue des livres d'un manufacturier*. Paris.

Pinceloup C.-C. 1993. *Histoire de la comptabilité et des comptables*. Nice: EDI-Nice.

Reymondin, G. 1909. *Bibliographie méthodique des ouvrages en langue française parus de 1543 à 1908 sur la science des comptes*. Paris: Société académique de comptabilité.
Reys du Sully. 1800. *Principes et cours pratique de comptabilité publique*. Paris.
Ricard, S. 1724. *L'art de bien tenir les livres de comptes en parties doubles à l'italienne*. Amsterdam: André Racle.
Rodriguès, M. 1810. *La tenue des livres ou nouvelles méthodes d'enseignement*. Bordeaux: André Racle.
Royer. 1840. *Traité théorique et pratique de Comptabilité rurale*. Paris: L. Bouchard-huzard.
Saussure (de), F. 1915. *Course in general linguistics*. NewYork: Philiosophical Library.
Trésor de la Langue Française Informatisé. http://atilf.atilf.fr/tlf.htm.
Vaganay, H. 1937. Pour l'histoire du français moderne. *Français Moderne* 5: 73.
Woronoff, D. 1998. *Histoire de l'industrie en France du XVIe siècle à nos jours*. Paris: Points Histoire.
Zimnovitch, H. 1997. Le calcul des prix de revient en France pendant la seconde industrialisation. Unpublished PhD dissertation, University of Poitiers.

Appendix

From the *Catalogue Collectif de France*, we drew up a list of books whose title includes either the phrase *tenue des livres* or the word *comptabilité*. We then collected all the definitions of *comptabilité* and *tenue des livres* that we found in those books. In this appendix, we present the original definitions (in French) mentioned in the article.

'Comptabilité'

First uses of the word comptabilité

Novembre 1750: 'Comptabilité des receveurs qui quitteront dans le courant de l'année' (p. 8).

'Les comptes dont nous venons de parler seront formés sous les yeux du directeur qui les vérifiera et mettra à la suite de la présentation VEU & VERIFIE, et signera. Cette comptabilité doit être entre les deux receveurs' (p. 9).

'Nous aurions attendu la fin de l'année de ferme que nous commençons pour vous entretenir de la comptabilité des buralistes et receveurs des départemens, si nous n'avions pas pensé que ce seroit donné plus sûrement l'intelligence du plan à suivre pour le recouvrement, que de le rapprocher, dès à présent, de celui de la comptabilité à laquelle il doit servir de principe' (p. 14).

Les fermiers des Aydes, *Circulaire de la Ferme générale proposant un mode uniforme de comptabilité*, Cote BNF FP-7297.

1759: 'Comptabilité du régisseur d'une terre' (p. 171).

Bellial des Vertus. 1759. *Essai sur l'administration des terres*. Paris: Hérissant. Cote BNF S-14790.

First definitions of the word comptabilité

1753: 'comptabilité est un terme nouveau dont on ne fait guère usage que dans les chambres des comptes : il signifie une nature particulière de recette et de dépense dont on doit compter ; par exemple le Trésor Royal, la marine, les fortifications, sont autant de comptabilités différentes' (p. 792).

Diderot D., et J. D'Alembert. 1753. *Encyclopédie ou Dictionnaire raisonné des sciences, des arts et des métiers*, tome III. Disponible sur http://gallica.bnf.fr/.

1798: 'obligation de rendre compte, état du comptable'.

Académie françoise. 1798. *Dictionnaire de l'Académie Françoise, Tome Premier A=K*. Paris : Smits et Cie. (5ème édition).

1814: 'Par le mot Comptabilité, on entend communément la manière de tenir les écritures et de rendre les comptes ; mais cette définition est incomplète. Nous devons donc comprendre sous ce terme générique les formes légales pour effectuer des recettes et des dépenses ; la connaissance des valeurs admissibles dans les caisses ; les transformations ou conversions que subissent ces valeurs par les échanges d'une caisse à l'autre ; l'art de la tenue et de la vérification des écritures ; la reddition des comptes, leur appurement et leur révision.'

Chalier, J. 1814. *Précis élémentaire de la comptabilité*. Paris: Libraires Emery, Delaunay, Baudoin Frères eandGoeury. Ref. BNF V-55685.

1824: 'le but de la comptabilité, dans toute gestion, doit être de montrer clairement à la fin de l'année, le profit ou la perte, dans l'année, non seulement sur l'ensemble de la gestion, mais sur chacun des détails qu'elle embrasse.'

Cazaux (de), L.-F.-G. 1824. *De la comptabilité dans une entreprise industrielle et spécialement dans une exploitation rurale*. Toulouse: J-M. Douladoure. Ref. BNF VP-7755.

Comptabilité générale – comptabilité auxiliaire

Comptes généraux – comptes particuliers

1786: 'on distingue, sur les Livres, deux sortes de comptes, savoir, les particuliers & les généraux. On appelle particulier, le compte que l'on ouvre sur ces Livres à celui avec lequel on est entré en liaison d'affaires. Les comptes généraux les plus usités dans le commerce, sont: le compte de fonds, le compte de traites & remises, le compte de caisse, le compte de marchandises générales, le compte de produits & pertes, & d'autres que l'on ouvre suivant la nature du commerce de chaque Négociant.'

Imhoof, J.-J. 1786. *L'art de tenir les livres en parties doubles, ou la Science de faire écriture de toutes les négociations de banque et de commerce*. Genève and Paris: Libraire Barde, Manget and Buisson. Ref. BNF V-6812.

1823: 'On ouvre des comptes aux individus et aux choses. Les comptes ouverts aux individus sont nommés comptes particuliers ou personnels. Les comptes ouverts aux choses forment deux classes: celle des comptes généraux, celle des comptes impersonnels, tels que meubles et ustensiles, ventes au comptant, voyages, foire de tel endroit, marchandise pour votre compte chez un tel, etc. etc.'

Dupuy, J.-B. 1823. *La Tenue des livres, ou Cours théorique et pratique de comptabilité commerciale à parties doubles, à l'usage des commerçans*. Lyon and Paris: Perisse Frères and Mequignon Junior. Ref. BNF V-37458.

1861: 'Ces comptes sont dits généraux ou impersonnels, pour les distinguer des comptes ouverts aux personnes et auxquels on donne le nom de particuliers ou de personnels. On les dits généraux, parce qu'on les rencontre, sous quelque dénomination que ce soit, dans tous les genres de commerce et d'industrie, et que tous les autres comptes ouverts sous des dénominations différentes n'en sont que des subdivisions, et rentrent, par conséquent dans l'une des cinq catégories de comptes.'

Barlet, C.H. 1861. *Tenue des livres appliquée à la comptabilité des mines de houille, des hauts-fourneaux et des usines à fer*. Paris : Librairies Lethielleux et Lacroix.

Comptabilité générale – comptabilité auxiliaire

1845: 'la comptabilité générale, celle représentée par les écritures, doit être purement financière, et s'appuyer de livres auxiliaires donnant tous les éléments du trafic, pour servir des tableaux périodiques.'

Helfenbein, P.L. 1845. *De la comptabilité des compagnies de chemin de fer*. Lyon : Léon Boitel. Ref. BNF V-41488.

1850: 'La comptabilité générale consiste à tenir un compte sommaire de recettes et dépenses; son résultat fait connaître la somme des bénéfices ou des pertes faits sur l'exploitation, pendant l'année. [...] Pour connaître positivement les avantages et désavantages de toutes les parties de l'exploitation, il faut recourir à la comptabilité de détail, qui consiste à ouvrir un compte particulier à chaque culture, à chaque espèce de bétail et à chaque genre de spéculation; de manière que chaque compte devienne débiteur de tout ce qu'il reçoit, et créditeur ou créancier de tout ce qu'il produit.'

Bahier, J.-L. 1850. *Manuel de comptabilité agricole à l'usage des fermes-écoles et des écoles primaires*. Saint-Brieuc: Imprimerie-librairie de L. Prud'homme. Cote BNF V-31209.

1865: 'Dans les grandes associations, la comptabilité générale, qui résume et montre la situation du travail à tous les moments, a pour point de départ la comptabilité auxiliaire, qui indique les mouvements journaliers effectués par le capital et l'analyse de leurs résultats.'

Guilbault, C.-A. 1865. *Traité de comptabilité et d'administration industrielles*. Paris: Librairie Guillaumin and Cie (1ère édition). Fonds Stevelinck Cote HC 0054.

1877: 'La comptabilité générale se tient au moyen des livres suivants, qui centralisent les opérations du commerçant:

1. Le journal
2. Le grand livre
3. Le livre des inventaires
4. Le livre des balances [...]

La comptabilité auxiliaire peut comprendre des livres en nombre illimité. Ce sont les besoins spéciaux de chaque commerce qui indiquent les livres dont il faut faire emploi. Pour les livres auxiliaires, nous citerons les principaux, qui sont:

1. Le livre de caisse ;
2. Le livre de magasin ;
3. Le copie de factures ;
4. Le copie d'effets à recevoir ;
5. Le copie d'effets à payer ;
6. La copie de lettres ;
7. Le carnet d'échéances ;
8. Les pièces comptables et les lettres des correspondants adressées au commerçant'.

Barré, J. 1877. *Cours complet de comptabilité*. Paris: Librairie de G. Masson. Ref. BNF 8-V-2238.

1887: 'Comptabilité générale, Description du Journal et du Grand Livre – La comptabilité auxiliaire ou spéciale recueille tous les détails possibles sur les opérations, qu'il s'agit en même temps de centraliser, de condenser à la comptabilité générale représentée principalement:

1. Par le Journal, où les opérations sont résumées en articles dans l'ordre chronologique;
2. Par le Grand Livre, ou livre des comptes'.

Barillot, A. 1887. *Cours de comptabilité*. Paris: Charles Delagrave. Ref. BNF 8-V-9377.

Comptabilité commerciale – comptabilité industrielle

Application of accounting to different economic areas

1827: 'les marchands de toutes classes [...] ont du chercher les moyens de se rendre compte à eux-mêmes, ou de rendre compte à leurs commettans' (définition de comptabilité commerciale).

Godard, P.-A. 1827. *Traité général et sommaire de comptabilité commerciale*. Paris: Librairie du Commerce. Ref. BNF MFICHE V-6838.

1847: 'Nous nommons comptabilité agricole ou agronométrie les calculs qui ont pour objet de faire connaître au cultivateur sa position pécuniaire passée et présente, et qui peuvent en même temps lui faire tirer des conjonctures plus ou moins vraies sur la situation à venire.'

Joubert, P.-Ch. 1847. *Agenda de comptabilité agricole, ou Registre comptable.* Paris: Cousin. Ref. BNF SP-1552.

1850: 'La comptabilité agricole est l'art de se rendre compte des recettes, des dépenses et de toutes les autres opérations d'une exploitation agricole. Le but que l'agriculteur se propose, en tenant une comptabilité, est de savoir si son exploitation est en bénéfice ou en perte. Il y a deux espèces de comptabilités: la comptabilité générale et la comptabilité de detail.'

Bahier, J.-L. 1850. *Manuel de comptabilité agricole à l'usage des fermes-écoles et des écoles primaires.* Saint-Brieuc: Imprimerie-librairie de L. Prud'homme. Cote BNF V-31209.

1853: 'La comptabilité agricole est l'art de constater les opérations d'une exploitation rurale de manière à en faire ressortir les résultats en perte ou en profit.'

Lefour, M. 1853. *Arithmétique agricole suivie de la comptabilité agricole.* Paris: Librairie agricole de la maison rustique. Cote BNF S-30072.

1856: 'La comptabilité commerciale est l'art de se rendre compte ou de justifier à des tiers des opérations ayant pour conséquence la transformation de l'argent en matières productives par leur vente, et de ces mêmes matières, rentrées en argent, dont le montant a dû donner un benefice.'

Hubert, F. 1856. *Cours de comptabilité commerciale.* Angoulême: Lefraise.

1857: 'la comptabilité commerciale est l'art d'inscrire, sur différents livres ou registres, toutes les opérations que fait un négociant en exerçant son commerce.'

Coulon, H. 1857. *Méthode générale de comptabilité et de correspondance commerciale.* Paris. Ref. BNF V-13775.

1859: 'La comptabilité commerciale (en partie double), considérée en elle-même, est cette série d'écritures que le négociant doit, selon la loi, tenir, avec la plus grande exactitude, jour après jour, sur des livres ad hoc, dans lesquels chaque article doit présenter une balance exacte entre le débit et le crédit, de toutes ses opérations commerciales.'

Matharan, P. 1859. *Réflexions critiques et morales sur la comptabilité commerciale.* Bordeaux.

Comptabilité interne – comptabilité externe

1861: 'La comptabilité industrielle présente deux phases: la première embrasse les opérations relatives à la fabrication jusqu'à l'achèvement du produit; la seconde, les opérations commerciales, c'est-à-dire, relative à la vente de ces produits. Le fabriquant devient alors marchand, et à sa comptabilité spéciale, il joint la comptabilité commerciale dont nous avons exposé les principes théoriques.'

Barlet, C.H. 1861. *Tenue des livres appliquée à la comptabilité des mines de houille, des hauts-fourneaux et des usines à fer.* Paris: Librairies Lethielleux and Lacroix.

1862: 'Les lois sur lesquelles reposent la comptabilité industrielle permettent en outre de suivre les matières premières dans leurs transformations, si simples ou si variées, si rares ou si nombreuses qu'elles soient, depuis l'heure où elles sont mises en œuvre, jusqu'au jour où elles peuvent être livrées au public.

Toute comptabilité industrielle a pour but de rendre un compte exact, par application, des sommes totales dépensées par la comptabilité financière.'

Heudicourt, F.-S. 1862. *Etudes sur la comptabilité industrielle*. Paris: Imprimerie De Cosse and J. Dumaine. Ref. BNF VP-11381.

1896: 'La comptabilité d'un industriel, d'un manufacturier, d'un fabricant, diffère nécessairement de celle d'un simple commerçant. La comptabilité commerciale constate directement, et par des procédés très simples, le prix d'achat et le prix de vente des marchandises achetées et revendues. La comptabilité industrielle constate bien directement aussi, et par les mêmes procédés, le prix de vente des produits fabriqués; mais ce n'est qu'indirectement, et par des procédés particuliers qu'elle arrive à en constater le prix de revient, qui pour l'industrie correspond au prix d'achat.'

Andoyer, M.J. 1896. *Traité théorique et pratique de comptabilité commerciale*. Paris: Belin Frères. Ref. BNF 8-V-26342.

1909: 'Prise en charge des matières; classement et répartition des dépenses concernant ces matières et leurs transformations qu'elles subissent dans les ateliers jusqu'à leur vente décomptée au prix de revient' (définition de comptabilité industrielle).

Bournisien, J. 1909. *Précis de comptabilité industrielle appliquée à la métallurgie*. Nancy: Feid and son. Ref. BNF 4-V-6925.

1911: 'La Comptabilité industrielle, tenue rationnellement, a pour but la comptabilisation de tous les mouvements des produits en fabrication.'

Edom, H. 1911. *Manuel théorique et pratique des prix de revient dans le Commerce et dans l'Industrie*. Lyon. Ref. BNF 8-V PIECE-17601.

Reform or renaissance? France's 1966 Companies Act and the problem of the 'professionalisation' of the auditing profession in France

Carlos Ramirez

HEC, Paris, France

This paper revisits an episode in the history of the auditing profession in France: the period that saw the 'professionalisation' of auditing in the late 1960s, almost 100 years after enactment of the law that had officially created the activity. Despite the existence of practitioners with a reputation for competency and despite the more stringent conditions imposed on the recruitment of these practitioners during the 1930s, certification of accounts had remained a 'function' rather than a profession. The reform of France's commercial code in 1966 thus gave auditors a second chance, making them a key component in an ambitious plan to modernise French financial markets. The paper considers this reform from the angle of the problem facing the reformers, that of 'professionalising the profession' of auditor. Two aspects of the problems are discussed. The first concerns the need to take into consideration the existence of another profession, the profession of the French chartered accountant (*expert-comptable*), which in the opinion of its leaders had a legitimate claim to a monopoly on auditing. The second concerns the fate reserved for pre-reform audit practitioners (*comissaires de sociétés*), not all of whom would be admitted as members of the new auditing profession.

Introduction

Auditing has been around in France for a long time. Its origins can be traced back to two Acts, one adopted in 1863 and, more importantly, the 1867 Act that founded French company law. These two Acts created the figure of the auditor responsible for verifying the accounts of limited companies (*sociétés anonymes*) and issuing a report on their audit to the shareholders (Mikol 1993). In regulating auditing, the lawmakers put France on an equal footing with countries such as the United Kingdom, where a similar desire to protect company owners by keeping them informed of how their investments were being managed had been expressed as early as the mid-nineteenth century. The increasing complexity of British commercial enterprises, which were growing considerably in size in certain sectors such as banking, insurance and the railways, fairly soon brought the days of the 'amateur' auditor to an end, leading ultimately to an association between the emerging accountancy profession and the auditing profession (Chandler, Edwards, and Anderson 1993). Although the appointment of a professional accountant as auditor only became a legal requirement in 1948, most large City of London firms were already audited by a member of a professional accountancy institute (generally the Institute of Chartered Accountants in England and Wales) by the end of the 1880s (Anderson, Edwards, and Matthews 1996; Edwards 1989; Jones 1981).

Curious though it may seem, especially from the Anglo-American point of view, in France it took a very long time for the association between the accountancy and auditing professions to be enshrined in law. The institutions for the two professions have also remained separate, even though members of the accountants' professional body, the *Ordre des experts-comptables,* have, since 1968, been eligible for ex officio registration with the auditors' professional body, the *Compagnie nationale des commissaires aux comptes*. This disconnection relates to a lack of regulation for the auditing profession after it was first created. Not until the 1930s was any specific requirement in terms of auditor competence or independence issued to complement the provisions of the Acts referred to above, so it is not surprising that auditing was seen more as a *function* than a *profession*, mocked in political and business spheres, and even by foreign professionals visiting France (Brown 1905). Every sensational scandal was seized on as an opportunity to point out that many auditors had little or no accounting knowledge, or were often hired because they were related to, or friendly with, the company's management (Lemarchand 1993).

The scientific literature contains several explanations for this contrasting situation in two countries which were economically similar, but where economic development had in one case led to an association between auditors and accountants, with audits of listed companies being carried out by ever-larger firms, while in the other it had resulted in audits being carried out by a miscellaneous collection of individuals, and considered in business and political circles as totally irrelevant. One of these explanations is the central role played by the capital markets in financing British and American economies (Matthews, Anderson, and Edwards 1998). Demand for auditing services brought with it a demand for associated economic and financial services, and professional accountants took full advantage of this, being less strictly regulated and less disdainful of the business world than the lawyers with which they were competing (Matthews, Anderson, and Edwards 1998; Sugarman 1995). In France, capital structures remained family-based for a long time, even in large companies, and financial resources were likely to come from ploughed back profits rather than from the capital markets (Bonin 1989). Also, French company law did not encourage professionals to take on large numbers of auditing engagements. In 1925, the SARL (*société anonyme à réponsabilité limitée*) limited company format was introduced, enabling owners of small and medium-sized companies to opt for limited liability without an obligation to have their accounts audited. Nationalisations after 1936 and 1945 led to direct control by the State and, thus, to further reductions in the number of large companies subject to a professional audit obligation (Fridenson and Straus 1987).

In the end, it was precisely the ambition of modernising financial markets as the development of the European common market intensified that obliged the French authorities to reform auditing in the late 1960s. Although the 1966 Companies Act and the 1969 decree on the organisation of the profession both directly concerned auditing, they were part of a series of laws that also includes the 1967 decree which created the stock market regulator *Commission des opérations de bourse*, and the 1968 Act reforming the accountants' body, the *Ordre des experts-comptables et des comptables agréés*. The modernisation of auditing thus took place within a broader movement which also involved modernisation of the accountancy profession. The 12 August 1969 decree placed clear restrictions on the recruitment of professionals and specified the scope of the auditor's task. It officially created the link between accountancy and auditing that already existed, either informally or formally, in many other industrialised countries.

And yet, this reform raised as many problems as it solved. Although the course had been set firmly towards the future, the transformation of French auditing could not escape the legacy of the past. That legacy was two-sided. First, another profession specialising in accountancy already existed. Its members were registered with the *Ordre des experts-comptables et des comptables agréés* (OECCA), the accountants' body set up in 1942, and a not insignificant number of them undertook auditing work. They thus swelled the ranks of the population of auditors (*commissaires de sociétés)* that had grown up since 1867. Within this population, some practitioners enjoyed certain privileges: since the late 1930s, auditors of publicly traded companies (*sociétés faisant appel public à l'épargne*) had been registered after (theoretically) passing an aptitude test. The existence of a population of audit practitioners was thus a second legacy inherited from the past, and the question of how to treat them was a tricky one. By no means all auditing practitioners were trained accountants or even specialised in accountancy. The reform of auditors' status therefore needed to be forward-looking and driven by the aim to develop credible auditing, based notably, as in other developed countries, on the affirmation of the link between accountancy expertise and auditing expertise. It would also have to take into consideration the legacy of the past as referred to above. The problem was how to define the 'new' professional who was to emerge from the reforms of the late 1960s. The designers of those reforms had to consider questions such as what link should there be between accountancy expertise and auditing and, in particular, should any auditing privileges be granted to members of the OECCA? Should all currently practising auditors be deemed competent to belong to the profession that would be born of the reforms? It was thus as if the modernisation of auditing meant a whole task of 'professionalisation'. Of course, professionalisation is not intended here in the sense with which it was endowed by functionalist sociologists (Wilenski 1964), that is to say the different steps that lead an occupation to become a profession. The paradox with auditing in France was that, from the beginning in 1867, it had acquired certain traits which would qualify it as a profession, and ever since audit practitioners had been working under a legal umbrella that defined – even though minimally – what their task was about. As we shall see further on, auditing was however deemed not professional enough and required the necessary 'professionalisation' measures to turn it into a fully-fledged profession, similar to that existing at the time of the reform in other European countries.

After a brief description of the development of accountancy and auditing in France up to the Second World War, this paper will analyse how the issues concerning the definition of the auditor's professional identity were handled. The question of the link between accountancy and auditing will be examined through the conflict of views between the accountancy and auditing elites over what auditing should be. The question of the fate reserved for pre-reform audit practitioners (*commissaires de sociétés*) will then be examined through the elimination of those considered unworthy of inclusion in the new profession. The 12 August 1969 decree organising the new auditing profession (*commissaires aux comptes*) set up administrative commissions in charge of accepting or rejecting applications for membership of the new profession from certain categories of practitioners. Based on the archives of those commissions, this paper investigates the definition of the notion of the 'competent professional', emphasising that in this case competence appears to have depended more on candidates' social attributes than the intrinsic quality of their work.

The auditing profession in France until the 1960s: limited regulation and a heterogeneous population of practitioners

The link between auditing and accountancy, which was established very early on in other countries either informally or in law, took some time to become established in France. Accountancy and auditing thus followed parallel roads to professionalisation. However, gaining a monopoly over auditing was naturally a key issue for accountants in their quest for official recognition of their profession. The accountancy profession had come into being in France for a reason completely unconnected with verifying the accounts of limited companies. When the *Ordre des experts comptables* was set up in 1942, Vichy government's technocrats' aim was to involve the accountancy profession in a social and economic rationalisation plan marked by corporatism, but more specifically focusing on production management and implementation of macro-economic tools to aid State intervention. Two Acts dated 3 April 1942 were the first to regulate the profession in France, granting accountants a monopoly on accounting services. The various sections of this Act were reaffirmed, after expurgation of the most anti-democratic provisions, in an Ordinance of 19 September 1945. The creation of the *Ordre* was thus contemporary with the introduction of the *Plan comptable général*, the general chart of accounts designed to standardise registration of companies' accounting and financial transactions (Fortin 1991; Standish 1990). However, it did not spring up out of nothing. Professional associations for chartered accountants (*experts-comptables*) had already been formed in the late nineteenth century in a spirit of elitism, aiming to make the profession independent of other forms of accountancy skills and creating an internal hierarchy within the accountants' world that placed independent practice at the apex. These associations were often modelled on British professional associations, with selective membership in theory if not in practice and a strict code of ethics to be respected by members. The earliest associations, such as the *Compagnie des experts-comptables de Paris* (1912), were often set up by members of the *Société académique de comptabilité*, which had been founded in 1881 (and became the *Société de comptabilité de France* in 1916) in response to the lack of organisation of official accounting education. The goal of the link established between professional excellence and independent expertise was to raise the standing of these practitioners among professionals. Assertion of this link was also intended to distinguish members of the independent accountants' associations from salaried accountants, whose status within the enterprise – notably compared to the status of engineers – was particularly low (Bocqueraz 2001; Ramirez 2001).

Prior to 1914, these associations' collective promotion campaigns, inspired by the actions of more prestigious professions, were doomed to failure, as independent accountancy remained a confidential (and essentially legal) activity at the time, fit only to attract those who had been less successful in other professional fields (particularly law and education). It was the post-First World War tax reforms that opened up a true market for chartered accountants. This market was an opportunity for the profession (providing it with a *raison d'être*) but also a problem, since it attracted all kinds of individuals, including total amateurs, and took little notice of the priority owed to the pre-war elites. However, those elites can still be credited with a certain influence, due to the not insignificant number of professional associations formed after 1920 based on the model of their predecessors. Their 'birthright' was to a certain extent acknowledged, as it was those associations with which the State negotiated over the creation of a chartered accountant (*brevet d'expert-comptable)* qualification in 1927, but the lack of interest in the profession hitherto shown by the authorities remained unchanged. Once formally qualified, the accountants were left to their own devices, and the low recognition of their qualification illustrates the limitations of institutionalisation without monopoly: it was not considered necessary to be an '*expert*' (whether qualified or self-proclaimed) to meet the needs of a clientele mainly comprised of small industrial and commercial businesses (Ramirez 2001).

The disparate nature of the population of accountants was a problem for the authorities when their professional association was created in 1942. A sufficiently large profession was needed to apply the country's economic rationalisation plans as mentioned earlier, and it needed high enough standing to be a regulated profession. The solution applied was to split accountants into two separate divisions, officially for technical reason, but in fact for reasons relating to professionals' respective social backgrounds. The association was thus born the *Ordre des experts-comptables et des comptables agréés* (OECCA), with a minority of *expert-comptable* (chartered accountant) members who undertook engagements involving 'monitoring and organising accounts', and a majority of *comptable agréés* members working as bookkeepers.[1]

Significantly, the auditing profession was untouched by the reform of 1942. It was only in 1966 that the Act amending French company law (and the 1969 decree organising the auditing profession) officially associated accountants with auditors. As mentioned earlier, the 1863 and 1867 Acts had provided for the existence of auditors (*commissaires de sociétés*) in charge of legally certifying accounts, but without any measures to guarantee their independence and competence. Since no formal qualification was required to carry out the function, auditor recruitment was probably based more on individuals' social standing than their competence in accounting techniques. In practice, to avoid any difficulty in obtaining certification, the auditors appointed were members of the managers' families or, perhaps, former executives of the company. Most auditors saw the statutory audit as a formal – and occasionally honorary – duty rather than a full-time job grounded in accounting expertise (Lemarchand 1993; Mikol 1993).

Ever since the creation of the pre-war *commissariat de sociétés*, auditing had been surrounded by controversy. Shareholders' associations used it as a pretext to call for stricter controls for corporate accounts (Lemarchand 1993), and proposals were often made to associate independent accountancy experts with those controls (Bocqueraz 2001; Ramirez 2001). This naturally became one of the key issues in the plans of the chartered accountants' associations to develop their profession, as a link between the two specialisations would have increased their members' chances of entering a network that extended across the business and political worlds. But the authorities appear to have turned a deaf ear to their attempts at lobbying: the minister for trade only thought of preparing a reform of the 1867 Act in 1917 (AN, F12 8165 and F12 8166), and a bill suggesting that accountants should be involved in statutory audits was not presented until 1926 (Documents parlementaires-Chambre 1926, 274–6).[2]

However, Parliament rejected these proposals (Documents parlementaires-Chambre 1927, 248–52), and it was only in the mid-1930s that the government took emergency action to bring in additional guarantees for auditing practices. The aim was not to rationalise, by totally rethinking auditing, the qualifications of auditors and the type of knowledge they would have to use. Instead, the move was a thorough response to a wave of financial scandals bringing disastrous political consequence in their wake. The primary aim of the people behind the decree-acts of 8 August 1935 and 29 June 1936 appears to have been to protect stock market investors – particularly small investors – rather than to 'professionalise' the auditing profession,[3] and the provisions introduced only concerned auditors of publicly traded companies. Although there is some concern in this legislation for improving auditing competence, no emphasis appears to have been placed on the need for any special knowledge, even less accounting knowledge. The 29 June 1936 decree thus brought in an examination to verify applicants' skills in accounting and financial techniques, but the task of recruiting auditors was delegated to the Courts of Appeal, without a single professional auditor on the examining boards.[4] Some of those boards even took the liberty of exempting certain candidates from the examination, clearly reflecting the idea that the essential qualities for recruitment lay outside the purely technical (Mikol 1993). Auditor recruitment was not therefore to be based on a systematic procedure but on the judgement of the examiners, who sometimes had little to do with the world of accounting. Consequently, the auditing profession remained open to individuals from very diverse backgrounds (engineers, lawyers, former civil servants, former employees or board members, etc).

There were thus no favours for the accountants in these new measures intended to increase the credibility of auditing. Some *experts-comptables* could become auditors, but they were appointed on a case-by-case basis. The decision depended on their reputation in the worlds of business or law, and took no consideration of their membership of a practitioners' association, since these associations had been granted no special privileges. Nor was there any preferential treatment for holders of the 1927 qualification referred to earlier (Documents parlementaires-Chambre 1936, 565–7). This refusal to associate the accountancy profession with the reform of auditing was not the only distinguishing feature of the 1930s reforms. As already noted, the decree-acts referred to above applied essentially to auditors of publicly traded companies (such auditors were referred to as 'registered with' or 'approved by' the Courts of Appeal). The State undertook no reforms to regulate auditing for other companies. As a result, an entire population of audit practitioners continued to exist alongside the registered auditors, auditing more modestly sized limited companies and subject to no criteria to guarantee independence and competence. In the late 1960s, auditing was still marked by the lack of a common denominator through which the population of auditors could be described in terms of professional qualifications. Apart from the great diversity in skills, auditors were no doubt even more diverse in terms of social status, since anyone could be an auditor for companies other than publicly traded companies.

The reasons why France saw no ambitious reform of auditing until the late 1960s, and particularly no reform that addressed the question of the links between certification of the accounts and accountancy itself, no doubt lie primarily in the authorities' long-standing distrust of accountancy specialists. In a country where social prestige often originates in State recognition,[5] the accountants' efforts to obtain a monopoly that would have included auditing were often frustrated by members of the government or parliament, on the pretext that they did not meet all the necessary requirements to deserve public trust. In response to arguments such as comparisons with the situation in the United Kingdom, where the professional associations were much more powerful and their power rested on a quasi-monopoly for audits of limited companies, the authorities replied that in terms of reputation, French accountants were still a long way behind their British counterparts and therefore no privilege of any kind could be envisaged. Given businesses' attitudes to the professionalisation of auditing, accountants had no hope of building up this reputation that seemed to be so cruelly lacking.[6] The authorities' distrust echoed the hostility felt by a whole section of French employers towards any reinforcement of the auditing profession, which would lead to greater interference into confidential company matters and, more importantly, increase the cost of the audit.

The problem of auditors' fees was an especially telling sign of the low esteem in which companies held their auditors' work. The low level of fees paid by companies underlined the deemed irrelevance of auditing and was often bemoaned in the professional press.[7] A fee scale had been fixed by decree in 1938 but generally went unapplied. The minutes of the 1948 annual general meeting of the *Compagnie des commissaires de sociétés agrées par la Cour d'appel de Paris* (page 3) note that some regional auditors' associations did not respect the tariffs imposed in 1938, often indulging in 'bid peddling'. The same minutes record that the fees paid for audits were generally very low and that it was difficult to stand up to certain company bosses. The official fee scale, which certainly did not reflect what happened in practice, was calculated based on the size of the entity being audited, not the hours actually spent on the audit (Archives National, hereafter AN, 612 AP 1).

To understand the lack of resources auditing specialists had to contend with, the information contained in a preparatory document for the 12 August 1969 decree on the organisation of the auditing profession is very illuminating, giving some idea of the range of opinions held by auditors regarding the work that should be done for an audit. The table below takes information from that document to report, for a selection of major French companies, the auditing fees actually paid, the fees that should have been paid in application of the official 1963 fee scale, and the fees that would have been payable following application of the scales proposed by the *Fédération des associations de commissaires aux comptes inscrits* ('Auditors' in the table), the *Ordre des experts-comptables et des comptables agréés* ('Accountants') and the major French employers' body, the *Conseil National du Patronat Français* ('Employers').[8] The figures reported are in thousands of current francs; figures in brackets show the number of days' work remunerated by the fees resulting from each project, on a basis of 750 francs per day.[9]

Prior to the reforms of the 1960s, auditing was thus primarily a *function,* and in order to obtain and exercise that function, 'social capital' was more important than good accounting knowledge. Statutory auditing was essentially carried out by individuals (some of whom, thanks to their network of contacts, acted as auditors for dozens of listed companies) with little resources. As fees for auditing were often low, the scope and depth of the work done did not appear sufficient to place auditing on a sound technical basis.[10] The elite of the accountancy profession took part in this activity (and were particularly active in auditors' professional associations) but still had to work alongside individuals from other professional backgrounds.[11] This was the situation inherited by the men who undertook a reform of French company law in the late 1940s, ultimately reaching fulfilment for auditing in 1969.

Preparing for the future: the reform of auditing, 'a necessary modernisation'

By the end of the 1960s, the most striking feature of the accountancy profession in France was the separation of accounting and auditing activities. When the OECCA was set up in 1942, the question of whether its members should be granted priority for auditing had been left unresolved.

Table 1. Fees paid for the audit of major French companies in 1968 and proposals to revise the official 1963 fee scale (in thousand current francs).

Company	Actual fees paid	1963 official fee scale	Auditors' proposals	Accountants' proposals	Employers' proposals
Rhône Poulenc	14 (18.6)	48.5 (64.7)	141.2 (189)	74.3 (99)	43.8 (57.4)
Ugine Kuhlmann	9 (12)	43.5 (58)	129.3 (172.4)	86.1 (115)	49.7 (66)
Pechiney	10 (13.3)	59.8 (80)	108 (144)	75.2 (100)	44.2 (59)
Compagnie générale d'électricité	10 (13.3)	31.2 (42)	82.6 (110)	57.6 (77)	33.5 (45)
Beghin	10 (13.3)	26 (34.6)	72 (96)	51 (68)	29 (38.5)
Ciments Lafarge	8 (10.6)	28 (37.3)	71 (95)	47 (62.5)	27 (35.5)
Kleber Colombes	5 (6.6)	22 (29.2)	59.4 (79.2)	42.4 (56.5)	23.9 (31.9)
Saint Gobain	12.8 (17)	82 (108)	137.6 (183.5)	81.6 (109)	47.4 (63.3)

Source: Document drawn up by the Association nationale des sociétés anonymes on 26 June 1968 (AN, 612 AP 1).

As was to be expected, the accountants would not simply let this situation lie; it had been a central claim in their pre-1940 struggle to achieve acceptance into the professional 'club'. Auditing at the time (*commissariat des sociétés*) remained split into two categories. Auditors of publicly traded companies were not strictly speaking 'auditing professionals', even if they had certain educational and social qualities. They were in a category separate from auditors of other companies, for which audits were totally unregulated and carried out by a widely disparate population. Although the Courts of Appeal responsible for registering auditors of publicly traded companies often looked favourably on applications from accountants, neither in the law nor in the collective consciousness was there any direct link between accounting expertise and the expertise necessary for auditing. The introduction of a series of ambitious reforms, with the progressively clear aim of adapting France for integration into the European Economic Community, was the perfect opportunity to overhaul the organisation of the accountancy and auditing professions.

As early as 1948, a commission for the reform of the French Commercial Code and company law met at the Ministry of Justice (Centre des archives contemporaines, hereafter CAC, 19950409, art. 103–4). This commission's work led to a bill in the early 1960s which finally found its way to the French National Assembly in June 1964, and was enacted on 24 July 1966. In the presentation of the grounds for the bill, the government referred to the complexity of the existing law, a consequence of the succinct nature of the provisions of the Commercial Code and the vast amount of superimposed legislation (31 amendments had been made since the last general Companies Act of 1867). It also stated, however, that renovation of company law had been made necessary by growing European integration and the development of international trade (Documents de l'Assemblée nationale 1964, 693).

Another stated reason for proposing the bill was that the result of the preliminary studies carried out showed that auditing in France had so many shortcomings as to be illusory. To rectify this situation, it was vital to provide auditors with a modernised professional organisation, increased resources for investigations, and clearly-defined responsibilities, 'with their remuneration fixed in proportion to the task required of them and the responsibilities they bear' (Documents de l'Assemblée nationale 1964, 696). After a transition period, only professionals registered on an official list would be authorised to audit a category of companies no longer restricted to publicly traded companies but now to cover all limited companies (*sociétés anonymes*). The lawmakers hoped this would enable auditors to acquire the 'competence, independence and prestige enjoyed by auditors of Great Britain's Institutes of Chartered Accountants, members of the American Institute of Certified Public Accountants, or German *Wirtschaftprüfer*' (Documents de l'Assemblée nationale 1964, 696). Age and good character requirements were laid down for audit practitioners (article 420 of the Act), the term of appointment and the auditor's attributions were defined, and his duties were extended. Publicly traded companies were obliged to have at least one auditor (article 419) immediately the Act took effect, and all companies limited by shares and large limited liability companies had to fulfil the same obligation within two years. The term of an auditor's appointment was increased to six years, i.e. the same as board members, to guarantee independence (article 713). Finally, the auditor was to certify that the company's position was truly and fairly reflected in the statement of assets and liabilities, the general operating accounts, the profit and loss account and the balance sheet (article 176), which 'considerably increased the responsibility of auditors, but was likely to provide greater security for shareholders'. The number and duration of verifications auditors could carry out (articles 176 and 177) without interfering in the company's management were also extended. Under article 181 of the Act, auditors bore no civil liability for breaches of law committed by directors, unless they were aware of them and had not revealed them in their report to the shareholders. Article 180 required auditors to reveal any criminal behaviour by company directors to the public prosecutor (Documents de l'Assemblée nationale 1964, 696).

However, most of the measures relating to the organisation of the profession would become applicable through issuance of a decree (article 168 of the Act), which only took place three years later on 12 August 1969. This decree exempted members of the OECCA from an examination to test their aptitude for the function of auditor (article 3). It also (Title 6 and article 7 of the decree, and article 218 of the 24 July 1966 Act) allowed firms to act as auditors, provided that at least three quarters of the partners were registered auditors. Admission to the list of registered auditors was governed by the Courts of Appeal through a regional commission, consisting of three judges of the Court, the regional tax inspector and the president of the regional auditors' association, the *Compagnie régionale des commissaires aux comptes* (article 8). Appeals against decisions by this regional commission could be referred to a national commission (article 15). The professional organisation consisted of a national association, the *Compagnie nationale des commissaires aux comptes*, and regional associations corresponding to the territories of French Courts of Appeal. These associations' council members were elected for four-year periods, and half of the regional council members were renewed or replaced every two years (article 31). The national auditors' council, the *Conseil national des commissaires aux comptes*, was located in Paris and consisted of delegates from the regional councils, elected for four-year terms, at the rate of one delegate for every 150 members (article 51).

Concerning the function of the auditor, the decree defined strict incompatibilities (in particular, auditors could not be directors or corporate officers under article 82). Article 66 also introduced a system for controlling the quality of a professional's work, in the form of an inspection conducted at least annually at regional level. A scale of auditing fees was drawn up. After widespread consultation, the government decided to impose flat-rate fees for the whole audit rather than time-based fees, as demanded, for example, by the *Commission des opérations de bourse* (COB), the stock market regulator.[12]

One of the novelties of the 1966–9 reform was that it gave the COB the right to monitor the activity of auditors of publicly traded companies.[13] Article 64 of the decree obliged auditors who were candidates for appointment by such companies to inform the COB, and article 67 entitled the COB to ask to see the auditors' working files. In so doing, the 1969 decree put the final touch to the system for audits of listed companies. The first report published by the COB in 1968 – that is, before the issuance of the decree on the organisation of the profession – took a highly disillusioned view of statutory audits:

> The way the auditor's mission has been conceived in France does not however meet the needs of the function auditors were supposed to exercise. In the most traditional auditing practice in France, the auditor operates alone, often for a large number of companies, restricting his work to superficial verifications that provide no guarantee, for himself or the shareholders, that he has detailed knowledge of the company's position. In such circumstances, even the most competent, most active men cannot carry out their task properly.
>
> (Commission des operations de bourse 1968, 39)

On page 40, the report noted the contrast with the 'principal industrialised countries' (without explicit reference to 'Anglo-American' countries): in those countries there were many powerful partnerships and in-depth verifications were performed, particularly for sensitive items such as stocks and accounts payable, and fees were commensurate with the level of service. The COB observed that 'the difference is so great that the subsidiaries of foreign companies use the services of auditors from their own country, while retaining a French auditor to meet their legal obligations'.

The designers of the 1960s reforms had clearly been driven by an aim to pull French auditing out of the state of affairs described by the COB. Auditing was reinforced in terms of guarantees of auditor competence and independence, the resources available for investigation, and auditors' responsibilities. The reform did take place, but there was no renaissance. Deficiencies in the legislation and regulations issued already formed an obstacle to auditing's future as a powerful, independent profession. The reformers had failed to address the very real lack of material resources French auditing needed to be internationally competitive, which reflected the non-existence of an 'audit culture' in France; in particular, they had not proposed any significant increase in auditing fees. Another reason why the profession's new status could not be considered a renaissance is that the past could not simply be swept away. The reformers found themselves obliged to work with the legacy of the auditing of the former *commissariat de sociétés*, developed a century earlier. Before reaching a conclusion on the true impact of the late-1960s reforms, we shall take a closer look at this legacy, which prevented unification of the accountancy and auditing professions around an accountancy-based professional identity.

The legacy of the past: the problematics of defining professional identity

Analysis of the 1966–9 reforms shows that their proposers were faced with the problem of defining the 'new' professional who would result from the application of the law. The idea was not to create a new profession from scratch, but to compromise with a population of practitioners already in existence by virtue of the 1867 Act, a section of whom had benefited from additional rights since the 1930s. This legacy complicated the reformers' task, particularly as the population concerned was extremely heterogeneous. The heterogeneity of the auditing community will be examined from two angles. It primarily concerned the professional elite. The principal reason for the government's inability – or unwillingness – to merge the auditing profession with the accountancy profession to form a unified accountancy profession and an instrument for modernisation of the French economy was that it took into consideration the rights historically acquired by auditors who were not accountants. Another reason, as we shall see, was that opinion in the professional world itself was extremely divided on the desirability of such a merger; the auditing elite of the time going so far as to deny any relationship between auditing and accountancy. But the heterogeneity of the auditing population also concerned the lowest strata of that population, the auditors of companies that were not publicly traded. At this level, the reformers were confronted with a different aspect of the problem of defining the 'new' auditor. They had to determine which of the 'small' practitioners were worthy of belonging to the new profession created by the 1969 decree. Here again, the selection process brought no privileges for professional accountants.

The 1968 Act relating to the accountancy profession and the rivalry between auditors and accountants

After the Second World War, the OECCA continued to lobby for a monopoly on auditing. As explained earlier, the authorities' aim in forming this organisation, bringing together existing practitioners, in 1942 was not to endow the country with a profession of specialists in accountancy and verification of accounts, but essentially to act as an instrument for application of the General Accounting Plan. The 1968 Act modifying the status of the OECCA followed the same modernising objective as the 1966 Companies Act. It was a just reward for the accountancy elite's campaign to convince the authorities that members of the OECCA could legitimately claim automatic access to the function of auditor. However, the hoped-for merger of the two professions did not come about, indicating the government's concern to avoid alienating auditors who were not OECCA members. Another factor was the dissensions between the auditing and accountancy elites which punctuated the discussions over the content of the laws that would reform their respective professions.

The 31 October 1968 Act changing the statutes of the OECCA essentially sought to modernise the accountancy profession and prepare it for development in an increasingly open European economic community.[14] In order to raise the qualifications of registered professionals, it was necessary to put an end to the quarrels that had undermined the institution since its creation. The two categories of accountants in the OECCA – *experts-comptables* and *comptables agréés* – were in conflict because the former, granted a monopoly by the 1942 Act and the 1945 Ordinance for organisation and monitoring of accounts, had a tendency to 'poach' on the territory of the latter, who had exclusive rights to bookkeeping services. Also, although there were many more *comptables agréés* than *experts-comptables*, they were under-represented in the OECCA's governing bodies.[15] The bill presented by the government thus discontinued registration of *comptables agréés* with the Order, while authorising equal representation in the representative bodies and allowing them to certify the balance sheets of companies for which they kept the accounts. *Comptables agréés* who were already registered would be able to become *experts-comptables* through a procedure described in detail in a decree of 1970. The attributions of OECCA members were consequently redefined: under article 1 of the 31 October 1968 Act amending the Ordinance of 19 September 1945:

> an accountant (*expert-comptable*) or auditor (*réviseur comptable*) as defined by this ordinance is any person whose habitual occupation is the review and assessment of the accounts of companies and organisations with which he is not linked through an employment contract. He is also authorised to certify the legality and sincerity (*régularité et sincérité*) of the balance sheets and profit and loss accounts.

The aim, clearly expressed through the stated grounds for the bill, was to modernise the French independent accountancy profession, and the new law opened up an opportunity for highly qualified technicians (companies' chief accountants, for instance) to become *experts-comptables*. The 1945 Ordinance had indeed introduced an examination for attribution of the title *expert-comptable*, although, according to the legislator, 'it should preferably be awarded in recognition of competence'. The bill also stated that technical progress (development of mechanisation with punch-card machines and computers) was bound to reduce bookkeeping work and increase auditing and interpretation of accounts. The application of the *Plan comptable général* through the publication of professional guides was also expected to simplify bookkeeping. Conversely, the growing importance of management techniques, the reform of auditing and the greater volume and complexity of verification procedures would make it necessary to recruit more professionals.

However, this modernisation did not include the granting of a monopoly of auditing to members of the renewed OECCA. The principal reason put forward by the government was that this demand could not be granted, as there were too many registered or independent auditors who were not part of the community of accountants (AN, 612 AP 29 and CAC, 19830740, art. 15). The initial draft of the 1969 decree included plans for a very broad recruitment of auditors. There would be no examination to pass, only a dissertation to submit and a training period of at least two years. Recruitment would be open to HEC business school graduates, people with degrees in law or economic science, holders of the *certificat supérieur de révision comptable* auditing certificate, and graduates of certain other business schools. A reduced six-month training period would be allowed for candidates aged under 60 years of age with ten years' experience, former magistrates from the judiciary and the Revenue Court (*Cour des comptes*), former members of the Council of State (*Conseil d'Etat)*, and former high-ranking civil servants of the Treasury.[16] Although, as seen earlier, the final version of the 12 August 1969 decree in fact required all new candidates to pass an examination, with exemption for members of the OECCA, the merger of the two communities representing the independent accountancy profession into a single large profession that could help France engage in European economic competition did not ultimately happen. And yet, the question of an official monopoly on auditing for *experts-comptables* had been raised by the OECCA's governing bodies from the earliest years of its existence. Such official recognition would have exempted *experts-comptables* and *comptables agréés* from applying for registration as auditors with the Courts of Appeal, which was not always granted.[17] Throughout the entire period from the Liberation to the 1966–9 reforms, the auditing and accountancy elites had been in conflict over the institutional form that should be given to independent, powerful auditing.[18]

The *experts-comptables* had argued that their technical expertise qualified them to verify accounts (and this was reasserted in the 1968 Act).[19] This expertise could easily be converted in practice into the legal certification of accounts (Ordre des experts-comptables et des comptables agréés, 1962). To promote this conversion, 1962 saw the creation of the *Comité permanent des diligences normales* under the auspices of an eminent member of the *Ordre*, Robert Mazars, with the declared aim of codifying auditing practice. The auditors made their own plans to counter the machinations of the chartered accountants. The various companies of auditors that had come into being with the application of the decree of 29 June 1936 had formed a federation, which started publishing a bulletin in 1964. In that bulletin, the federation's president, Jean Trial, railed against the opponents of re-creation of the profession of auditor given that the profession of accountant already existed:

> Why did they not react before? Why did they not criticise the 1867 Acts and the decrees of 1935, 1936 and 1937? Why did they not attack the auditors of agricultural cooperatives or mixed-economy companies registered on the prefectoral lists?[20] Why did they not sue the experts registered with the Courts who carry out accountancy engagements without being chartered accountants?
>
> (*Bulletin de liaison de la fédération des associations de commissaires de sociétés inscrits par les cours d'appel*, March 1965, no. 2: 7)

In Trial's opinion, plans to make the OECCA the professional body for auditors, whereas 'more than a third of registered auditors are not *experts-comptables*', were mere dreams (*Bulletin de liaison de la fédération des associations de commissaires de sociétés inscrits par les cours d'appel*, March 1965, no. 2: 7).

In an article also published in the March 1965 edition of the *Bulletin* (pages 10–14), the Federation's general secretary Jean Sigaut admitted that, in its thinking on auditing, the Federation had fallen well behind other organisations 'which are more dynamic due to the way they operate'. He reminded his readers of the fundamentally different nature of the accountancy and auditing professions: the auditor is a censor, whereas accountants are advisors. The auditor's work took place at a higher level than simple accounting technique, and the accounts were merely reflections of legal obligations, the auditor's job being to check that they fulfilled requirements. Sigaut raised the question of the legislators' intentions – some thought the aim was to transpose 'Anglo-American auditing methods' to France – and recognised that it would be necessary to define standard audit diligence 'but without losing sight of the fact that the certification of sincerity, which expresses a conviction, draws its value from conscientious work and reliable judgement, not the number of tick-marks made by junior employees' (*Bulletin de liaison de la fédération des associations de commissaires de sociétés inscrits par les cours d'appel*, March 1965, no. 2: 13).

In another article published in the Federation's bulletin in November 1965 (pages 9–13), Sigaut returned to the OECCA's idea of creating a committee for audit standardisation. In his opinion, French accountants and auditors had nothing to be ashamed of compared to their foreign counterparts, as they had the same technical competence:

> The difference lies primarily in the value of their signature, for which they have successfully gained recognition. There is much talk of the rules established by foreign professional associations, but most of these measures apparently tend towards standardisation of accounting, which is achieved in France by other methods [. . .] the code of diligences cannot be a mere list of material checks, because checking is not a purely material activity.[21]

In February 1966 (*Bulletin de liaison de la Fédération des associations de commissaires de sociétés inscrits par les cours d'appel*, February 1966, no. 5: 6), it was Jean Trial's turn to discuss the definition of audit standards, because most work in that field was 'only translation of foreign texts, which causes confusion'. Robert Mazars, for instance, in *La Vie française* (no. 1979, 28 January 1966, *Les experts-comptables se penchent sur la certification des bilans* [Accountants examine the issue of certification of balance sheets]) used the term 'auditing' (*révision*) for a general verification with the aim of assessing whether accounts give a true and fair view of the company's position. In Trial's opinion, 'just as an Englishman only has to issue an 'opinion', a Wirtschaftprüfer issues a *Bestätigungvermerk*, in other words a formal certification (because the law imposes presentation rules and the task of German professionals is to certify respect of those rules)'. There was therefore no need for hasty transposition of foreign customs into French practice, which had its own specificities (*Plan comptable général*, the tax influence on the formation of the accounting position, the obligation to report any illegal behaviour). Trial reasserted the need to have rules for auditing developed 'by, and only by, those who practice auditing'. From this position came the decision to set up a commission to study the standards applicable to the auditor (general meeting of the Federation on 19 January 1965).

Behind the hostility towards 'imported' methods expressed by the leading figures of French auditing lay the fear that the community of *experts-comptables*, who were more accustomed than auditors to practising their profession in collective structures, could more easily apply these methods and thus gain a dominant position in the new profession of auditing. Sigaut had complained bitterly about article 218 of the 24 July 1966 Act, which allowed the function of auditor to be exercised by individuals or professional partnerships founded by individuals. In particular, firms registered with the OECCA were entitled under the Act to accept appointments as statutory auditors. In Sigaut's opinion, auditing work was likely to go to firms where chartered accountants worked 'under the instructions of people foreign to the profession' or people who could sell services concerned by the rules on incompatible engagements (AN, 612 AP 31, Letter from Sigaut dated 28 September 1971). He was referring particularly to the *sociétés fiduciaries* and the best-known of such companies, *Fiduciaire de France*. These companies had grown up in France after the First World War, based on the model of Swiss and German *Treuhadgesellshaften*. They offered a clientele of mainly small- and medium-sized businesses a full range of services, from bookkeeping to legal and tax advice (Ramirez 2001).

The 1966 Act and the preparation of the 1969 decree had thus been an opportunity for the professional elites to confront one another with their views on the notion of the competence of the auditor, and in the end the position of the representatives of auditing associations prevailed. Although the link between accountancy and auditing had been established, the legislator had not wished to affirm the connection between the two bodies of technical knowledge by granting a monopoly to the chartered accountants. The visible division between members of the elites, some of whom had been involved in the governing bodies of both professions, certainly gave the authorities no encouragement to combine them into a single institution.[22] More broadly, another key factor was the division expressed through the significant number of practising auditors who were not from the accounting world. The heterogeneous nature of the auditing community also raised a further problem for the authorities when it came to deciding what to do about its smallest members. In the next sub-section, we therefore turn our attention to a second aspect of the 'professionalisation' of auditing, the issue of professional competence. After considering the problem of legal definition of the auditor's professional competence, examined from the angle of the relationship between accountancy expertise and auditing expertise, we will look at the issue of assessing the competence of certain practitioners in order to determine whether or not, after the reforms, they were worthy to remain in the profession.

The reform of auditing and elimination of the 'small practitioners'

Article 179 of the decree of 12 August 1969 stipulated that each regional commission set up by article 8 of the same decree (see above) would establish the first list of auditors on its territory as at 1 January 1970. All persons registered as auditors of publicly traded companies by virtue of the decree of 29 June 1936 would be automatically included in this list, provided they had exercised as auditor for at least one company since 1 October 1968. Persons who had held at least three engagements as auditors for four years prior to 1 October 1968 could, under article 180 of the decree, submit an application for inclusion on the list. This application would be examined by the regional commission, and it was possible to appeal against its decision before a national registration commission set up under a Ministry of Justice decision of 7 November 1969, comprising Jean Portemer, judge at the Supreme Judiciary Court (*Cour de cassation*) as head of the commission, two members of the Revenue Court, two law professors and two senior civil servants of the Treasury (from the *Inspection des finances*). The members of the profession represented at the national registration commission were Jean Trial, President of the *Fédération des compagnies de commissaires de sociétés inscrits près les cours d'appel*, Ferdinand Martin, honorary president of the *Compagnie des commissaires de sociétés inscrits près la Cour d'appel de Paris*, and Jean-Paul Fargette, Chairman of the *Association nationale des commissaires aux comptes de sociétés* (ANACACI).[23]

On 1 January 1967, there were 3597 auditors registered under the decree of 29 June 1936, including 1,567 in Paris (approximately half of these had been registered for more than ten years). Outside Paris, no company of auditors set up under the same decree had more than 300 members: Lyon had 251, Douai 200, Aix 284 and Agen only 15 (AN, 612 AP 29). The auditing elite discussed earlier were thus to be found in Paris, which had the greatest concentration of companies whose accounts were supposed to be audited by auditors of publicly traded companies. Some idea of the nature of this elite can be gained from examining the composition of the governing boards of these auditors' associations, especially that of the *Compagnie* of auditors registered with the Paris Court of Appeal. From the notice of the general meeting to be held on 24 May 1948 to replace 13 members of the board, we see that those 13 members included six *experts-comptables*, a former paymaster general, a general secretary of a bank, a head of department in a limited company, and two graduates of the *Polytechnique* and *Ecole Centrale* prestigious engineering *grandes écoles*. One year later (5 April 1949), 16 board members were to be replaced, including eight *experts-comptables*, a *Polytechnique* graduate, a retired member of the Revenue Court, a senior executive from an industrial company, a head of department in a listed company, an assistant manager and deputy manager of the Comptoir d'escompte bank, and an honorary general inspector from the Banque de France. The addresses stated in the minutes are all in the most desirable areas of Paris: the 15th, 16th, 17th, 8th and 7th *arrondissements* (AN, 612 AP 1).

Alongside this elite was a host of unregistered auditors working for small companies, most of whom were eliminated in the late 1960s reforms. It is difficult to gain an impression of these 'small auditors', particularly because there were no collective organisations representing them.[24] The process for establishing the new lists of auditors instigated by publication of the August 1969 decree indicates a sample of this population: the French National Archives' Centre for contemporary archives contains the papers relating to would-be auditors who appealed to the National registration commission following rejection of their application by the regional commissions (CAC, 19910775, art. 1–23 and 19910594, art. 1–54). These papers thus only concern auditors who considered themselves worthy of inclusion in the new auditing profession but had initially been refused registration. They do not include auditors who never applied to join the list, nor those who had been admitted to the list by the regional commissions, sometimes by virtue of their age.

We examined one hundred cases, randomly selected from approximately one thousand. The results were then compared with the summaries prepared by the national registration committee as stored in the national archives (AN, 612 AP 30). For each candidate, the decisions by the National registration commission have an attached file containing the following information: date of the application, decision by the regional registration commission and grounds for that decision, applicant's age and place of residence, applicant's character and any comments on his criminal record, applicant's titles, qualifications and membership of associations (such as the ANACACI), and the applicant's professional activities. Any documents provided by the applicant (auditor's reports, references) are also attached. Of the candidates in the selection, some 10% were retired, often from the tax authorities or banking, and the others consisted of roughly equivalent proportions of salaried accountants, *comptables agréés* (often former salaried accountants) and legal and tax advisors. The average age of the last two categories was just over forty, and the population was essentially male (only three female *comptables agréés* were noted). In three-quarters of cases, the qualifications held by candidates who were *comptables agréés* and legal and tax advisors were very modest, and apart from a few law diplomas had not been issued by higher education establishments. In terms of geographical area of origin, the Paris area is fairly clearly over-represented. The auditors in the sample studied worked as auditors for small businesses (in trade and light industry). The police file attached to the application for registration shows that for most applicants, auditing was a secondary source of income and they had other sources, being in some cases relatively well off with assets, often in the form of a second home (in 25% of the cases examined, the main home was also the auditor's place of work).

We observed that, in practically 75% of cases, the national commission upheld the decisions of the regional commissions, suggesting that the aim of the recruitment process was indeed to eliminate a large number of 'unworthy' candidates. The selection process thus also reveals the grounds on which the authorities decided to include candidates in, or exclude them from, the new profession. The definition of professional competence adopted appears to have relied more on social criteria than technical criteria. Being unable to assess candidates' expertise given the lack of professional standards, and without direct access to those candidates' working papers, the grounds for rejecting an applicant often concerned the applicant's modest social background, particularly the fact that he had only been appointed as auditor to small or unimportant companies. One interesting factor is the importance the national commission members appear to have attached to dual training in both accountancy and law, which should in theory be the background of the new auditor. Legal and tax advisors were therefore rejected on the grounds that their accounting knowledge was certainly too superficial, whereas *comptables agréés* were rejected because of their supposedly imperfect expertise in the legal aspects of the auditor's task. In appeals, the Commission generally took an indulgent line with candidates holding a degree and retired civil servants (who were sure not to remain auditors for long). This was the case of an auditor from Morlaix (in Brittany) born in 1911. He had graduated from the tax school *Ecole nationale des contributions directes et de l'enregistrement* in 1931, then worked as a tax inspector from 1942 to 1966, when he retired and became an independent tax advisor. Another successful applicant was a Polytechnique graduate, born in Nice in 1914 and now living in Paris. He had worked for the Bull computer company, then at the consultancy firm Planus as an engineer and subsequently as a manager and financial advisor. He was a registered expert witness and had worked as auditor to top-ranking companies: *Delmas Vieljeux* from 1956 to 1957, and *Promodès* in 1958–60. Another case concerns an applicant, born in 1914, who had neither qualifications nor any past engagements as auditor, but 'excellent references and worked at the *Société fiduciaire française d'expertise comptable* [accounting and auditing firm] from 1946 to 1954, then from 1954 to 1970 as sales manager at the *Compagnie européenne de révision et d'expertise comptable* [accounting and auditing firm]' (AN, 612 AP 30).

However, the commission showed no mercy for *comptables agréés* (many of whom had only vocational qualifications) and young legal and tax advisors, who were asked to prove their abilities by sitting the examination to test their aptitude for the profession of auditor. For example, 22 cases were examined at the meeting of the national registration commission of 14 October 1971, including seven from outside the Paris area (CAC, 0019910594, art. 53). The Parisian candidates included: a 44-year-old public sector employee with degrees in literature and law (rejected), a 33-year-old holder of the BEPC (French equivalent to the GCSE – rejected), a 70-year-old chief accountant with three appointments as auditor (rejected), a 29-year-old *Ecole supérieure de commerce de Paris* business school graduate (decision adjourned), a 38-year-old chief accountant with five appointments as auditor (rejected), a 63-year-old head of accounts and administration departments with three appointments as auditor of companies with average turnover of 350 million francs (accepted), a 55-year-old holder of a vocational qualification and nine appointments as auditor (rejected), a 53-year-old holder of a basic law diploma (*capacité en droit*), who had been a chief accountant since 1953 and had held one appointment as auditor (rejected). The provincial candidates included: a candidate from Lyon with seven appointments as auditor (accepted), a 67-year-old holder of the *baccalauréat* with three appointments as auditor (accepted), a 44-year-old holder of the BEPC with two appointments as auditor (rejected), a 42-year-old holder of a basic law diploma (*capacité en droit*), who had passed the first and second preliminary examinations for the qualification as *expert-comptable*, had been registered as a *comptable agréé* in 1955, was a trainee chief accountant and ex-serviceman (rejected), and a 51-year-old *comptable agréé* with seven employees and one appointment as auditor (rejected).

Conclusion

It was not until the end of the 1960s, i.e. very late in the comparative history of the accountancy profession in France and other industrialised countries, that there were any significant legislative and regulatory moves to modernise auditing in France. This modernisation took the form of 'professionalisation' of a profession that was already more than a century old. We have reviewed the problems encountered by this professionalisation; although it paved the way for the future by creating a new type of auditor, it was unable to shake off the legacy of the past, particularly the difficult relations between accountants and auditors, and the heterogeneous nature of the community of audit practitioners.

In clarifying the relationship between accountancy and auditing and raising the general level of the profession, the 1966 Act and the 1969 decree provided an opportunity to create a powerful independent accountancy profession developed around a renewed definition of what auditing was. Stricter recruitment and working requirements, formation of a professional organisation, greater resources for auditing, but also greater auditor responsibility; all these measures seemed to be converging towards the end of the much-lamented 'illusory' and 'irrelevant' auditing. For all that, was this a true renaissance? In fact, the laws and regulations simply made a new kind of professional possible, rather than endowing existing professionals with the powers and resources necessary to carry out their new functions. The new auditors of 1970 were weighed down by the legacy of the past: in creating the substance of their profession, they could rely neither on past practices, which had been flagrantly lacking in resources, nor on doctrinal texts, which were nothing more than an idealised, highly 'legal' vision of effective auditing. But the 1966 Act and its application decree carved the profession a path which would by no means bring them closer to the practices and the status of British chartered accountants as mentioned by the lawmaker in the foreword to his bill of law.

The 24 July 1966 Act and 12 August 1969 decree did have the merit of helping to strengthen the influence of the French independent accountancy profession, chiefly by asserting the link between accountants and auditors, if not between accountancy expertise and auditing expertise. However, more time was to pass before the various stakeholders in auditing, especially company managers, acknowledged that reliable accounting information came at a price, and the official fee scale did not correspond to that price. While waiting for official recognition of the auditing profession to be reflected in an increase in auditing fees, the late 1960s laws helped to put the status of the auditor on a level with other professions. The aim of the stricter incompatibility rules intended to preserve the dignity of the function, and the greater responsibilities making the auditor a censor with civil and criminal liability for illegal behaviour by managers if he failed to report offences that came to light, was to confirm the auditor's independent professional status and his reliance on his own judgement. The Act and decree thus contributed to a conception of professionalism that remained attached to the 'sole practitioner' or 'small group of practitioners' model as the only model able to guarantee accountants the same regard as the longer-established professions, starting with the legal profession (Ramirez 2001, 2003).

And yet this conception was not to form the basis of professional elitism in the two decades that followed the reform. A new definition of professionalism was to emerge from the market and globalisation of business and capital flows, in the form of expansion in France by the large Anglo-American auditing firms. These firms offered a different model of professionalisation, founded on collective organisation of auditing practice and early internationalisation (Ramirez 2003). The changes of the late 1960s for French auditors thus constituted, in our opinion, a reform but not a renaissance, since the market for auditing as a professional service remained to be constructed, and the idea that market and profession could be compatible had yet to penetrate thinking in France.

This paper thus acknowledges the explanatory power of the 'financial markets' variable to account for the late development of the French auditing profession, but considers the French case as a sort of mirror-image of the British and American case, not only by focusing on the smaller role played by financial markets in the French economy and the actual lack of demand for audits, but also by stressing the impact of this low demand on the quality of the service provided by French auditors.

In the American and British context, the importance of reliable accounting information for the investor probably greatly influenced the leading firms' development of sophisticated audit techniques based on analytical reviews and sampling procedures (Matthews, Anderson, and Edwards 1998; Power 1992; Previts and Merino 1997). In turn, professional institutes used these methodologies to nourish the audit standard-setting process. Although France's auditing institute, the *Compagnie nationale des commissaires aux comptes*, set up its own programme of compulsory auditing standards in 1971, it was impossible to apply them fully with the level of audit fees that continued to prevail until the mid-1980s. It was only in 1985 that a new scale for audit fees was set, this time based on hourly rates. The growing internationalisation of French companies and the modernisation of the Paris Bourse in the middle of the 1980s no doubt helped to foster an 'audit culture' among French businessmen but, ironically enough, the benefit was essentially reaped by the large Anglo-American firms who now had the opportunity to expand in what had become a profitable market. The success of the now Big Four, in France as elsewhere, is indicative not so much of the superiority of market economies *per se* than of the fact that credibility is a commodity that takes time to produce. The ancestors of today's multinational audit firms were born in economies where financial markets are central, in societies in which the professions are powerful and enjoy considerable independence of the State. By the time the French audit profession had become effectively 'professionalised', these firms already had long years of experience behind them and, most importantly, had been able to use the credibility built up at home to export their services beyond their Anglo-American preserve. The edge that the 'Big' Anglo-American firms had on their French counterparts did not primarily derive from superior personnel or methodologies, but rather from the fact that they were vital parts of the economic system in which they operated and that they had contributed to its internationalisation.

Notes

1. This division effectively split the profession along the lines of the social origins of its members. From 1942 onwards, the *experts-comptables* included the 600 holders of the 1927 *brevet* qualification (most of whom had been exempted from actually sitting the examination) and candidates with sufficient educational qualifications for ex officio registration as *experts-comptables* (law graduates, HEC business school graduates, and some graduates of the prestigious *Ecole Polytechnique*). In contrast, few of the *comptables agréés* had been in higher education. Although it was logical from a social point of view, this division soon became difficult to manage from an economic point of view, particularly for the 'small' *experts-comptables* without the necessary social connections to obtain engagements that would enable them to earn a living from monitoring accounts. Poaching on the *comptables agréés*' territories was all the more intolerable because although the registered accountants made up the majority of members, they had only minority representation under the statutes of the OECCA (see below). No less than ten bills of law were filed between 1950 and 1965 seeking either to divide the OECCA in two, or merge the two categories. Ultimately, a 1968 Act put an end to recruitment of *comptables agréés* and offered to them the opportunity to join the Order as *experts-comptables* (this is discussed later in the paper).
2. In 1921, another bill had sought to oblige French companies to have at least one accountant among their auditors, but only mentioned accountants as individuals (and *experts-comptables* as expert witnesses for the courts), rather than a professional category. However, the 1926 bill, brought by members of the Left, suggested creating a body of accounting specialists in charge of overseeing the introduction of accounting standards in businesses.
3. Further measures were added to the provisions of these decrees in October 1935, July 1937 and August 1937 (see Mikol 1993).
4. The January/June 1950 issue of the auditors' journal *Revue de la Compagnie des commissaires de sociétés agréés par la Cour d'appel de Paris,* page 86, describes how auditors insisted they should be members of these boards.
5. For an illustration of this idea in the study of professions, see Krause (1996).
6. Regarding the attitude of certain employers' representatives towards auditing, it is interesting to consult the Chambers of Commerce and Industry's reports on the proposed auditing reforms. These reports generally repeat the arguments put forward in the parliamentary reports of the 1920s and 1930s, advising against granting a monopoly on auditing on

the general grounds that professional accountants lack 'reputation', and more particularly that only a small number of them, for instance the qualified chartered accountants (*experts-comptables)*, have any real technical abilities. In the Paris Chamber of Commerce and Industry archives, one major source is cote III-3.33 (18), *commissaires aux comptes* 1926–8.

7. Only with the issuance of a decree on 3 July 1985 did professionals come to be paid on an hourly basis.
8. In a letter to the French Minister of Justice on 22 July 1968, Henri Courbot, president of the Paris Chamber of Commerce and Industry, returned to the question of the rules on auditors' fees: 'While there is no doubt that auditors should receive remuneration that guarantees their work will be done conscientiously, care must be taken that their remuneration does not become too large an expense for companies in addition to all the other charges already incumbent upon them'. In Courbot's opinion, the proposed new tariffs for audits did not meet this requirement. The Chamber of Commerce even found them 'exorbitant' (CAC, 0019910594, art. 52).
9. It is also interesting to note that the CNPF's proposals included an upper limit of 50,000 francs regardless of the basis used, and no increase in fees if there was a second auditor. Furthermore, the cost of any experts or assistants who worked with the auditor was not covered. A few international comparisons indicate the low level of resources available to French auditors to carry out their engagement. One good illustration is the *Papeteries de Navarre* affair in 1971, which concerned one of the leading figures of the profession, Jacques Frinault. A graduate of France's prestigious *Polytechnique* engineering school, Frinault was at the head of a large firm serving a clientele of big listed companies and co-auditor of the major paper manufacturer *Papeteries de Navarre*. With his colleague Michel Descazes (aged 77 at the time), he was accused by the buyers of *Papeteries de Navarre* of having erroneously approved accounts showing profits, whereas a private audit by the British firm Cooper Brothers commissioned by the same buyers concluded that the company was several million francs in the red. Apart from accounting quibbles, Frinault argued in his defence that auditing in France suffered from a 'tragic' lack of resources. Descazes summed up the 'tragic' aspect of the situation by comparing the 2500 (current) francs he had received for auditing in 1969 with the 700,000 (current) francs paid to the British firm for their audit (CAC, 0019910594, article 54. Décisions de la chambre nationale de discipline des commissaires aux comptes de sociétés – Année 1972).
10. Although many auditing textbooks had been published since the start of the twentieth century, the question remained to what extent the auditors had sufficient means to apply the methods proposed. The 'legal' tendency of the French-style conception of auditing can be contrasted with the 'economic' conception held by the British and Americans, based on statistical techniques that meant audits required more time and resources (Power 1992). For a comparison between French auditing in the late 1960s, when it was still essentially a matter for individuals, and the 'Anglo-Saxon' full audit as carried out by firms, see Archavlis (1961) and Wisner (1967).
11. The 8 August 1935 decree-act required auditors who had been registered by a Court of Appeal to establish an association to represent their interests, within the jurisdiction of the relevant Court. In 1938 a national structure to federate the existing regional bodies emerged as the *Fédération nationale des commissaires de sociétés agréés par les Cours d'Appel*. Given the distribution of the population of auditors in France, the only one of these associations with any real bargaining power was the Paris association, *Compagnie des commissaires de sociétés agréés par la Cour d'appel de Paris.* For some time, the only professional publication that existed was the also Paris-based *Bulletin des commissaires de sociétés agréés par la Cour d'appel de Paris,* which published highly technical articles essentially aimed at listed companies' auditors. In 1964, the decision by the *Fédération nationale des commissaires de sociétés agréés par les Cours d'Appel* to start publishing its own bulletin probably resulted from the need to combine forces to negotiate with the government over the future of the profession (see below). Several directors of the professional auditing organisations had also held important positions in the *Ordre des experts-comptables et des comptables agrees.* Jean Trial, for instance, the first president of the *Compagnie nationale des commissaires aux comptes*, the auditors' association that was born with the 1969 reforms, had also been president of the OECCA council (*Conseil supérieur de l'Ordre)* in the early 1960s. Source: Memo to the French Minister of Justice of 19 May 1969, nomination of Trial, Fauconneau and Sigaut for appointment to the French National Order of Merit (CAC, 0019910594, art. 52).
12. The COB had been involved in the preparatory work for the 1969 decree. When the flat-rate fee system was chosen, the COB insisted that it should be possible to go above the upper limit in certain circumstances (AN, 612 AP 29).
13. The Ordinance of 28 September 1967 set up the regulator *Commission des opérations de bourse* (COB) to provide information to securities holders and report on certain stock market transactions. Seeking to encourage long-term investment through better public information and to enable the financial market to play an international role, the government had formed an institution that was fairly similar to the SEC (Securities Exchange Commission) in the US. It is important to remember that the stock market's situation had been in constant decline during the 1960s: the lower number of investors and falling prices made it more difficult for companies seeking financing to attract investors (Bonin 1989).

14. Statement of the grounds for the bill. Preparatory documents for the bill of 31 October 1968 (CAC, 19830740, art. 15).
15. The *comptables agréés* had been attributed one-third of seats in the representative bodies, although they outnumbered the *experts-comptables* by three to one.
16. Visibly the government's original plan was to retain auditing's nature as a function (even though it was to be enhanced by admission of candidates with high social and cultural standing) rather than to make it a profession, i.e. a full-time activity exercised to the exclusion of all others, for which the professional had specific training (AN, 612 AP 29).
17. The editorial of the November 1948 *Bulletin de la Compagnie Nationale des experts-comptables brevetés* complained that the registration commissions at the Courts of Appeal did not automatically recognise the competence of *experts-comptables* to become auditors. In particular, the President of Rouen Court of Appeal refused automatic registration of accountants already registered with another court, systematically obliging them to take the examination introduced by the June 1936 decree. A monopoly was thus necessary, as 'verification of an account is inseparable from its preparation'. In a letter dated 15 February 1962 (CAC, 0019910594, art. 52), the Minister of Education informed the Minister of Justice that 'great confusion currently reigns over the ways in which the different Courts of Appeal proceed for registration on the lists of auditors of publicly traded companies. Some register all applicants without exception, others require all candidates to sit the examination, and others (the majority) admit most candidates and only require them to sit the examination in a very few cases'. The same letter pointed out that since 1945, the number of candidates for the examination had never exceeded 50 (there had been 859 in 1936 when the first list was established). Thirty to fifty per cent of those actually took the examination and the results were poor (in 1955: 28 candidates, 13 present at the examination, 5 passes; in 1956: 24 candidates, 14 present at the examination, 7 passes; in 1957–8: 49 candidates, 12 present at the examination, 3 passes; in 1959: 37 candidates, 12 present at the examination, 5 passes; in 1960: 39 candidates, 12 present at the examination, 6 passes; and in 1961: 39 candidates, 15 present at the examination, 6 passes).
18. The divergence of views predated the period covered in this article. Even in the early twentieth century, the accounting world was divided over the possible amendments to the 1867 Act. Some auditors such as Gustave Doyen, who was also President of the *Compagnie des experts-comptables près le tribunal de première instance de la Seine*, accepted that the formation of professional associations with a monopoly on auditing was 'pure fantasy' (Ramirez 2001).
19. In their negotiations with the government, some chartered accountants hoped that the monopoly on accounting would be reserved for an elite in the renewed *Ordre*. Pinceloup (1976) quotes a letter sent on 6 January 1966 to their peers by ten *comptables agréés* who were resigning from the Council of the *Ordre*, denouncing manoeuvres since the Nantes congress (1964) to prevent the *comptables agréés* from holding appointments as auditors.
20. The auditors of agricultural cooperatives and mixed economy companies were governed by different regimes from the standard laws on auditing of company accounts.
21. In a tract dated 2 December 1970 (AN, 612 AP 31), Sigaut rejected the idea of merging 'Anglo-Saxon' style and French auditing: 'we will not accept the assumption that the methods are good because they are American'.
22. On this point, see note 16 above.
23. The ANACACI had been formed in 1968 to defend the interests of auditors who were not on the lists created by the decree of June 1936. It included many *comptables agréés*, auditors of small businesses who were keen to assert their rights, particularly after the reforms of the status of the OECCA that now allowed them to certify balance sheets (AN, 612 AP 29).
24. As noted earlier, the ANACACI was formed solely for the purpose of defending applications from auditors who considered themselves the most suitable for inclusion in the new profession.

References

Primary sources:

Archives:

Assemblée nationale, Paris:

Documents parlementaires-Chambre, séance du 25 février 1926, Proposition de loi Chastenet *et al.* No. 2668, 274–6.

Documents parlementaires-Chambre, séance du 17 novembre 1927, Rapport Angoulvant No. 5065, 248–52.

Documents parlementaires-Chambre, séance du 10 mars 1936, Rapport Evain No. 6883, 565–7.

Documents de l'Assemblée nationale, annexe no 1003, 2ème session ordinaire de 1963–4, séance du 23 juin 1964.

Centre d'Accueil et de recherche des Archives nationales, Paris (AN in the text):
Série 12 Ministère du Commerce et de l'Industrie
F12 8165 Contrôle des sociétés anonymes (1905–21)
F12 8166 Réforme de la loi sur les sociétés. Experts-comptables
Série 612 AP Fonds Jean Portemer
612 AP 1 Formules et modèles d'actes notariés établis pendant le stage de Jean Portemer. 1928–31; 1937–69. Les commissaires aux comptes de la 1ère réforme: décret-loi du 8 août 1935 et décret du 29 juin 1936. (1937–69)
612 AP 29 Président des commissions de préparation du décret du 12 août 1969 sur les commissaires aux comptes
612 AP 30-31 Président de la Commission nationale d'inscription et de la Chambre nationale de discipline des commissaires aux comptes

Centre des archives contemporaines, Fontainebleau (CAC in the text):
Fonds Justice – Direction des Affaires Civiles et du Sceau – Sous-direction du droit économique – Bureau du droit commercial
19910775 Art. 1–23 Commission nationale d'inscription des commissaires aux comptes, chambre nationale de discipline, équivalence de diplôme et recours en application du décret 69-810 du 12 août 1969, années 1970–87, dans l'ordre alphabétique.
19910594 Art. 1–54 Commission nationale d'inscription des commissaires aux comptes: dossiers d'appel des décisions des commissions régionales en application du décret 69-810 du août 1969, années 1969–77 dans l'ordre alphabétique
19950409 Art. 103–104 dossiers de législation, réglementation et codification en matière de droit commercial (classement thématique): 1843, 1897, 1913–90
Premier Ministre – Secrétariat Général du Gouvernement – Service Législatif
19830740 Art. 15: Dossiers de préparation des lois janvier 1967–janvier 1973. Troisième législature: projet de loi modifiant le statut de l'ordre des experts-comptables et des comptables agréés. N 427 Ministère de l'économie et des finances. loi 68.946 du 31 octobre 1968 JO 258 1er novembre 1968

Periodicals:

Bulletin d'information de la Compagnie nationale des experts-comptables brevetés par l'Etat (1946–62).
Bulletin de liaison de la Fédération des associations de commissaires de sociétés inscrits par les cours d'appel (1964–68).
Revue de la Compagnie des commissaires de sociétés agréés par la Cour d'appel de Paris (1948–69).

Secondary sources

Anderson, M., J.R. Edwards, and D. Matthews. 1996. A study of the quoted company audit market in 1886. *Accounting, Business & Financial History* 6, no. 3: 363–87.

Archavlis, E. 1961. Current trends in auditing in limited companies. [Tendances actuelles en matière de commissariat aux comptes dans les sociétés anonymes]. *Economie et Comptabilité* 55: 2707–12.

Bocqueraz, C. 2001. The development of professional associations: The experience of French accountants from the 1880s to the 1940s. *Accounting, Business & Financial History* 11, no. 1: 7–27.

Bonin, H. 1989. *L'argent en France depuis 1880: Banquiers, financiers, épargnants dans la vie économique et politique*. Paris: Masson.

Brown, R.C.A. 1905. *A history of accounting and accountants*. Edinburgh: Jack.

Chandler, R., J.R. Edwards, and M. Anderson. 1993. Changing perceptions of the role of the company auditor, 1840–1940. *Accounting and Business Research* 23: 443–59.

Commission des opérations de bourse. 1968. *Rapport annuel de la Commission des opérations de bourse. Année 1968*. Paris: La Documentation française.

Edwards, J.R. 1989. *A history of financial accounting*. London: Routledge.

Fortin, A. 1991. The French accounting plan: Origins and influences on subsequent practices. *The Accounting Historians Journal* 18: 1–25.

Fridenson, P., and A. Straus, eds. 1987. *Le capitalisme français XIXe–XXe siècle: Blocages et dynamismes d'une croissance*. Paris: Fayard.

Jones, E. 1981. *Accountancy and the British economy 1840–1980: The evolution of Ernst & Whinney*. London: Batsford.

Krause, E.A. 1996. *Death of the guilds: Professions, states, and the advance of capitalism, 1930 to the present.* New Haven, CT: Yale University Press.

Lemarchand, Y. 1993. *Du dépérissement à l'amortissement: Enquête sur l'histoire d'un concept et de sa traduction comptable.* Nantes: Ouest éditions.

Matthews, D., M. Anderson, and J.R. Edwards. 1998. *The priesthood of industry: The rise of the professional accountant in British management.* Oxford: Oxford University Press.

Mikol, A. 1993. The evolution of auditing and the independent auditor in France. *The European Accounting Review* 2, no. 1: 1–16.

Ordre des experts comptables et des comptables agréés. 1962. *Le commissaire aux comptes dans les sociétés françaises: aspects juridiques et techniques de l'exercice du mandat. Actes du congrès de Dijon de l'Ordre des experts-comptables et des comptables agréés.* Paris: Ordre des experts-comptables et des comptables agréés.

Pinceloup, C. 1976. *Comptes et comptables contemporains: Un siècle d'histoire de la comptabilité dans son contexte politique et économique.* Unpublished manuscript (available for consultation at the library of the *Ordre des experts-comptables*).

Power, M.K. 1992. From common sense to expertise: Reflections on the pre-history of audit sampling. *Accounting, Organizations & Society* 17, no. 1: 37–62.

Previts, G.J., and B.D. Merino. 1997. *A history of accountancy in the United States: The cultural significance of accounting.* Columbus, OH: Ohio State University Press.

Ramirez, C. 2001. Understanding social closure in its cultural context: Accounting practitioners in France (1920–1939). *Accounting, Organizations & Society* 26, no. 4–5: 391–418.

Ramirez, C. 2003. Du commissariat aux comptes à l'audit – Les Big 4 et la profession comptable depuis 1970. *Actes de la Recherche en Sciences Sociales* 146–7: 62–79.

Standish, P. 1990. Origins of the Plan comptable général: A study in cultural intrusion and reaction. *Accounting and Business Research* 20: 337–51.

Sugarman, D. 1995. Who colonised whom? Historical reflection on the intersection between law, lawyers and accountants in England. In *Professional competition and professional power: Lawyers, accountants and the social construction of markets*, eds. Y. Dezalay and D. Sugarman, 226–37. London and New York: Routledge.

Wilenski, H.L. 1964. The professionalization of everyone? *American Journal of Sociology* 70, no. 2: 137–58.

Wisner, J. 1967. Reflections on the mission of the auditor [Réflexions sur la mission du commissaire aux comptes]. *Revue des sociétés*, October–December, nos 10–12: 371–8.

Accounting for triangular trade

Cheryl S. McWatters[a] and Yannick Lemarchand[b]

[a] *University of Alberta, Edmonton, Canada;* [b] *Université de Nantes, Nantes, France*

This study complements our investigations into the use of accounting manuals as representations of commercial activities. Our previous work focused on the *Guide du Commerce* of Gaignat de l'Aulnais and the slave trade in eighteenth-century France. We broaden our scope with cross-sectional archival evidence to examine the extent to which the methods and operations in these sources point to a collective knowledge shared amongst traders and those engaged to conduct the slave trade on their behalf. Of particular interest is the prevalence of standardised methods, documents and terms of trade, all of which point, in a similar way to that of the *Guide du Commerce*, to the slave trade's technical contributions to capitalism (Pétré-Grenouilleau 2004, 352). The archival evidence illustrates the rationalisation and institutionalisation of an economic system, albeit a particular outlier, and its progressive sophistication in terms of operating processes, creating thereby the illusion of a rational business model.

Introduction

Our earlier research into the history of, and accounting for, the slave trade has examined accounting manuals as representations of commercial activities. This research has prompted us to expand the scope of our studies to incorporate current themes within the history of slavery, as well as prevalent themes in maritime history. The present study questions to what extent the accounting for triangular trade exemplified a shared collective knowledge amongst *armateurs*, ship captains, investors, African traders and colonial agents. The accounting and trading system, as we first encountered it in the *Guide du Commerce*, was both rational and standardised. We began to question whether or not this representation was an anomaly, the author's own invention. Our earlier research provided initial evidence that the systems and practices outlined in this work conformed to eighteenth-century practices. These findings provided a means to link our research to the techno-rationality arguments provided by scholars of the history of slavery and maritime trade more generally.

To further our knowledge, we have undertaken archival research to develop a cross-sectional analysis of ship owners, vessels, voyages and captains from a number of trading cities of eighteenth-century France. From these 21 cases, we attempt to demonstrate that the accounting for triangular trade exhibited the same rationalising tendencies as other forms of capitalism.

The French slave trade has been described as a lottery that operated within the broader sector of maritime and international trade and colonialism. The trade offered the possibility of high potential returns but also exhibited high risk. Yet, its attraction lay in the ability to take advantage of these high returns to offset lower returns from trade in other areas.[1] To some degree, high barriers to entry were evident, as the cost to mount such a venture was considerable and the venture's success depended partially on luck but also on the skill of the vessel captain and crew. Risks also were related to the length of the voyage, the unpredictability of the weather, health concerns and international relations. Captive and crew mortality varied greatly. The question of risk sharing is an important one in relation to the returns generated. We focus on the three main parties concerned: the *armateur*, who undertook and raised the capital for the venture, the ship's captain, and the colonial agent, who acted on commission to sell the captives to colonists as slave labour.

The *armateur* had his personal capital at risk in these ventures as part of his overall business operations. Given the financial commitment, these voyages, including the vessel, were subdivided into parts shared across a network of diversified investors. While risk sharing reduced exposure in an individual voyage, the *armateur* confronted the reality of time lags and market uncertainty with respect to the sale of colonial goods. The *armateur* also earned commissions for transactions on behalf of other associates, including insurance arrangements. Risk diversification was prevalent within the slave-trade market, across the maritime trade sector more generally and in other business interests. As noted by Gaston-Martin (1993) and Meyer (1999), *négociants* did not specialise in the slave-trade but included this sector in their broader business and investment portfolio.

The ship's captain stood to benefit substantially from a slave-trade venture. Not only did the captain receive wages well in excess of those earned in less risky shipping operations, he frequently earned additional sums from bonuses and incentives provided to align further his interests with those of associates.[2] He sometimes had the dual role of being an agent on behalf of the *armateur* and the other associates, as well as being an associate in the venture which he commanded. The returns from this trade provided the means to move up the social ladder within the trading community.

The colonial agent was responsible for the sales of the captives in the colonies. The *armateur* generally provided the name of the colonial agent to whom the captain was referred and in many cases an alternate should the trade location change. Colonial agents worked on a commission basis, and their ability to attract trade depended to a great extent on the reputational effects of their business conduct and their frequent links to the French trading community through family ties. They became known for their business skill, especially in their ability to attract colonists who would be firm in their financial commitments, along with their understanding of the market situation for both captives and the colonial merchandise for which they were exchanged.

We proceed as follows. The next section presents an overview of the trade operations, including differences in the French *versus* English system, after which we outline our sample and sources. The following two sections examine the instructions to vessel captains and the control and incentive systems utilised. We conclude the study with summary comments and suggestions for further research.

Triangular trade

The triangular pattern of the slave trade was reflected in the accounting process. First, the vessel was outfitted to leave France. This process or *l'armement* included all costs prior to departure. The pre-departure costs (*la mise-hors*) were divided amongst the associates according to their respective share. After leaving the French port, the vessel travelled to trading locations on the African Coast. The vessel captain purchased captives at various locations in Africa (Coast of

Guinea, Coast of Angola, Mozambique) in exchange for the merchandise sent from France. Once the captives were acquired, the vessel made its 'middle passage' across the Atlantic to the colonies. Upon arrival in the colonies, the captain addressed himself to the designated colonial agent through whom the sale of captives took place. The terms of trade were cash, bills and letters of exchange, and colonial commodities (primarily sugar, tobacco and indigo). The vessel then returned to France with goods and funds, while the captain frequently remained in the colonies to manage this part of the venture. He also was required to provide various reports to the *armateur* in France, along with similar reports provided by the colonial agent. The laying up or *le désarmement* of the vessel took place in France, and included payment of outstanding wages, duties and other fees upon arrival to dock and unload the vessel. The series of shipments of colonial goods continued as the colonists repaid their outstanding debt through these shipments. The sale of these goods resulted in a series of *retours* or net proceeds that were divided amongst the associates according to their respective shares.

Differences between the French and the English trade

As noted elsewhere (see Daudin 2004; McWatters and Lemarchand 2006; McWatters 2008), the organisation of the slave trade in France differed significantly from the English case, which has been the subject of more extensive research. The reasons for these variations included the following:

- French vessels were relatively inefficient compared to those from England and other countries due to state requirements resulting in higher staffing ratios (crew to tonnage).
- The French government tended to provide more support to colonists compared to counterparts in other countries, especially in terms of debt repayments.
- The credit and banking system in France was less developed relative to those in other parts of Europe, including the financing and liquidity of state debt.
- The French government provided specific incentives to promote the trade (such as a bonus for slaves introduced, the elimination of duties on colonial goods) or to receive funds (through the imposition of duty payments on each captive introduced), in the latter case gaining financially and directly from the trade.
- The commissions received by colonial agents were much less in the French case compared to those in England (in the English case, the colonial agent bore the risk of non-payment by colonists, whereas in France it was the *armateur)*; the commissions earned in each context reflected these differences in risk – English agents often received 10% but French counterparts earned only 1–2%. In the French trade, colonists paid for slaves with hard currency or more usually with the exchange of colonial merchandise sent to France for sale by the *armateur* on the open market. The colonial agent was not responsible for debt collection. In the English case, the slave market and the goods market were not linked in this way, with the commission agent bearing responsibility for debt collection. Thus, the commissions earned in each context reflected these risk differences (Darity 1985; Daudin 2004; Richardson 1976).

The captain had a much greater and multi-faceted role in the French context, especially with respect to sales, the selection of colonial merchandise, sales terms, and arrangements with the colonial agent. The captain was selected for his versatility, often staying in the colonies to collect debts and oversee the affairs of the vessel. For example, in the declaration to the admiralty upon the return of *La Jeanette* to Nantes in 1741, the second captain Adrien Chapy noted that he had taken command of the ship in order that the captain could remain in Saint-Domingue to manage the affairs of the vessel (‘*gérer les affaires du navire*’) on behalf of the *armateur* Darrèche (A.D. L.-A. B4789). In the captain’s instructions of *La Bonne Société*, Article 17 outlined that the captain would stay in Port au Prince if the colonial agent had died and until such time as new instructions were received. As well, the Article specified the captain’s expenses during this stay that were to be charged on account to the vessel (Bibliothèque Municipale de La Rochelle, hereafter, B.M. La R., Ms 2290).

Theoretical underpinnings

Before proceeding with our analysis, we situate the slave trade and its organisation within the broader context of social and trading networks. These networks also provide a practical demonstration of communities of practice. We then adopt insights from institutional economics and agency theory to illustrate how these networks became institutionalised and formalised in practice. As with communities of practice, institutional mechanisms incorporated diffusion mechanisms with respect to organisational learning and processes.

Social and trading networks

Business and commercial interests in France were reinforced by links through family, religious and social ties. Those involved in trade or investment had established strong networks throughout the country and internationally. These networks had a commercial as well as a social dimension. An important means to foster strong business links was via their parallelism in family relations. In the case of the French colonies in the Caribbean, many families had interests there, both in plantations and as commercial agents. Some of these holdings resulted from investments made to facilitate control and oversight, but many also resulted from assets received as partial debt repayment by colonists. Trading families sent family members to manage and oversee operations in other European cites and overseas. Younger family members went abroad, to other parts of Europe to acquire business and language skills, or to the colonies as a means to provide career opportunities to offspring. Many of the latter would send their own children to France and other parts of Europe to be educated or to enter the commercial trade.

Networks offered competitive intelligence, financial and investment support and opportunities, and a means to lever one’s own business skill and capital. The business correspondence of the *armateur* Deguer underscores the value of networks. For example, in 1772, concerns about the credit worthiness of the Labatut interests in Saint-Domingue led to court action. It also created a ripple effect through the entire business network, as other associates and *négociants* were made aware of this situation and concerns were expressed about business links with this family in Bordeaux (A.D. L.-A. 8J7). Letters to business partners, potential investors and family members demonstrate the constant need to maintain strong relations with those whose support and credit would be important. These letters also confirm the degree of familiarity within these networks. Correspondence dealt with business matters but also spoke to other aspects of their relationships, be it family ties, health matters, travel, etc. Recommendations for investments and personnel, along with self-promotion, were frequent topics.

In maritime trade, these networks provided additional means to recruit labour, especially ship captains. The latter often remained with the same *armateur* for many voyages and a number of years. They also were ‘recruited’ by others, even in different cities, having established their reputation and being recommended by *armateurs* and investors. They frequently were members of the *armateur's* family, offering a means of control for the *armateur* and on-the-job training for the family member. Others rose through the ranks, both in terms of their trade and, importantly, in terms of family circles and social linkages. Captains could do well financially through their own trading, leading to entrées into the commercial and social milieu.

The armateur milieu

Armateurs were a close network linked through their business interests, family, social and cultural context. Networks facilitated repeated contracting and fostered long-term relationships. The reputation of the individual members was the key to co-operation, decreasing both contracting costs and reducing opportunism. Membership in this context resulted from the trust and reputation as a result of prior activities and exchanges. These exchange mechanisms were long-standing in nature and reinforced by their sharing of cultural, social and family ties.[3] As noted by Pétré-Grenouilleau (1998, 113): 'Trade, is therefore, above all, a set of gestures, behaviours, ways of thinking, in brief, the expression of an original culture ... Even within families, everything therefore worked for the maintenance of the professional, mercantile and bourgeois values of the milieu'.

Free Masonry *(la franc-maçonnerie)*

The role of membership in the Free Masons, while not necessarily a dominant feature of the social milieu, was an important integrating mechanism. Nevertheless, during the eighteenth century prior to the French Revolution, membership of the Free Masons and the number of lodges were increasing. As noted by Masseaut (2000), this aspect of commercial society was expressed in any number of ways, including the naming of vessels which were part of commercial fleets. Vessel names, such as *Les Coeurs Unis* and *L'Harmonie*, were also names of Free Mason lodges in Nantes. Other names symbolised Free Masonry values, including *La Vertu, La Parfaite*, *La Paix* and *L'Union*. Free Masonry linked traders across various commercial centres, with lodges being established in the major port cities. It also brought together commercial interests across Europe, especially as they reinforced other linkages such as those which linked Jacobite sympathisers with their counterparts in other parts of Europe. Religious ties were not limited to Catholics, but similarly Protestants, who were well established in various cities, including Nantes, La Rochelle and Bordeaux, were closely tied to commercial interests in Holland, with whom they shared their religion.

However, Free Masonry networks were a supplement (and a useful, perhaps necessary one) to *existing* networks. In the eighteenth century, commercial success was measured on an international scale. Being part of these international networks was necessary, and inserting oneself into the requisite social and commercial contexts was obligatory. Social mobility, be it from small trader to *armateur*, or from ship's captain to ship owner, was possible, but required both financial and social credit.

The ideas of Free Masonry echoed those of the philosophy of the period. The '*siècle des Lumières*' and the belief in science, rational thought and progress were of great interest to the commercial elite. Self edification was one reason. Such knowledge and understanding also were important in terms of business itself. The eighteenth-century salon and library meant art and literature but also mathematics, medicine and science. Such knowledge could bring important returns if it led to improvements in business operations. Masseaut (2000) outlines this interlocking relationship, along with its reconciliation with what appears to us today as the 'unspeakable traffic' of slavery.

Ship captains

As noted earlier, captains were highly sought after, and their reputations, good or bad, followed them. The captain of a trading vessel was expected to be multi-talented. Not only did he have to possess all the requisite technical and navigational skills (for which he had been admitted to the rank of captain), but also possess business acumen, the ability to manage a diverse crew, and the understanding of the terms of trade in both Africa and the Caribbean. The *Guide du Commerce* outlines this versatility briefly (Gaignat de l'Aulnais 1771, 310), where the author describes this difficult trade and the necessary knowledge required of the captain: what sort of merchandise, what quantities, their assortment, differences related to geographic location and levels of competition, etc. The terms of exchange changed, as did the preferences of buyers and sellers. Upon reaching the rank of captain, many individuals stayed with the same *armateur* for a long time. Given the diverse trade undertaken by most *armateurs*, captains were involved in a variety of voyages, some involving the complete circuit of triangular trade, others dealing only with *les voyages en droiture* between the colonies and Europe, and others as part of trade operations within European networks.

Given the mutual dependence of *armateur* and captain, a certain familiarity is noted in correspondence between them (Hervé 1999, 52). Such correspondence also indicates that, in reporting to their *armateur*, captains provided up-to-date information regarding the trade situation, competitors, merchandise preferences and prices. While attaining the rank of captain represented upward social mobility, some captains came to this profession via established commercial families. Other captains came from the ranks of the nobility, in part, to forge commercial links that were considered (and in some cases legislated) to be otherwise outside the domain of these social groups.

The slave trade's social organisation suggests an interesting parallel between organisational networks and communities of practice. We adopt the concept of community of practice in the sense of a group of individuals who undertake a craft or practice with particular emphasis on the role of social capital and social relations which develop around their activities (Barlatier and Thomas 2007; Cox 2005; Dupouët, Yildizoglu, and Cohendet 2003). Learning in these communities can be formal, such as within a guild or apprenticeship, or informal. In our case, we consider two potential communities of practice, one composed of the *armateurs* and one of the ship captains. The two groups and their practices were interlinked and membership was not restrictive in the sense that captains could move into the *armateur* circle as a result of financial success and family ties. Both groups learned by doing, through imitation, and observation. As part of a social network, this learning also included how to act and conduct oneself, along with the performance of the actual work or business activity.

Institutional economics and agency theory[4]

The slave trade was part of the overall system of maritime trade, and thus incorporated, adapted and utilised the norms and practices long established in trading operations. Many of these were formalised in, and reinforced by, legal and state requirements, such as those required by the *Ordonnance de la Marine* (1681). The social and organisational networks in which this trade was conducted further institutionalised norms and practices, and provided important diffusion mechanisms through which ways-of-doing and modes of action were reinforced.

Similar to other long-distance trading operations, the slave trade demonstrated the customary features of principal-agent relationships: moral hazard, opportunism, adverse selection. Thus, our research analysis draws upon the relevant literature of institutional economics and agency theory, as well as network analysis as applied to maritime trade.[5] As noted earlier, we focus on the three main parties involved, the *armateur*, the ship's captain and the colonial agent.

The *armateur* engaged the ship's captain and also the agent in the colonies to act on his/her behalf and on behalf of the other associates to whom the *armateur* was accountable. Imperfect information across and amongst all groups meant that possibilities existed for opportunistic behaviour and adverse selection in all areas. The interests of all parties (e.g. *armateur*, associates, captain and colonial agent) were not necessarily aligned. It could be expected that the captain would operate in his own interest, given that his actions could not be observed, and the conditions of his contract with the *armateur* left him room to take advantage of the trading situation to his own benefit. The possibility existed for shirking by the captain and his productivity was difficult to measure in that his work was unobservable. The *armateur* only learned of the trade situation in both Africa and the colonies after the fact. Some control existed due to the surveillance role of other crew members and of the colonial agent who reported to the *armateur*. Shirking was mitigated by the captain's own self-interest to complete the voyage successfully and safely. It also was reduced through the use of incentives: bonuses to the captain and officers for captives safely introduced to the colonies (referred to as the *prime par tête* or '*par-tête*'); the system of *les pactotilles* or *port-permis*[6] that had long been established in the shipping trade; sales commissions such that it was in the captain's interest to get the best price in the colonies on the best terms, in some instances including a commission on credit recoveries; and the captain's share interest in the voyage.

The captain was responsible for the selection of captives, the final decision on trade locations and the exchange terms (despite specific indications dictated in the *armateur*'s instructions and the requirement to consult on these decisions with other officers aboard the vessel). A certain amount of competition existed within the sector. Nonetheless, captains who commanded slave ships tended to be more specialised in this area, while not all who were recruited into this role were successful.

While the *armateur* could not observe the captain once he left port, he could obtain information through other means: reports sent to France via other ships; observation of the captain by crew members (the crew sometimes included members of various *armateur* families); reports on the captain's conduct in the colonies via the colonial agent, etc. However, this information was costly to obtain and not timely. Hence, various control mechanisms and incentive structures, both informal and formal, were developed over time to reduce transaction costs. As indicated in the *Ordonnance de la Marine*, the captain was obligated to consult regularly with his officers about navigational matters and, more generally, about all important decisions affecting life on board.[7]

The colonial agents also had opportunities to turn situations to their advantage, as their counterparts in France relied on their knowledge and expertise to select a clientele that would meet its financial commitments. An element of control was possible in that the market was not a monopoly; thus, if agents did not perform well, they could be replaced. Yet colonial agents did not bear the same level of risk as did investors in France, and were compensated accordingly. The colonial agent also performed an important role in providing the necessary reports to government (as stipulated in the *Ordonnance*) and to the *armateur*, which at the same time assured the accountability of the captain and of the *armateur* to other associates.

Institutional economics suggests that formal mechanisms are preferred to informal or social contracts. Thus formal mechanisms will replace social controls as societies and norms evolve over time. Greif (1994) broadens this analysis to incorporate cultural and context-specific factors, yet concurs that over time networks based on mutual trust will be replaced by those based on contract. However, as argued by Forestier (2005), and as we further examine here, the slave trade utilised both formal and informal mechanisms in combination to reduce transaction costs. While the mechanisms became more formal over time, they did not eliminate the significant role played by social, cultural and business networks.

Formal mechanisms included the *armateur's* instructions to the captain, the agreed-upon contract between the captain and the *armateur* (including wages, bonuses and other perquisites), and the mandated reporting to the admiralty (prior to departure, on return and upon arrival in the colonial port). These formal mechanisms incorporated specific accounting controls that ensured the accountability of the captain, the agent and the *armateur* to the government and to various partners and associates.

Informal mechanisms included the reputational effects of the *armateur*'s and agent's conduct, the importance of repeat contracting, the social (including family) relations amongst the *négociants*, captains and others, and the ability, through trading success, to climb the social ladder. Social control was an important factor in facilitating trade.

Sources and sample

Our research examines 21 voyages undertaken by vessels whose port of registry was one of the five principal centres of the French slave trade (Table 1). These voyages represent less than 1% of the expeditions carried out from these cities in the eighteenth century. The paucity of available sources explains in great measure the limited sample size, but we make no claims here as to its exhaustiveness. We are far from having managed to locate all of the available documents. Moreover, we have had to abandon the study of some sources due to difficulties in terms of access and the practical constraints of time. Nonetheless, a fairly extensive review of the prior literature and of the catalogues of specific archival collections, supported by the very comprehensive overview of the sources for the study of the slave trade undertaken by Mettas (1975), reinforces our opinion that it would be difficult to exceed a sample size of roughly 30 voyages.

Depending on the voyage, our study was based on primary sources (Archives Départementales de Loire-Atlantique and de Charente-Maritime, Archives Municipales and Bibliothèque Municipale de La Rochelle, the Belgian State Archives in Ghent) and/or using a variety of works by historians (see Table 2). In particular, we draw upon two works of Rinchon (1938, 1964) which

Table 1. Departure point of the voyages examined.

Port of Registry	Number of voyages (1713–92)	Sample (1731–84)
Nantes	1402	10
La Rochelle	423	6
Bordeaux	393	3
Saint-Malo	214	1
Vannes	12	1
Total	2444	21

Source: Mettas (1984).

Table 2. List of voyages studied and sources drawn upon.

Vessel	Port	Dates	Archives	Secondary sources
Le Diligent	Vannes	1731–32	Beinecke Rare Book and Manuscript Library, Yale University, Gen Mss Vol. 7	Harms (2002)
L'Affricain	Nantes	1738–40	A.D. L.-A. B 5004	Mousnier (1957, 19–126)
La Reine des Anges	Nantes	1741–2	A.D. L.-A. 16 J 9	Boulanger (1970), Rinchon (1964, 81–4)
Le Saint-Édouard	Nantes	1741–	A.D. L.-A. B 4789	
La Bellonne	La Rochelle	1741–2	A.D. C.-M. E 512	
Le Jason	La Rochelle	1742–4	Private archives not located	Coupleux (1983)
La Jeannette	Nantes	1743–5	A.D. L.-A. 2Mi 886, B 5006	Boulanger (1970)
La Reine de France	Nantes	1743–5	A.E.B. Gand. Fonds d'Hoop 965	Rinchon (1964, 84–93)
La Levrette	Bordeaux	1748–9	A.D. L.-A. 2Mi 886, B 5006	Mousnier (1957)
La Diligente	Nantes	1749–50	A.D. L.-A. B 5004	
La Perle	Saint-Malo	1755–7		Vignols (1930)
Le Télémaque	Nantes	1763–5	A.E.B. Gand. Fonds d'Hoop 965, 969, 970	Rinchon (1964, 95–123)
Le Roy Guinguin	Nantes	1764–6	A.D. L.-A. 16 J 1	
L'Africain	Nantes	1766–8	A.E.B. Gand. Fonds d'Hoop 969, 971–974, 982	Rinchon (1938, 141–239; 1964, 137–222)
Le Pompée	Nantes	1769–70	A.E.B. Gand. Fonds d'Hoop 975–976, 982	Rinchon (1964, 223–91)
Le Roi Dahomet	La Rochelle	1772–4	A.M. La R. Ms E 282	Yacou (2001)
Le Duc de Laval	La Rochelle	1773–6	A.E.B. Gand. Fonds d'Hoop 965, 969, 977, 982	Rinchon (1964, 293–331)
La Suzanne-Marguerite	La Rochelle	1775–6	A.M. La R. E 280	Yacou (2001)
Le Pactole	Bordeaux	1777–8	A.E.B. Gand. Fonds d'Hoop 965, 969	Rinchon (1964, 347–58)
Le Pactole	Bordeaux	1783–84	A.E.B. Gand. Fonds d'Hoop 965, 969	Rinchon (1964, 359–67)
La Bonne Société	La Rochelle	1783–84	B.M. La R. Ms 2290–2291	

exploited the very rich archival collection of the captain Van Alstein, held in the Belgian State Archives in Ghent, and the works of Yacou (2001), Harms (2002) and Vignols (1930).

The data provided in Mettas (1984) have enabled us to supplement those at our disposal in the documents examined and the volumes previously cited. Constituted essentially from the files of the admiralty archives, this valuable catalogue provides various details for each voyage: the vessel (e.g. tonnage, *armateur* and captain), the progress of the expedition (e.g. date of departure, main ports of call, return date, incidents, etc.) and commercial operations (e.g. number of captives bought and sold). Moreover, in order to place these 21 voyages in the overall context of the French eighteenth-century triangular trade, we have drawn upon the work of Masseaut (1992), which was carried out for Nantes and built on the data initially gathered by Mettas. We also have made use of the Voyages Database of the Trans-Atlantic Slave Trade Database (accessible online at http://www.slavevoyages.org).

In the course of our research, we began first with accounting documents, analogous to those in the list provided by Gaignat de l'Aulnais (1771, 310) in his *Guide du Commerce*:

> The manner by which to manage this trade is not very difficult. Four principal books (a trade journal, a journal of the sale of Blacks and of the purchase of return merchandise from America, an invoice book and a general ledger) are sufficient to provide an account of one's management, both at the Coast for the trade in Blacks, purchase of gold powder, etc, and in America for the sales there and the purchase of return merchandise.[8]

We supplemented these sources with two important documents to which Gaignat makes no reference at all as they do not form part of the accounting records. These are the instructions provided to the captain by the *armateur* and the ship's log book. The *Ordonnance de la Marine* (1681) stipulated the requirement for a log book to be kept in which were to be recorded all events related to navigation, transactions, as well as incidents linked to life on board. In principle, it was to be maintained by the captain, or by the ships' scrivener *(l'écrivain)*[9] if there was one, as in the case of a certain Dam Joulin, who we encounter on the *Affricain* (1738), *La Jeannette* (1743) and *La Levrette* (1748), in the latter case engaged as the second captain.

Complete sets of document for the same voyage have been impossible to come by, and hence our research is focused on incomplete records (see Table 3). Frequently only one of the documents for a voyage is found, for example, the ship's log book, because it has been kept in the admiralty archives for a particular reason, such as litigation related to the vessel. Sometimes it is the descendent of a captain who has undertaken to publish the ship's log of his distant ancestor as a fictionalised account (Coupleux 1983), or better, by providing a faithful transcription of it (Plasse 2005). Yet all of these sources remain very partial. A few private archival collections, those of *armateurs* or captains, housed in public institutions, contain more significant sets of records. None exists, however, in which we find together the accounts for the outfitting and laying up (*l'armement et le désarmement*) of a ship created by the *armateur* and the complete management documents of the captain, which would allow us to calculate and analyse the return from a specific voyage.

Instructions to captains

We focus our analysis in this section on the sub-set of our sample for which the instructions to captains are available. Even if the relatively few instructions examined are dispersed over time – 45 years separates the first voyage from the last – and if their format and details vary somewhat, the same type of instructions generally are found. The sample data are summarised in Table 4. These instructions can be divided into two categories: maritime and commercial instructions; and

Table 3. List of documents available for each voyage.

	Instructions to captains/*Instructions aux capitaines*	Ship's Log Book/*Journal de bord*	Trade Journal/*Journal de traite*	Recapitulation Table of the Trade/*Tableau récapitulatif de traite*	Sale of Captives/*Vente des captifs*	Invoice of the Return Cargo/*Facture de la cargaison de retour*	Remarks
Le Senaut			X	X	X	X	Artificial example of Gaignat
Le Diligent		X					
L'Affricain	X	X					
La Reine des Anges	X		X	X			
Le Saint-Édouard				X	X	X	
La Bellonne				X			
Le Jason							Novel
La Jeannette		X					
La Reine de France			X		X	X	
La Levrette		X					
La Diligente		X					
La Perle					Summary		
Le Télémaque				Fragment	Fragment	Fragment	
Le Roy Guinguin			X	X Summary			
L'Africain	X	X	X	X	X	Various details	
Le Pompée	X	X	X	X	X p. 281	X	
Le Roi Dahomet		X	X		X		
Le Duc de Laval	X	X			Some details		
La Suzanne–Marguerite			X		X		
Le Pactole			X	X			
Le Pactole		X					
La Bonne Société	X		X	X	X	X	

Table 4. Instructions to captains.

			Archives	Secondary sources
L'Affricain	Nantes	1738–40	A.D. L.-A. B 5004	Mousnier (1957, 19–29)
La Reine des Anges	Nantes	1741–2	A.D. L.-A. 16 J 9	Rinchon (1964, 81–4)
L'Africain	Nantes	1766–8	A.E. B. Gand. Fonds d'Hoop 982	Rinchon (1938, 158–70)
Le Pompée	Nantes	1769–70	A.E. B. Gand. Fonds d'Hoop 982	Rinchon (1964, 239–46)
Le Duc de Laval	La Rochelle	1773–6	A.E. B. Gand. Fonds d'Hoop 982	Rinchon (1964, 296–8)
La Bonne Société	La Rochelle	1783–4	B.M. La R. Ms 2291	

contractual terms related to the incentives given to the captain and to ship officers over and above their salaries. The first category is examined here, while the second is explored more fully in the next section devoted to incentive systems.

Some of the maritime and commercial instructions (the only ones that are truly instructions in the proper sense of the term) deal with the entire voyage. Amongst the orders of a more general nature, four of the six cases recommended, in varied but more or less equivalent terms, the use of the greatest economy (‘*d'user de la plus sage économie*’), as stated in the instructions for *La Bonne Société*). Other instructions dealt only with one of the three stages of the voyage: the trade along the coast of Africa, the middle passage from Africa to the West Indies, or the stay in the Antilles.

The trade along the African coast

Once the part of the African coast along which the vessel was to undertake its trade was determined (coast of Guinea or coast of Angola), the precise choice of trading locations generally was left to the captain as the opportunities arose. The instructions next indicated what was anticipated in terms of purchases. In the case of the captain of *L'Affricain* (1738), it simply was stated to procure the greatest number of captives that it was possible for the ship to carry.[10] The instructions for other ships, however, set quantified objectives in terms of the value of the merchandise cargo of *la mise-hors*: a range of 400 to 500 captives for *Le Pompée* (1769); from 480 to 500 for *Le Duc de Laval* (1773). The two vessels loaded respectively only 390 and 393 captives, after both had spent more than eight months along the coast of Africa. A minimum number of 400 was stipulated for the captain of *La Reine des Anges* (1741): ‘if contrary to our expectations the trade is long and lingers, to avoid the wasting away of his cargo, he [the captain] will leave the coast as soon as he has acquired four hundred strong and good slaves on the account of the vessel’.[11] This order was scrupulously observed, as the vessel left Africa with 407 captives after spending six months and five days on the coast. Moreover, it underscores two key elements in the success of the undertaking: the speed of the trading campaign and the quality of the loaded ‘cargo’.

The sojourn on the African coast, if the trade dragged on beyond what was anticipated, could become particularly trying, not only for the captives but also for the members of the crew due to poor climatic conditions, the insalubrious nature of the vessels, as well as the risks of revolt. According to the statistics compiled by Masseaut (1992, 18) for the eighteenth-century Nantes trade, the annual average duration of the stay on the African coast was three to eight months,

Table 5. Voyage duration and mortality rates.

	Voyage dates	Trade duration (days)	Duration of the crossing (Africa–Antilles) (days)	Total number of captives traded	Number of captives sold	Mortality Number	Percentage
L'Affricain	1738–40	179	122	323	292	31	10
La Reine des Anges	1741–2	188	104	407	269	138	34
Le Saint-Édouard	1741–	125	58	232	183	49	21
La Reine de France	1743–5	134	146	440	404	36	8
La Perle	1755–7	150	64	603	588	15	2
Le Télémaque	1763–5	170	64	342	320	22	6
L'Africain	1766–8	124	64	386	377	9	2
Le Pompée	1769–70	246	34	390	325	65	17
Le Roi Dahomet	1772–74	139	62	424	406	18	4
Le Duc de Laval	1773–6	262	53	393	346	47	12
La Suzanne-Marguerite	1775–6	259	92	567	393	174	31
Le Pactole	1777–8	202	80	690	609	81	12
La Bonne Société	1783–4	100	165	425	350	75	18
Average		175	85	432	374	58	14

depending upon market conditions and the competence of the captain. We find related figures for a sub-set of 13 of the 21 voyages for which we have all of the necessary data at our disposal. The shortest trade duration was three months and nine days (*La Bonne Société* 1783); the longest was eight months and 18 days (*Le Duc de Laval* 1773), with an average stay of five months and 23 days. As Table 5 indicates, the ships which experienced the longest sojourns on the African coast were often those for which the mortality level was the greatest; the correlation coefficient between the mortality rate[12] and the duration of the trade is 0.38. However, the small size of our sub-set and the statistical non-significance of our observed coefficient make it impossible to draw reliable conclusions from these data, especially as the causes of death are many.

Therefore, to obtain more robust results for captive mortality, in relation to the influence of several variables examined in this section, we downloaded all French voyages listed in the Trans-Atlantic Slave Trade Database that took place between 1711 and 1790, in effect, 3,043 voyages. Next, we extracted sub-samples in terms of the data necessary to undertake analyses of mortality rates. In this case, based on our final sample of 802 voyages, the resulting correlation coefficient between the mortality rate of captives and the duration of the trade campaign in Africa is only 0.11 (significant at the 1% level), which is very small.[13]

While the average stay in Africa increased throughout the first half of the century, during which the trade was more itinerant in nature and competition intensified, it decreased in the following period (Masseaut 1992, 19–20). This decrease resulted, in part, from an improved organisation of the trading system which led to a concentration of the supply side of the trade at a few specific points along the coast: Juda (Ouidah) on the coast of Guinea and Cabinda on the coast of Angola.

The graph in Figure 1 (calculations based on 1467 voyages from the Trans-Atlantic Slave Trade Database) confirms for France overall the observations of Masseaut (1992) for Nantes. Moreover, the comparison of the two curves – that for the average duration of the trade campaign and that for the number of voyages by period – indicates the progress in terms of the trade's organisation during the last quarter of the eighteenth century. In effect, from 1711–15 to 1766–70, a

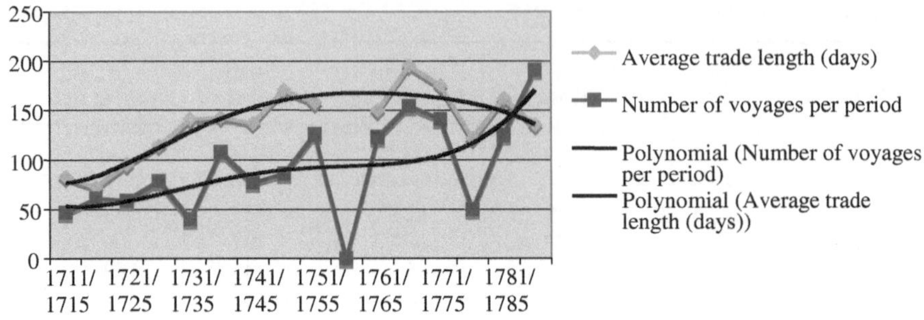

Figure 1. Average trade length (days) and number of voyages 1711–90 (five-year periods). Source: The Trans-Atlantic Slave Trade Database (figures calculated for 1,467 voyages).

growth in competition translated into a substantial increase in the average stay, with a correlation coefficient of 0.75 between the two series (significant at the 1% level); whereas afterwards, a general downward trend in the trade duration is in evidence, despite significant growth in competition during the last two periods – the number of voyages and the total number of captives boarded increased from 125 to 191 (+53%) and from 48,917 to 65,655 (+34%) respectively between 1781–5 and 1786–90.

The 'quality' of the captive cargo, in essence, good health, good looking and youth, was frequently noted in connection with the need to protect it throughout the voyage. Captains were instructed to select the best and youngest, and to trade as few women and young girls as possible. As stated in the instructions of *L'Affricain* in 1738:

> Above all, strive to find good-looking captives and prefer young ones. Besides the fact that they will withstand better the fatigue of the crossing, you will be able to sell them more advantageously in America. Before trading the Blacks, have your surgeon visit them. Take as few women and little children as you can.[14]

One notes a preference for men who would be immediately productive; in effect, the life expectancy on the plantations was very short at the time, and the natural replacement of the slave population was not particularly sought after by plantation owners. Captains were expected to provide market updates as frequently as possible via other ships such that those in France were advised of changes to the terms of trade, competition, etc.

The middle passage from Africa to the West Indies

While the duration of this crossing could be from three weeks to four months, the average time was between two and three months during the entire century (Masseaut 1992, 23). We find comparable figures for our sub-set, from one extreme of one month and four days (*Le Pompée* 1770) to that of five months and 13 days (*La Bonne Société* 1784); the average being two months and 24 days. To make their crossing, the vessels needed to take advantage of the trade winds. To leave the Gulf of Benin, ships travelled south of the equator to encounter the south-east trade winds, passing via the Île de Principe, where ships frequently made a port of call as much to rest and refresh the cargo as to await favourable winds. A skilful captain was essential, as the route to the Antilles passed through a zone in which dead calm alternated with violent thunderstorms, and the risks of a vessel coming to a complete standstill were not inconsiderable (Masseaut 1992, 21–2).

This crossing clearly could be very trying for the captives, and all the instructions examined devoted a paragraph to their care. As the century progressed, a certain humanism even began to be exhibited. One cannot express it better than did the *armateurs* of *La Bonne Société* in 1783: the captives were to be

> well fed, carefully cared for and observed and guarded adequately to eliminate the danger of revolt; familiarity with female captives was to be avoided to prevent negative consequences; finally, captives were to be shown humanity and kindness matched with the necessary prudence.[15]
>
> (B.M. La R. Ms. 2290)

Portier, the *armateur* of *L'Africain* (1766), devoted no less than five articles of his instructions to this matter, setting out specifics related to the food, water, daily visits by the ship surgeon, hygiene, and the necessary vigilance. On the latter point, he recommended the advisability of engaging some young Negroes as spies ('*négrillons espions*') while prohibiting their negative treatment. As revolts amongst the captives were rare, it was equally unnecessary to provoke them, as it was dangerous to be taken by surprise by them. The articles of *La Bonne Société* (1783) reiterated this tone:

> However, in case of an unfortunate accident, put your records in order such that we can provide ourselves with recourse against our insurers. If, God forbid, you experience some sort of revolt amongst the Negroes, do not forget to insert in your statements that they were in irons.[16]
>
> (B.M. La R. Ms. 2290)

Nonetheless, the mortality rate remained of major importance. Only two vessels out of a total of 1,427 ships recorded as having left Nantes during the eighteenth century did not report any loss of captives. The largest number of deaths was recorded by *La Fleur Américaine*, which took more than four months to cross the Atlantic, 325 of the 384 African captives aboard dying during the voyage (Masseaut 1992, 23). Of the sub-sample examined, the average is 14%, with a minimum of 2% (*La Perle* and *L'Africain*) and a maximum of 34% (*La Reine des Anges*). The correlation coefficient between the mortality rate of captives and the duration of the crossing is only 0.19 and not statistically significant, but the data from the Trans-Atlantic Slave Trade Database bear witness to this variable as a decisive factor. For 802 voyages undertaken from 1711 to 1790, we report a correlation coefficient of 0.41 between the captive mortality rate and the duration of the middle passage (significant at the 1% level).[17]

Captive mortality, whose evolution is presented in Figure 2 for the same sample of 802 voyages, was a fundamental element that the *armateurs* took into account in their provisional calculations. In 1770, in a letter in which the *armateur* Deguer of Nantes proposed to his close relatives their participation in the financing of a voyage that he was about to launch, he estimated this mortality rate to be 10% (A.D. L.-A. 8J6, Folio 3; Rinchon 1956, 52–3). This estimation corresponds to the average rate that we observe at the end of the 1760s, prior to evidence of a resurgence that could be attributed potentially to the weakened health of captives due to greater competition and an overall increase in the number of captives boarded.

The West Indies

Once the crossing had taken place, it was important to find the best location in the islands to sell the captives. Depending on the final destination, Saint-Domingue, La Martinique or even Guadeloupe or Guyana, the captain usually was provided with a number of agents, depending

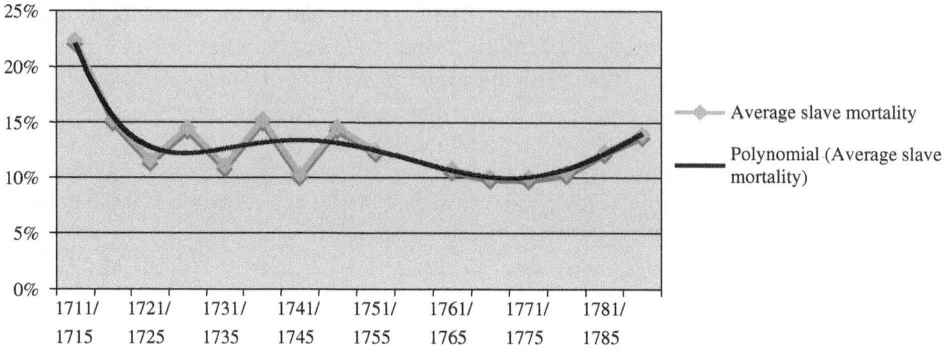

Figure 2. Average slave mortality 1711–90 (five-year periods).
Source: The Trans-Atlantic Slave Trade Database (figures calculated for 802 voyages).

upon the ports in which he was likely to disembark. These agents helped him in making his final choice in light of the market situation, and then would provide advice and guidance during the sale. The most successful sale was not necessarily the one which was achieved at the highest prices. Rather, it was the one that resulted in the most hard currency, and for the remainder, credit-worthy buyers and short credit terms. The words to this effect varied little. For example, those of *L'Affricain* (1738) stated that the captain was 'only to sell to sound debtors and to obtain as much as he could in hard currency [. . .] But as we anticipate that it is not easy to sell all for cash, you should sell on the shortest terms that you can'.[18] To motivate sales, there was no hesitation to lower expectations: 'lower even the prices of your Negroes to obtain [cash] or reduce the payment terms' (*L'Africain* 1766, and *Le Pompée* 1769). Credit recoveries were such a crucial matter that in the case of two vessels, both outfitted by les Portier, it was arranged that the captain would remain in the Antilles to take care of business while the second captain would return the vessel to Nantes. Unfortunately, we do not have sufficient data at our disposal to enable us to estimate the operating profitability of the vessels in our sample, even in a partial way based on the conclusion of the sales of captives.

The progressive decrease in the duration of expeditions and the reduced risks as measured in terms of mortality rates made the trade more attractive than it had been at the beginning of the century. Many of these 'improvements' were due to changes in operating methods such as vessel size and design, better hygiene, training, as well as the result of knowledge transfer amongst market players. The slave-trade ventures offered enviable professional opportunities to the maritime populations that took advantage of them. The number of captives tripled in the eighteenth century compared to the previous one, yet this increase required only twice the number of expeditions (Masseaut 1992, 46). Vessel dimensions grew but the overall number of crew decreased: between the periods 1711–30 and 1771–90, the average vessel tonnage rose from 175 to 267 tonnes (+53%), while the total crew size fell from 46 to 36 (–24%).[19] The potential return from an expedition, as measured by its net proceeds, clearly improved over the course of the eighteenth century, in no small measure due to improved operating methods and industry knowledge.

Control mechanisms and incentives

Controls and incentives included both formal and informal mechanisms. We analyse these mechanisms in terms of our sample data, and draw on additional source materials to provide further confirmatory details.

Formal controls related to prescribed documents and reporting, as well as established patterns of action within maritime trade and the slave trade in particular. As per the *Ordonnance de la Marine* (1681) and as outlined in the *rôle d'armement* for each voyage, captains and the *armateurs* had a number of formalities with which to comply. First, this document outlined the voyage in terms of location, purpose, crew and the name of the *armateur*. It was signed on departure by the captain, *armateur* and admiralty officials, including the acceptance by the captain of funds to provide the two-month advance paid to the crew. The document also attested to the duty to report to port authorities within 24 hours of arrival in the port of final destination.

Besides this reporting obligation, vessel captains had to comply with colonial formalities related to their arrival in port, cargo, duty payments and the attestation of events such as the death of crew members. The captain also was required to prepare sales reports on the trade in Africa and the sales in the colonies, in writing, to both the colonial agent and the *armateur*. The colonial agent also had a duty to report to the *armateur*, thus implementing an extra measure of accountability by requiring that both agents reported to the *armateur* and therefore each serving as a check on the other.

Instructions to captains, which were signed by both parties (the *armateur* as principal, and the captain as agent), detailed their agreement as to the nature of the voyage, destination(s), number of expected captives, along with the specific terms of the wage payment and incentive structure. As noted earlier, wages on slave-trade voyages provided a premium for the risk undertaken and the extended nature of these voyages relative to other maritime shipping. This contract established the responsibilities of the captain, and often included a statement about penalties to be paid if the captain acted otherwise. For example, the instructions of *La Bonne Société* included a penalty if goods or captives other than those authorised as *port-permis* were boarded on ship. In the case of *L'Affricain*, the *armateur*, Charles Trochon, required a daily record of expenses incurred during the trade period in Africa, along with other records.

Articles in the instructions to captains (and other sources) indicate that the various incentives offered became more systematic and institutionalised over time. More incentives were developed and used in different and differing combinations (*port-permis*, bonus, commissions and share interest) as indicated in Table 6. Experience with various incentives (such as *les port-permis*) led to their use in combination with, or replacement by, others (such as sales commissions, commissions on *les retours* – to enhance the captain's long-term perspective). Officers were frequently included in these incentive arrangements such that their interests were aligned and joint effort was motivated. For example, ship's officers, especially the medical officer

Table 6. Types of incentive and frequency of use.

Incentive type	One incentive used	Two incentives used	Three incentives used	All four incentives used	Frequency of use
Port-permis	5	1	3	2	11
Par-tête	1	1	3	2	7
Commission (%)	0	2	3	2	7
Share interest	0	0	0	2	2
Number of voyages where incentive used	6	2	3	2	13

(*le chirurgien*), received a bonus '*par-tête*' for each captive safely introduced and sold in the colonies.

Acquiring a share interest in the vessel was a long-established practice in maritime trade, offering the captain another means to gain financially. Forestier (2005, 26) has calculated the percentage of voyages where this occurred at 21.33% for the 211 ventures from La Rochelle between 1763 and 1792 (i.e. 45 ventures). Jolin (1999, 101) calculated this at 11% for the 259 voyages from Nantes between 1717 and 1738 (i.e. 29 voyages), which he stated as comparable to other studies undertaken for La Rochelle.[20] In our sample, captains held a share interest in 9.5% of the voyages. We have traced further examples of this share interest in the records of other vessels not included in our sample. For example, the records of the *armateur* Deguer indicate that the captain frequently had a share interest ranging from 1/40th to 1/4 (see McWatters 2008). It became more frequently used as an incentive in the latter stages of the eighteenth century, in Deguer's case for ventures undertaken after 1763. A share interest was not an innovation of the slave trade, as it was used in other shipping ventures, but its more prevalent use in this sector in later years suggests the evolving nature of controls and incentives over time. A share interest placed the captain in the position of an associate, thus on a similar level to the other investors, all the while being an agent in terms of his role in commanding the vessel and overseeing the conduct of business. Finally, the captain had to raise funds to finance his share, and this financing was often through a loan for which the *armateur* acted as guarantor or lender.

Certain incentives had a more immediate line of sight, such as the *port-permis* and especially the commission, in that the recipient could readily determine the amount and the relationship between performance and the payment. From the *armateur*'s point of view, these types of incentives were a better tool with which to measure productivity and efficiency. These incentives were short-term in nature such that they were paid once the performance had been completed – they were calculated on arrival in the colonies.

Other incentives, such as the percentage paid on '*les recouvrements*', i.e. the recovery of funds at a later date (two cases of this mechanism in our sample), and an ownership share were long-term in nature. If the captain received funds from this type of incentive, he bore more risk in that the payment of these incentives resulted from actions and factors not under his control. For example, the recovery of funds owed in the colonies and the net returns produced from the sale of colonial goods depended, amongst other things, upon the prevailing market situation, the colonists' credit standing and often political factors (such as the forgiveness by the French state of certain colonial debts to appease colonists at the expense of French merchants). While this type of incentive would align the captain's interests more closely with those of associates, its long-term value would not be as easily determinable. For the agent who wished to finalise the voyage and move on to other opportunities, a continued share interest would not offer that possibility as readily. For the *armateur* and agent (captain) who re-contracted on other voyages, it might be more enticing as a way of fostering this longer-term relationship. For example, the records of the *armateur* Deguer provide a number of examples in which the captain held a share interest and was re-contracted on a series of voyages. In our sample, the captain Van Alstein held a share interest in two voyages (*Le Pompée* and *Le Duc de Laval*), but not his last voyage (*Le Pactole*), perhaps as he anticipated his final days as a captain and a shift to a passive investor. As noted in Rinchon (1964), Van Alstein did take up a share interest of 6,000 *livres* in the subsequent voyage of *Le Pactole* but not its command.

As noted, accountability and control were augmented by a system of informal controls. While the *armateur* could not observe the actions of the captain once he left port, he did have other means by which to acquire information. For example, the instructions to captains often included the request to provide updates via other ships. The officers were to be consulted on matters related to changes in itinerary or routing, but also had the responsibility to account to the authorities and the *armateur* in the case of deemed negligence or similar misconduct on the part of the captain.

Positive reputational effects and the ability to make use of them and financial gains to move up the social ladder were integral to the trade's smooth functioning. Captains who were deemed unsuccessful were replaced and this information followed them. Successful captains were sought after and highly esteemed by *armateurs*, with whom they often had family connections. In our sample, Captain Van Alstein built on his marine success to enter into the social milieu of Nantes, leaving the trade for a life of relative ease. During his career, he was noted to be a dependable and highly successful captain, and his recognition led to recruitment in various port cities (Nantes, Bordeaux and La Rochelle).

Both *armateurs* and captains operated within settings that display features typical of communities of practice. *Armateurs* undertook their affairs within systems of accountability in which specific methods, including those of accounting, provided control and standardised norms of behaviour. The accounting reports and records used across the sector became more standardised over time. The complexity of incentive systems in the trade increased as *armateurs* shared their knowledge with like-minded traders and investors. Information about the trade, its participants and markets was shared across the network and resulted in joint action to promote shared interests.

Similarly, vessel captains undertook their voyages as members of a maritime community who learned by doing and by sharing information. Captains rose through the ranks, and by doing so gained knowledge and experience of maritime operations. They also gained knowledge of accounting and reporting systems that provided control mechanisms and accountability to the *armateur*, the State and to other crew members. We know that Van Alstein 'practised' his trade by studying the log books and trade journals of earlier voyages, including that of *La Reine de France*. The *Guide du Commerce* of Gaignat de l'Aulnais (1771), published as a commercial guide to strategic success in maritime trade, including the slave trade, recreated the world of maritime commerce by recopying and supplementing the records of earlier voyages. Traders and vessel captains could acquire through this manual an understanding of the methods necessary in the trade and how accountability relationships functioned and were maintained.

Network relationships were an important dimension of the control system in a milieu where social, business and family ties were intertwined at many levels. Families operated together in business and reinforced these links through marriages. Investments and financial backing were provided by others in the same social circle. Yet this circle was more accurately a set of expanding ones, as networks operated within the local community, across France and other parts of Europe, and extended to the colonies.

We find evidence of these network ties in our sample. Georges Eustache, who outfitted *Le Saint Edouard* in 1741, was the uncle of Van Alstein and the person to whom Van Alstein first addressed himself on his arrival in Nantes from Antwerp. This family connection likely facilitated Van Alstein's introduction into local networks. The Grou family, whose operations included *La Diligente* and *Le Télémaque*, also was distantly related to Van Alstein, which might further explain his ability to move within these networks. Van Alstein's personal records note a life of social and economic comfort amongst the *négociants* of the city. He commanded a number of the vessels in our sample, was recruited by different *armateurs* in different port cities, thanks to his highly favourable reputation that was shared across the network. He served as captain of two of the voyages, *L'Africain* and *Le Pompée*, undertaken by the Portier family. Charles Trochon, *armateur* of *L'Affricain*, belonged to an established business family in Nantes and was linked to the Portiers through marriage and business ties, including insurance syndicates.

Family and social ties also extended across various port cities. For example, the Nairac family operated in both La Rochelle and Bordeaux, in our case outfitting *La Suzanne Marguerite* and *Le Pactole* respectively in these cities. Business dealings with the Nairacs figure frequently in the accounts of other *armateurs*, either for merchandise, insurance or referrals to their colonial agent. The Nairacs also had business connections in Saint-Malo with whom various *négociants* in Nantes associated. It was through these extended networks that Van Alstein was recruited by Garesché to be captain in La Rochelle where he commanded *Le Duc de Laval* in 1773. Van Alstein later was recommended by Garesché to a member of the Nairac family in Bordeaux as captain of *Le Pactole* (Rinchon 1964, 296, 335).

Families also were established in the colonies as plantation owners and colonial agents, facilitating business relationships. For example, the Rozée family (linked to les Portier through business and marriage) held a share interest in Forget, Lecompte and Bourret in la Martinique (A.D. L.-A. E II 354, 18-7-1745). We see similar colonial ties with the Chaurand family, who also were related to the Portiers, as Honoré Chaurand had married Marie Portier de Lantimo in 1748. At their marriage, an attestation of his personal fortune included a half-interest in property in la Martinique (Meyer 1999, 190, fn.1). The Nairac family also maintained ties with colonial agents. For example, the records of the *armateur* Deguer indicate that he often engaged the Nairac's agent in Saint-Domingue, De Russy. De Russy had family in Saint-Malo, and the Saint-Malo branch in turn invested in Deguer's business. Garesché operated a branch network in Saint-Domingue, referring Van Alstein to these family members when he reached the colonies.[21] These family and business networks reduced transaction costs and offered an efficient way to monitor behaviour and reduce opportunism (Boyce 1995; Forestier 2005). As well, given the financial interests shared across members of these elites, the financial gains (and losses) were distributed across the sector. Opportunistic behaviour and the consequent loss of reputation were quickly transmitted across the various local, national and international networks.

Conclusions and future research directions

This research study provides further insights into the nature and operations of the French slave trade in the eighteenth century, including the role of accounting in the standardisation of its practices and techniques. The French case offers a useful example of how trade patterns differed across states and adapted to political, economic and social forces. While our sample size is small, we present evidence that the system became more routinised and refined as business interests sought to obtain market returns, while also attempting to minimise, as much as possible, the risks undertaken.

The accounting system was based on procedures long established in maritime trade. Yet these procedures were enhanced through the introduction and greater use of a variety of incentives that supported other mechanisms to control the slave trade. The series of articles which outlined the instructions to captains became more comprehensive, as *armateurs*, captains and associates gained more experience in the trade, its rewards and its pitfalls. The slave trade also contributed to the globalisation of the market economy as trade links were established across a number of continents. Accounting supported these new network relations through its reporting mechanisms, which both reinforced and reflected existing social and family ties.

The records that we have examined to date provide us with further indications as to how accounting knowledge was transmitted and how these ways-of-doing became accepted norms of conduct and action. The trade was not organised as a guild, but knowledge transmission was guild-like in nature. As noted earlier, the trade displays features common in communities of practice, including the importance of social capital and shared understandings of their milieu. Business interests shared market intelligence, invested in each other's operations and worked jointly to create sustainable trade networks. Likewise, captains learned through doing, including frequent consultation with fellow captains and crew and the study of documents from earlier voyages.

An avenue for future research is the specific examination of the slave trade's contribution to capitalism. Based on this research sample, we see the emergence and use of a number of formal incentive and control mechanisms, adopted in complementary fashion with a series of informal ones. The complementary use and the choice of particular incentive combinations are a singular feature of this trade sector, adopted subsequently in other commercial activities. Their adoption is clear evidence of their value in reducing the negative features inherent in agency relationships.

Future research could develop this line of reasoning to provide a model that specifies the circumstances under which such incentives tend to be employed and in what particular combinations. Initial results suggest that certain conditions favour their emergence and adoption: management at a distance across space and time; high-risk ventures; and slow circulation of working capital. We intend to explore these patterns further, including the examination of these business networks in other maritime sectors with similar risk/return profiles, including the trade of *les corsaires* and the privatisation of war.

Notes

1. Further analysis of profitability is discussed in Daget (1990), Daudin (2002a, 2002b, 2004), Gaston-Martin (1993), Meyer (1999), Pétré-Grenouilleau (1998, 2004) and Rinchon (1956); in the English context, Anderson and Richardson (1985), Darity (1985), Inikori (1983, 1981) and Thomas and Bean (1974).
2. A sample of *les rôles d'armement* for vessels leaving Nantes between 1735 and 1743 (Archives Départementales de Loire-Atlantique, hereafter, A.D. L.-A., 180 J 351 to 374) indicated a wage premium for captains of slave-trade vessels of 38.3% relative to those paid to captains in other areas of maritime trade. The premium for the lieutenant and *contre-maître* was 18.1%. Chouteau (1994) analysed voyages from Nantes in 1784 and reported the following premiums: captains, 42%; second captain, 44%; surgeon, 71%; and *contre-maître*, 22%. The premium for the surgeon underscores the importance of this role in slave-trade voyages. Incentives provided to the surgeon also encouraged careful attention to the well-being of captives.
3. These arguments are more fully developed in Boyce (1995).
4. A review of agency theory and its use in accounting history is provided in Bricker and Chandler (1998).
5. In the course of our research, we learned of complementary research by Forestier (2005) which examines the slave trade at La Rochelle, also adopting this theoretical approach and providing important confirmatory details.
6. Private cargo (*pacotille* or *port-permis*) were items that the officers and some members of the crew were allowed to transport for their own use, over and above the ship's normal cargo. The captives became the personal property of the officers. These incentives motivated officers to ensure cargo arrived safely at its destination.
7. The pertinent articles are Titre I, Article 15 and especially Article 25; Titre III, Article 3.
8. '*La manière de gérer cette traite n'est pas bien difficile. Quatre livres principaux qui sont, un journal de traites, un journal de la vente des noirs et de l'achat des marchandises en retour de l'Amérique, un livres de factures et un grand livre, suffisent pour donner raison de sa gestion, tant à la Côte pour le troc des nègres, achat de poudre d'or, etc. qu'à l'Amérique pour la vente d'iceux et l'achat des marchandises en retour*'.
9. The *Ordonnance de la Marine* (1681) stipulated the maintenance of a log book by the captain in Livre 2, Titre 1, Article X: '*Sera tenu [le maître] d'avoir un registre ou journal cotté et paraphé en chaque feuillet par l'un des principaux intéressez au bâtiment, sur lequel il écrira le jour qu'il aura été établi maître, le nom des officiers et matelots de l'équipage, le prix et les conditions de leur engagement, les payemens qu'il leur fera, sa recette et sa dépense concernant le navire, et généralement tout ce qui regarde le fait de sa charge, ou pour raison de quoy il aura quelque compte à rendre, ou quelque demande à faire*'. Alternatively, it could be kept by the ship's scrivener as set out in Livre 2, Titre III, Article 1: '*L'écrivain sera tenu d'avoir un registre ou journal, cotté et paraphé en chaque page par le lieutenant de l'amirauté, ou par deux des principaux propriétaires du navire*'.
10. '*Votre cargaison est assez forte pour pouvoir charger le plus de noirs que vous pourrez dans le navire*'.
11. '*Si contre notre attente la traite était longue et traînait en longueur, pour empêcher le dépérissement de sa cargaison, il partira de la côte sitôt qu'il sera rempli de quatre cents beaux et bons esclaves pour le compte du dit navire*'.

12. The mortality rate is calculated by expressing the difference between the number of captives traded and the number of captives sold as a percentage of the number of captives traded.
13. In actual fact, it was the crews who seemed to suffer from a long stay on the African coast, with a correlation coefficient between the crew mortality rate and the trade duration of 0.19 (calculated on a sub-set of 713 of the 802 voyages and significant at the 1% level).
14. '*Sur toutes choses, attachez-vous à prendre de beaux captifs et préférez les jeunes. Outre qu'ils résistent mieux à la fatigue de la traversée, vous les vendrez plus avantageusement à l'Amérique. Avant de traiter les noirs vous les ferez visiter par votre chirurgien. Prenez le moins de femmes et de négrillons que vous pourrez.*'
15. '*Bien nourris, convenablement soignés et suffisamment observés et gardés pour n'avoir point de révolte à craindre*'; '*empêcher de même la fréquentation des blancs avec les négresses ce qui souvent a de fâcheuses suites*'; '*au surplus, nous vous recommandons l'humanité envers tous les captifs et de les traiter avec toute la douceur qui pourra s'allier avec la prudence*'.
16. '*En cas de fâcheux accidens mettez vos procès-verbaux en règle afin de nous ménager notre recours contre nos assureurs. Si par malheur, ce qu'à Dieu ne plaise, vous éprouvez quelque révolte des nègres, n'oubliez pas d'insérer dans vos procès-verbaux que les noirs étoient aux fers*'.
17. Again, the average mortality rate of the crew was higher than that of the captives – 18.7% compared to 12.4% for a sample of 702 voyages. We observe a correlation coefficient of 0.10 (significant at the 1% level) of the crew mortality rate with the duration of the middle passage. It was, therefore, the sojourn on the African coast that was the most problematic for sailors, but the *armateurs* seemed to have adapted to this situation without difficulty as no allusion is made at all to it in the captains' instructions.
18. '*Ne vendre qu'à de bons débiteurs et le plus que vous pourrez en argent comptant* [...] *Comme nous prévoyons qu'il n'est pas facile de tout vendre au comptant, vous vendrez au plus court terme que vous pourrez*'.
19. Figures calculated for 1467 voyages extracted from the Trans-Atlantic Slave Trade Database.
20. For further details of the La Rochelle trade, the interested reader is directed to Deveau (1990).
21. Forestier (2005, 16) examines the networks emanating from La Rochelle. She notes that about 50% of the *armateurs* in her study had relatives in the colonies. Twenty-nine per cent had family relations to which they directed their ventures upon reaching colonial ports.

References

Primary sources

Archives Départementales de Charente Maritime, La Rochelle

E 512 – Comptes du navire *La Bellone*

Archives Départementales de Loire-Atlantique, Nantes

Amirauté de Nantes:

B 4789 – Livre de bord du *Saint-Édouard*

B 5004 – Livres de bord de Dam Joulin (*L'Affricain*, *La Diligente*)

B 5006, 2Mi 886 – Documents concerning *La Jeannette* and *La Levrette*

E II 354 – Fonds notariaux, étude Boufflet

8 J – Fonds Delaville-Deguer

8 J 7, 8 J 6 – Correspondence

16 J – Fonds Bertrand de Cœuvres

16 J 1 – Journal de traite du *Roy Guinguin*

16 J 9 – Journal de traite de *La Reine des Anges*

180 J 351 to 374 – Rôles d'armement

Archives Municipales de La Rochelle

Ms E 280 – Journal de traite de *La Suzanne-Marguerite*

Ms E 282 – Journal de navigation du navire *Le Roi Dahomet*

Bibliothèque Municipale de La Rochelle

Ms 2290 – Papiers relatifs au navire *La Bonne Société*

Ms 2291 – Journal de traite de *La Bonne Société*

State Archives in Ghent (Belgium)

Fonds d'Hoop 965, 969, 970, 971-974, 975-976, 977, 978, 982 – Papers of Captain Van Alstein

Trans-Atlantic Slave Trade Database

http://www.slavevoyages.org

Secondary sources

Anderson, B.L., and D. Richardson. 1985. Market structure and the profits of the British African trade in the late eighteenth century: a rejoinder rebuttal. *The Journal of Economic History* 45, no. 3: 705–7.

Barlatier, P.-J., and C. Thomas. 2007. Savoir-voir collectif et développement de capacités réseau. *Revue Française de Gestion* 33: 173–90.

Boulanger, A. 1970. Deux négriers nantais de la première moitié du XVIIIe siècle d'après leurs journaux. 1741–1742, 1743–1744. Unpublished master's thesis, history, Université de Nantes.

Boyce, G. 1995. *Information, mediation and institutional development: The rise of large-scale enterprise in British shipping, 1870–1919*. Manchester: Manchester University Press.

Bricker, R., and N. Chandler. 1998. Accounting theory in historical accounting research. *Business and Economic History* 27, no. 2: 486–99.

Chouteau, C. 1994. L'armement de traite nantais: 1782–1788. Unpublished master's thesis, history, Université de Nantes.

Coupleux, A. 1983. *Moi, Pierre Tessier, capitaine du Jason*. Paris: Pierre Belfond.

Cox, A. 2005. What are communities of practice? A comparative review of four seminal works. *Journal of Information Science* 31, no. 6: 527–40.

Daget, S. 1990. *La traite des noirs: Bastilles négrières et velléités abolitionnistes*. Nantes: Éditions Ouest-France Université.

Darity Jr., W. 1985. The numbers game and the profitability of the British trade in slaves. *The Journal of Economic History* 45, no. 3 (September): 693–703.

Daudin, G. 2002a. The quality of slave trade investment in eighteenth century France. Working Paper No. 2002-06, Observatoire Français des Conjonctures Economiques, Fondation Nationale des Sciences Politiques, Paris, France.

Daudin, G. 2002b. Comment calculer les profits de la traite? *Outre-Mers: Revue d'histoire*, 336–337: 43–62.

Daudin, G. 2004. Profitability of slave and long-distance trading in context: The case of eighteenth century France. *The Journal of Economic History* 64, no. 1: 144–71.

Deveau, J.-M. 1990. *La Traite rochelaise*. Paris: Karthala.

Dupouët, O., M. Yildizoglu, and P. Cohendet. 2003. Morphogenèse de communautés de pratique. E-GOST TSER Contract of the European Union HPSE-CT-2002-50026 (Thematic Network), Strasbourg, France.

Forestier, A. 2005. Principal-agent problems in the French slave trade: The case of Rochelais armateurs and their agents, 1763–1792. Working Paper no. 13/05, London School of Economics, Department of Economic History.

Gaignat de l'Aulnais, C.-F. 1771. *Guide du commerce*. Paris: Despilly, Durand and Valade.

Gaston-Martin. 1993. *L'ère des négriers (1714–1774), Nantes au XVIIIe siècle*. Paris: Éditions Karthala.

Greif, A. 1994. Cultural beliefs and the organization of society: A historical and theoretical reflection on collectivist and individualist societies. *The Journal of Political Economy* 102: 912–50.

Harms, R. 2002. *The Diligent. A voyage through the worlds of the slave trade*. New York: Basic Books.

Hervé, B. 1999. Quelques aspects de la traite négrière nantaise. *Cahiers des Anneaux de la mémoire* 1: 45–57.

Inikori, J.E. 1981. Market structure and the profits of the British African trade in the late eighteenth century. *The Journal of Economic History* 41, no. 4: 745–76.

Inikori, J.E. 1983. Market structure and the profits of the British African trade in the late eighteenth century: A rejoinder. *The Journal of Economic History* 43, no. 3: 723–8.

Jolin, N. 1999. Les capitaines négriers – Nantes pendant la période 1717–1738. Unpublished master's thesis, history, Université de Nantes.

Masseaut, J.M. 1992. Les équipages de la traite atlantique au XVIIIe siècle, à travers les rapports de voyage des capitaines nantais des navires négriers répertoriés par Jean Mettas. Unpublished master's thesis, sociology, Université de Nantes.

Masseaut, J.M. 2000. Symbolique des noms de navires négriers. *Cahiers des Anneaux de la mémoire* 2: 293–312.

McWatters, C.S. 2008. Investment returns and *la traite négrière*: Evidence from eighteenth century France. *Accounting, Business and Financial History* 18, no. 2: 161–85.

McWatters, C.S., and Y. Lemarchand. 2006. Accounting and the slave trade: The *Guide du commerce* of Gaignat de l'Aulnais. *The Accounting Historians Journal* 33, no. 2: 1–37.

Mettas, J. 1975. Pour une histoire de la traite des noirs française: Sources et problèmes. *Revue française d'histoire d'outre-mer* 62, no. 226–7: 19–46.

Mettas, J. 1984. *Répertoire des expéditions négrières françaises au XVIIIe siècle*. Paris: Société française d'histoire d'Outre-mer.

Meyer, J. 1999. *L'armement nantais dans la deuxième moitié du XVIIe siècle*, Vol. I and II. Paris: Éditions de l'École des Hautes Études en Sciences Sociales.

Mousnier, J. 1957. *Journal de la traite des noirs*. Paris: Éditions de Paris.

Ordonnance de la Marine. 1681. http://gallica.bnf.fr/ark:/12148/bpt6k95955s (accessed 19 October 2007).

Pétré-Grenouilleau, O. 1998. *Nantes au temps de la traite des Noirs*. Paris: Hachette Littératures.

Pétré-Grenouilleau, O. 2004. *Les traites négrières. Essai d'histoire globale*. Paris: Gallimard.

Plasse, J.-P. 2005. *Journal de bord d'un négrier*. Marseille: Editions le Mot et le reste.

Rinchon, D. 1938. *Le trafic négrier d'après les livres de commerce du capitaine gantois Pierre-Ignace-Liévin Van Alstein*. Brussels: Éditions Atlas.

Rinchon, D. 1956. *Les armements négriers au XVIIIe siècle*. Brussels: Académie royale des Sciences coloniales belge.

Rinchon, D. 1964. *Pierre-Ignace-Liévin Van Alstein capitaine négrier. Gand 1733–Nantes 1793*. Dakar: Institut Français d'Afrique Noire.

Thomas, R.P., and R.N. Bean. 1974. The fishers of men: The profits of the slave trade. *The Journal of Economic History* 34, no. 4: 885–914.

Vignols, L. 1930. La campagne négrière de ≪La Perle≫ (1755–1757) et sa réussite extraordinaire. *Revue historique* 55, no. 163: 51–78.

Yacou, A. 2001. *Journaux de bord et de traite de Joseph Crassous de Médeuil de la Rochelle à la côte de Guinée et aux Antilles (1772–1776)*. Paris: Karthala - CERC.

Environmental turbulence and the functions of budgetary control

Nicolas Berland

Abstract

While budgetary control is a potentially significant tool when the economic environment is unstable and unpredictable, the analysis of its development demonstrates that its use has dramatically expanded over the time since companies have been able to run forecasts. In order to help them develop budgetary control, companies have implemented strategies that have reduced risks and hence improved their ability to make accurate forecasts. Such strategies have taken many forms and varied from one firm to another. They materialized as various types of agreement, including cartels, through strategies to effect market leadership, or via policies of nationalization. In those companies where the environment was stable and risk limitation was not important, budgetary control could be used for various internal purposes. In this respect, the analysis of the management of companies helps us to identify the purposes for which budgetary control is utilized. It is found that budgetary control allows for greater expansion opportunities and provides the means to strengthen the control of management within major companies. Our observations highlight a contradictory aspect of budgetary control: while it is relevant within an unstable environment, it performs best in an environment which is highly managed.

Introduction

In France, budgetary control has been developing from the 1930s onwards (see Berland, 1998a). It is a management technique which consists of comparing activity forecasts, broken down into objectives or standards, with the corresponding achievements, and the variances between the two figures then being interpreted in terms of good or bad performance. The first stage of the budget process therefore comprises the drawing up of forecasts through some form of planning process. Indeed, budgetary control can be equated with short-term planning, where short-term generally means one year, and can be integrated in more ambitious five- to ten-year plans (Mintzberg, 1994).

The efficiency, and thus the utility, of budgetary planning partly depends on the ability of companies to run more or less accurate forecasts. However, it seems that budgetary planning in France developed in a predictable world. The first companies to implement it managed, one way or another, to reduce the uncertainty they faced, either thanks to deliberate strategies or by taking advantage of opportunities resulting from the economic situation. Our first aim is then to demonstrate that budgetary control and the planning which stems from it are management tools adapted to routine conditions.

To that end, we examined, from a historical standpoint, certain companies which had developed budgetary planning in order to better understand the type of environment facing these companies. Our study is based on the examples of Saint-Gobain, Pechiney, Electricité de France (EDF), Alsthom, Total, Le Printemps, the Paris-Lyon-Méditerranée (PLM) railway and Le Matériel Téléphonique. This investigation shows that these companies all developed budgetary control while operating in a stable environment.

The second aim of the paper is to examine the ways in which budgetary planning enables companies to perform when their environment becomes routine. It is found that, first, it provides them with the means to optimize what can be planned, by isolating the production activity from environmental changes and by reducing internal uncertainty. Second, it allows increased decentralization by making it easier to control the work of subordinates.

Environment and planning

Recent research in management has shown that turbulent environments make it difficult to plan ahead. Budgetary control, since it relies on accurate forecasting, can therefore be seen to be an outdated management tool. But, before this view can be accepted, it is necessary to clarify what is meant by the concept of environmental turbulence.

Environment as a contingency factor

The impact of environment on budgetary control and planning is multi-faceted. First, a predictable environment makes it easier to plan, as evidenced by previous historical studies which have shown the importance of stability for the development of certain management practices.

Difficulties in planning

Mintzberg (1994) deals with how difficult it is to plan ahead. His approach is all the more interesting as it links budgetary control to planning in an integrated whole, insisting sometimes that the two concepts are very closely related. He puts forward the idea that strategic planning is all the more efficient when it operates in a stable, certain or untroubled environment. According to him, most of the time companies are unable to plan ahead. Their forecasts for the future are limited to an extrapolation from the present. As long as this relatively simple projection works well, i.e. as long as the future can more or less be inferred from the present, then companies manage to run planning systems properly. He then concludes that planning seems more appropriate as a means of sustaining, in the long term, stable operations aimed at efficiency.

The 1960s thus seem to have been an ideal time for the development of strategic planning since economic trends were more stable, or at least more favourable to the corporate world.

An historical point of view

The development of management tools in the US provides a landmark for our study. Thus, Chandler (1977) showed how railway companies had to work together to build a national network at the end of the nineteenth century. Within the framework of agreements, companies are always seeking maximum activity in order to make their investments profitable. Variations in their levels of activity are resented since they entail uncertainty and can lead to bankruptcy. Companies therefore seek a guaranteed level of activity. For Chandler, corporate co-operation increases the professionalism of executives. Administrative co-ordination becomes stronger than market co-ordination, and enables the company to enjoy a regular flow of activity. The integration and development of administrative co-ordination thus seems to be mainly a form of protection from market turmoil. Executives were able to develop tools to rationalize flows because the economic background became more stable thanks, at first, to agreements and then to integration. Being in a predictable environment made possible cost savings, thanks to new administrative techniques.

Chandler also recalls the type of environment faced by Dupont de Nemours. As horizontal agreements were replaced by vertical integration, company managers tried to ensure a steady activity. To that end, they refused to be in a monopolistic situation, which would have forced them to face big fluctuations in the explosives market. They kept alive less efficient, and therefore harmless, competitors to cushion market fluctuations. Johnson and Kaplan (1987) reach the same conclusion. According to them, this strategy gave Dupont the means to work at full (or almost full) capacity on a regular basis. The environment shaped by the company thus must have been a key factor in the birth of Dupont's management tools (Hopper and Armstrong, 1991).

There are countless other examples. The main concern for companies is to obtain stable flows which are easier to manage and which enable an increase in the use of their investments. The steadiness of the environment seems to be a beneficial factor for the development of greater rationalization.

An outdated management tool

From this standpoint, budgeting looks like an old-fashioned tool, devised for problems which are no longer faced by companies. This topic sometimes resurfaces in the management literature. Thus, in their assessment of the traditional tools of management control, in which they include budgetary control, Bunce *et al.* (1995) point out that the new feature of today's environment is turmoil. In contrast, traditional management tools were devised for relatively stable environments dominated by producers. The traditional budgeting process would thus correspond to an old-fashioned conception of management. According to these authors, the decisions were top-down, built on a closed and rigid hierarchy, and their main purpose was to check on the expenses of employees in the field. The current environment encourages managers, on the contrary, to think in terms of process rather than of function.

In the same way, Hopwood (1974) investigates the conditions of budget use depending on the environment. He points out that budgets, which are easy to formulate in stable and predictable environments, would be very useful in unstable environments in which there is a strong need for control. However, the more useful budgets are, the more difficult they are to formulate and so the less reliable and relevant they may become.

Historians of Anglo-American management and control often underline the important part environment plays in the development of accounting tools. Johnson and Kaplan (1987) considered changes in the environment as one of the six possible explanations for understanding the contemporary criticism of the approach to management based on a consideration of figures of return on investment (ROI) (see Kaplan, 1984). Changes in the competitive environment, in the macro-economic environment and in the world-wide development of new technologies are among the explanations for what is sometimes seen as the lack of accuracy, and hence relevance, of present management tools. This irrelevance might be due to the changes which have occurred since these tools were first developed.

Though he is not an accounting historian, Mévellec (1994) has also noted the importance of environment in the shortcomings of current management tools. According to him:

> problems arise more from the difficulty in re-modelling the environment, i.e. market structures and factors determining value, than from the inability of accounting to adapt. The shift from a supply economy to a demand economy deeply altered the relevance of accounting traditions.
>
> (Mévellec, 1994: 24)

Environment and its characteristics

Environment as a concept has been often studied and, consequently, is defined in a variety of different ways. Before selecting a particular definition it is necessary to review those which have already been offered.

The contribution of the contingency writers

Many famous studies have emphasized the importance of environment (see Rojot and Bergmann, 1989) and, while the concept is easy enough to grasp intuitively, it has been given numerous definitions. According to Burns and Stalker (1966), the environment of a given company is made up of two key variables: scientific technology and the market for a product. Lawrence and Lorsch (1967) carried out one of the most famous studies which took into account the environment. They define environment as the rate of growth of a company's market and the number of products in the market. Uncertainty is measured via three items: the rate of change in the environmental conditions, the degree of certainty of acquired information, and the amount of time required to know the outcome of decisions. In Thompson (1967) environment is considered to comprise four items: clients, suppliers (of material, work or capital), competitors and regulatory groups (government, trades unions, etc.). Duncan (1972) criticizes these approaches and thinks that environment is poorly delineated. He defines it in relation to two dimensions: the number of physical and social factors to be taken into account in decision making and their degree of change.

The work of Weick (1969) represented a major breakthrough in environment studies, drawing a line between the objective environment facing individuals and the subjective environment perceived by actors who react to it.

Environment in this study

A definition in terms of components and attributes, such as those of Thompson (1967) and Lawrence and Lorsch (1967), to mention only the best known, seems to be the most operational. Like these authors, we consider environment under different aspects, but we adapt our definition to the specificity of the chosen data-collection method. The intensity of the competition between the actors in a market, their type of competition (through prices, innovation, etc.), the growth rate in their sector, the trust of individuals in the information they collect are the items examined systematically in order to define the environment of each of the companies studied.

The variability of the environment is seen in a classical way (in the sense of Child (1972), quoted in Kalika (1988)) through many dimensions: frequency/rhythm of change of the different aspects of the environment, scope/importance of the modifications carried out after each change and the variability of change. An unstable environment is one that is undergoing strong, irregular and unpredictable modifications. On the other hand, an economy which exhibits a strong but regular growth rate, say 10 per cent per annum, will not generate an unstable environment since the rate of growth is easily predicted. Our definition of uncertainty is borrowed from Govindarajan (1984): it is the unpredictability of the actions of clients, suppliers, competitors and regulating groups which belong to the external environment of a company.

Lastly, Mintzberg (1982) points out that we are interested in the real environment of the organization, not in the way it is perceived nor, for example, in the description which may be given by the Chief Executive Officer who has ticked a series of boxes in a questionnaire which has been mailed to them. He thus rejects Weick's proposal to take the actors' perception into account. We follow his lead.

French companies, uncertainty and planning

Recent research by Berland (1998b) has shown that, in France, budgetary control generally developed within an environment which facilitated 'objective' planning.[1] Companies were found to establish the use of budgets when they were able to undertake effective forecasting, and several factors were found to have contributed to such a situation.

Mechanisms for limiting uncertainty

Several mechanisms enable firms to reduce the uncertainty they face. Some of them are deliberate (such as the establishment of agreements and the formation of monopolies), others stem from economic opportunities (a high growth rate or administered prices) and some are the outcome of an estimated activity (especially jobbing).

Deliberate strategies

During the twentieth century, French markets have been partly structured by producers' agreements. These have taken very different shapes depending on the time period and product concerned, and their influence has varied widely. Some sectors have been regulated by cartels, which define not only the links between companies but also their links with markets. For others, agreements have been more of a source of trouble, since the agreements have not worked very well and have sometimes led to bad relations between the various actors in the economy. International agreements have sometimes been added to national ones. All told, these corporate agreements have contributed to shaping competition and influencing corporate management styles.

Let us try to draw a quick outline of the main agreement patterns that have existed historically in France. Agreements can, first, define privileged selling areas, as was the case for the coalmines. Agreements can set the volume of exports for each company without capping national output, which is a kind of geographical spread. This was the case for steel. The agreement could be limited to common price setting, as was the case for nitrogen, for instance, and for glass and mirrors. Agreements can definitively set the output volume and split it between the various players, as in the example of aluminium. The limitation of over-capacity can also be a stated objective. The textile industry is a good example of this, rationalization of the industry being effected by the Woollens Committee which purchased companies merely to close down their productive capacity (Braudel and Labrousse, 1980). Actually, without explicitly saying so, agreements in some sectors can share production out between companies by product categories. Thus, in respect of chemicals, French companies seem to have reached a situation which 'avoids' competition since each company has its own market niche. These networks of agreements, by setting up a particular organization of the French economic landscape, had an important bearing on management habits (Dyas and Thanheiser, 1976). They contributed to reinforcing the stability and predictability of economic activity.

Moreover, some companies obtained a monopoly position by dint of government action. In this framework, which can be considered as an extreme case of producers' agreement, forecasts are easier than in a classical competitive system. In a monopoly situation, the producer does not have to worry about the reactions of competitors (in the short term at least). Such a case is not so much a choice in favour of deliberate stability by the company as a choice of the government of the time. Thus, in cases such as PLM and EDF, a monopoly was created by the government because the classical competitive system had failed.

Economic opportunities

The economic situation is a key factor of corporate environment and variations in growth rates give rise to differing conditions faced by economic actors. The research of Carré *et al.* (1972) offers a comprehensive overview of French growth up to the early 1960s and, utilizing the rates of growth of industrial output and of gross domestic product (GDP) as relevant indicators, they delineate five main periods of growth between 1896 and 1963 (see Table 1).

For the purposes of this study, given that budgetary control was largely unheard of before 1929, it is the last three sub-periods delineated by Carré *et al.* which are of significance. The first two of these three periods exhibited a great deal of uncertainty. Negative growth caused by the economic crisis of the 1930s was followed by the upheavals of the Second World War and the immediate post-

Table 1 Growth of the French economy (1896–1963)

	Average annual growth rate	
Periods	*Industrial output*	*GDP*
1896–1913	2.4	1.9
1913–29	2.6	1.7
1929–38	−1.1	−0.4
1938–49	0.8	0.9
1949–63	5.3	5.0

Source: Carré *et al.* (1972: 32).

war boom. Hence, little development of budgetary control was possible because the future was unpredictable. Only from 1949 did this situation change, as economic growth became steady and sustained, though the degree of environmental stability varied as between different sectors of the economy. The fastest and most stable growth rates after the war were experienced by the refining and distribution of oil and gas sector (9.5 per cent), and by the chemical industry, ore and non-ferrous metals (aluminium) sector (7.9 per cent). Given the importance of environmental stability, it is not surprising to find that it was in industries such as oil and chemicals, as well as metal working, transport and trade, that budgetary innovations can be observed (Berland, 1998b). In sectors which were declining, or where future prospects were less predictable, such as in coal production, textile, clothing and leather, few examples of firms adopting budgetary control can be found.

In addition to the opportunities for improved forecasting afforded by stable economic growth, the ability to control prices also aided the development of budgetary control. The price of a product – a core element in the classical competitive system, where it is normally set by the point at which demand matches supply – was sometimes determined either by cartels or by the State. Price variation was therefore limited, thus increasing the predictability of economic conditions. In France, prior to 1936, prices were regulated either by the market or by cartels, where such existed. In the cartels, prices were set jointly by the various players in a market. From 19 August 1936, however, the State began to implement price control through the creation of a national committee on prices (*Comité national de surveillance des prix*). Powerless at first, this committee developed a stronger role in 1937 following the enactment of legislation against unjustified price increases. Far from being temporary, this policy remained in operation until recently. State control covered not only product prices but also wages, that is, the price of labour.

After the Second World War, as a means of combating inflation, an order dated 30 June 1945 defined four price-setting systems: 'total freedom, which was planned to be exceptional; supervised freedom, in which the producer was required only to inform the administration; controlled freedom, in which case the State had only a two-week time limit to invalidate a proposed price; and, finally, a price freeze in which the price level is set in an authoritarian way' (Braudel and Labrousse, 1979: 808). Officially, wages were regulated up to 1950, when management/union negotiations returned, but in practice regulation continued until the late 1950s. The efficiency of these measures, or the real power of the State, can be debated, yet the rigidity of adjustments through prices undoubtedly influenced the outlook of economic actors on their environment. Clearly the environment was not completely unpredictable.

The boom period after the Second World War therefore seems to have been crucial for many companies in establishing their planning processes (both short term and long term). During this period, growth was relatively constant and hence planning was easy, since future trends could be inferred from past data. Government price controls in this period also increased predictability.

Jobbing

Some companies which work to order have their production activity planned ahead. The order book sets the volume of activity and the latter can be planned several weeks or months ahead. The task of production planning is then greatly simplified, even though the planning of future orders still raises a difficulty. As long as the order book is full, it is possible to implement planning procedures and thus use budgetary control.

Let us now examine the situation of the various companies in our sample in the light of these mechanisms.

Companies and uncertainty

The companies which developed budgetary control did so after they were able to formulate reliable forecasts (Berland, 1998b). Depending on the cases studied, one or several of the mechanisms described above operated to reduce corporate uncertainty. The situation of each company examined is summarized in Table 2.

All the companies in our sample seem to have developed budget forecasts from the time when they were able to plan. As soon as forecasting became impossible, for instance because of a change in the economic environment, companies stopped using budgetary control. A lack of archival evidence in the cases of Total and Le Printemps prevents us from being categorical in these two cases, but it appears that both companies operated in an environment of excess demand, enabling the companies to operate at full capacity, thus making forecasting a simple operation.

Such a situation enables us to understand better why, in the companies studied, budgets were more often than not applied to production alone, with no account being taken of the sales department. When excess demand exists, plants can be run at full capacity, and forecasts merely comprise a statement of the capacity of the plant, incorporating any planned increases. Forecasting is simple when the rate of utilization of the plant can be known with accuracy, especially when this is the normal capacity of the production plant. Situations of excess demand and their associated full-capacity utilization enable the rational management of a company to start at the shopfloor level, where knowledge is certain.

Companies thus implemented uncertainty reduction strategies so as to reach a better rationalization of their activity. We shall now examine the way in which budgetary planning is adapted to a stable environment.

The relevance of budgetary control in a stable environment

We focus here on the functions that budgets hold in relation to a stable environment. First, companies try to shut themselves off from the external environment in order to optimize their internal management, be it to organize production better or to reduce the complexity of political bargaining over resource allocation

Table 2 Summary of the environment (economic background) facing major companies and their development of budgetary control

Firm	*Economic background and ability to make forecasts*	*Development of budgetary control*
Saint-Gobain, glass and mirrors (before 1940)	Very turbulent market in the 1930s. Cartels were weak and unstable; their regulation did not allow forecasts to be made.	Attempt at introduction.
Saint-Gobain, glass and mirrors (1940–53)	State-run war economy, followed by troubled markets up to 1953, and cut-throat competition. Departments unable to plan.	Attempts to implement forecasts and budgetary control, but given up in 1946 due to difficulties departments had in planning. Limited to main office expenses between 1946 and 1953.
Saint-Gobain, glass and mirrors (after 1953)	Very high growth rate of demand which saturates production capacities. More and more stable cartels. Easy to plan.	Important development of budgetary control.
Saint-Gobain chemicals (1940–7)	Chemicals are left aside. State-run war economy, then markets are very turbulent until 1949, prices and production conditions vary widely. Departments find it impossible to operate forecasts.	No attempt at budgetary control before the war. Implementation of forecasts and budgetary control during the war, but latter given up in 1946 due to difficulties departments faced in planning.
Saint-Gobain, chemicals (from 1949)	Market growth becomes unstable. Development of cartels and agreements lead to the use of forecasts.	Development of precise financial forecasts as early as 1949. Then very quick transition/shift to budgetary control from 1856.
Pechiney (before 1939)	High market growth, systematic promotion of aluminium, cartels spread production between companies.	Implementation of budgetary control from 1933.
Pechiney (after 1945)	Market conditions become more steady. Return to the pre-war system: strong demand and regulation by cartels.	Re-implementation of budgetary control as early as 1948.
EDF-GDF	Monopolistic situation, with very high demand which supply was unable to meet until 1950.	Implementation of forecasts and budgets as early as 1947.
Total distribution (from 1956)	Development of the national network of Total in France and wide development of distribution abroad. No distributors' agreements; many independent distributors; the main competitors are English or American.	Implementation of budgetary control for the distribution networks from the mid-1950s.
Le Printemps (from early 1930s)	Little information	Development of budgetary control in the 1930s.

Table 2 Continued

Firm	*Economic background and ability to make forecasts*	*Development of budgetary control*
Alsthom (from early 1930s)	Heavy electrical supplies: long-term orders enables planning of expenses. Small equipment: little information; 'stock' production.	Development of budgetary control in the 1930s.
PLM (from mid-1930s)	Goods traffic: forecasts are easier since the traffic is booked in advance. Passenger traffic: rough estimates thanks to the economic situation.	Development of budgetary control in the 1930s.

(to optimize the predictable). The budget is then fully significant within the framework of a predictable environment. The second point enables us to understand delegation, which depends on the environment. Indeed, do people delegate because the environment is stable or because it is turbulent? We shall seek to demonstrate that it is easier, through budgets, to delegate in a stable environment (delegating in safety). Thus budgets enable the management of more complex entities.

Governing in a world which can be planned

A budget is an appropriate tool for a routine environment. We can interpret this routine in different ways but a budget seems to be adapted to each of them, as is clearly shown by the typology of Emery and Trist.

Budget: the tool of a stable environment

Emery and Trist (1963) distinguish four types of environment:

- The random quiet environment, characterized by a low degree of uncertainty and a marked repetition of events. The various situations faced by the firm are grouped at random.
- The grouped quiet environment is also fairly stable but the dangerous or favourable situations are no longer grouped randomly. A good knowledge of the environment is thus necessary to survive.
- The moving reactive environment is similar to the preceding one but it is much more dynamic. It requires the ability to be able to take into account the behaviour of the other actors at play in the market.
- The turbulent environment is complex, dynamic and uncertain. As it is ever changing, it makes forecasting difficult, if not impossible.

Budgets are adapted to the first two types of environment. In the random quiet environment it is possible to know the future states of the environment in a precise way through studies. In this case, setting objectives is simplified. Past achievements are the best possible estimate of the future, given the inertia of the environment, such as was the case at Le Printemps and the PLM. The environment is thus easy enough to predict when it is routine. Forecasting can then be delegated to operational staff who must formulate the forecasts since they are closer to the market. This was no doubt the case at Total.

In the grouped quiet environment, the top managers can take a hold of the setting of the objectives to be reached. They can set up departments of economic studies (EDF), trust inter-company agreements (Pechiney, Saint-Gobain) or plan actions through long-term contracts (Alsthom). As soon as the environment gets more turbulent, as soon as it is important to take into account the behaviour of the other players in a market, such as the State, competitors, partners who breach their word or unreliable suppliers, forecasting becomes difficult, even impossible. Budgetary control must then be given up. Indeed, its continued use might trigger adverse effects, such as the making of incorrect decisions, generate poor motivation, etc.

To avoid uncertainty, firms develop specific strategies or take advantage of opportunities. A decrease in uncertainty can be obtained in many ways. In some of the cases studied, it was achieved through acting on the environment or by opportunism: monopoly,[2] cartels, high growth. But in other cases, such as that of Total, it appears that decentralization enabled the simplification of what is perceived as the environment.[3] This works, providing the environment does not become too turbulent. The operational staff and the management must be able to define objectives likely to be used again later on. The simplest thing, for example, is to take the past year's achievements and increase them by a few percentage points.

Efficiency of a budget

Competition between companies could be expected to enhance the development of increasingly sophisticated performance-enhancing tools, such as budgetary control, so as to limit the chances of failure and increase the profitability of invested capital. Yet this is far from true if we examine the different cases at hand. Companies developed budgetary control in a context of weakened competition and very imperfect markets, such as under state control in the case of post-war France.

This implies that some management innovations help to boost corporate performance when companies are operating in a relatively safe environment. Company managements devise tools which are adapted to the environment they face. When budgets appeared, the environment was quiet, so companies were able to apply flow-optimization methods, both financial and physical. Much later, in the 1970s, the environment turned out to be much more turbulent. The globalization of competition and the degree of economic turmoil made it impossible, or at least extremely difficult, to try to plan or optimize. The ability to react, intuition and the 'management of ambiguities' became the new buzzwords (Peters and Waterman, 1982).

The analysis of McArthur and Scott (1970), which focused on the links between industry and management systems, produced results similar to those found in this study. According to them, inter-company agreements limited competition since they froze the position of each firm involved. The main concern for companies was no longer to gain market share, but to push costs down as much as possible. This way, they maximized their unit margin. The only room to manoeuvre for top management lay in the optimization of a frozen production system. Since the outlets were known, the issue was how to make as much profit as possible from them. Budgetary control provided a solution to this problem. According to McArthur and Scott, this was the reason why French companies laid stress on production rather than on marketing, a tendency which was even more pronounced for those companies operating in a monopoly situation. In their view, this clearly showed that management's concern was with the market structure, in particular the need to eliminate competitive pressures, rather than with the issue of planning internal management. Inter-company agreements provided a safe environment for each company, since they reduced competitive risks and ensured that a company's growth would be close to that of the industry as a whole, but simultaneously allowed them to take risks in other directions, such as the launch of new products: 'Big companies tended to diversify a lot, and . . . inter-corporate agreements gave them the means to rise to numerous challenges' (McArthur and Scott, 1970: 197).

These results partly match our conclusions. Planning was eased by inter-company agreements for instance but, at the same time, McArthur and Scott add that those companies which did not carry out forecasting, though able to survive, nevertheless suffered lower profitability. Their survival was not put into question since they were protected by the French market. However, it should be pointed out that, in spite of the cartel organization of the steel market, because companies shared a single sales organization, budgets did not develop in this sector. Being able to plan in a market is not a sufficient condition for the development of budgetary control if the management does not have the will to do so. However, a routine market makes it easier to run forecasts and thus to plan ahead.

We have seen that budgeting is especially useful to companies operating in a stable economic environment since it enables them to perform better. We now have to shed light on the way in which budgetary control increases the efficiency of these companies.

How to optimize the predictable

To the extent that the future can be planned, thanks to a stable economic environment, companies can optimize their work flow, since there is no need to have to respond to external fluctuations. As a consequence of the separation of internal planning from external fluctuations, the political mechanisms of resource allocation between the company's agents become easier.

Isolating production

Thompson (1967) and Hayes (1977) bring an interesting contribution to the management of organizations depending on their environments. Hayes (1977) carried out a study in which he demonstrates that the performance of the different departments of a company depends on different variables. Thus, in the production department, performance is mainly accounted for by in-house variables and to a lesser degree by the interdependence of the various units within the company. In the research and development (R&D) department, the level of interdependence between research units and the environment provides the best explanation for their performance. Lastly, the environment plays a key role in the results of the commercial department. Hayes points out that costs are not a good performance indicator for commercial or R&D departments. Indeed, their performance is influenced by variables they do not control and which can be found in the environment. Unlike the production departments they do not have the means to act fully on their costs. Conversely, production departments can use financial elements to assess their performance, provided that the environment does not de-stabilize production too much. Hayes takes up a hypothesis put forward by Thompson[4] which suggests that companies develop strategies to isolate their production activity from the environment; to that end they implement 'buffer' strategies to soften shocks from outside. Companies can choose from many strategies. They can develop long-term contracts, sign alliances or anticipate market fluctuations by setting up survey departments. Once the core business of the company has been isolated, optimization processes can be implemented more easily, for instance, to make sure that machine use is optimal.

Among the companies examined in our study, it is found that the head offices of EDF, Saint-Gobain and Pechiney implemented risk-lowering strategies or took advantage of favourable economic conditions, but were not always aware of doing so. In any case, they never had in mind to act on the environment to ease the development of budgetary control and planning, which appeared because these companies had the opportunity to implement them and had an interest in using them. Budgets first developed in production services, then a few years later they were extended to commercial departments.

This supports the findings of Hayes (1977) and Thompson (1967), namely that companies try to isolate themselves from the external environment. It enables them to implement new tools to manage this situation. Once the system is closed, the company can then devote itself fully to optimizing the internal flows which run through it. It is all the easier since technology is routine and creates very few exceptions. If the link between ends and means is well known, then the process will be all the easier to supervise (Thompson, 1967). Technology is no doubt a key factor in the development of budgetary control. We can also point out that EDF, Saint Gobain and Pechiney have continuous-process technologies or long-link technologies in Thompson's terminology. The programming of production entailed by that type of technology enhances the predictability of corporate actions. In a few cases, such as for Total and Le Printemps, it is possible to see them in terms of mediation technology

(Thompson, 1967); however, the lack of information on these companies prevents us from developing this point further.

Curbing internal uncertainty

In addition to being a rationalizing tool in a stable environment, budgets make resource allocation simpler in an unchanging economic situation. Cyert and March (1963) analyse the budget as a tool enabling the curbing of uncertainty inside a company while underlining that budgets are not the only tools companies have at hand to reduce external uncertainty. According to them, inter-company agreements also do this. It can be suggested that budgets create an internal negotiated environment which complements the external negotiated environment. In very complex situations budgetary control can lead to a quasi-settlement of conflicts. The latter can be carried out in different ways. Companies do not try to optimize the situation, which they are probably unable to do anyway. They have to arbitrate between the objectives of the various coalitions making up the organization. Budgeting then provides a framework defining work processes and the way resources are allocated. Year in, year out the political puzzle of contribution allocation is simplified by carrying forward the objectives defined for each coalition. This then accounts for the carrying forward of the budget balances reached beforehand. Minor adjustments are worked out to take the changes in each coalition's situation into account. However, this is possible only if the balance struck over a period of time is not fundamentally undermined by economic changes in the company's environment. If the latter is relatively stable or predictable, contribution sharing can run smoothly and use the prior results which have been frozen in budgets.

The minor adjustments worked out by companies and the under-optimization implied in budgets lead to an excess of resources which are not indispensable to the good working of the organization. That is what is called organizational slack. It enables budgets to work and to adjust to the marginal changes in the environment. In growth periods, operational staff ask for more resources than they need: these resources are then used in difficult times or for re-structuring. When the environment becomes unpredictable, operational staff are ill-equipped to run complex forecasts and can survive only with minor adjustments of the organizational slack. In times of unexpected growth the management can feel left out, whereas, in a recession, operational staff resent a situation unfair to them. Once more budgetary control extends the low uncertainty of markets to the internal side of the company.

Secure delegation

The curbing of external uncertainty enables the budget to be used to simplify internal corporate relations. The reduction of such uncertainty enables the management of more complex activities since the actions of a greater number of subordinates can be analysed. Local reasoning systems to achieve performance can then be synonymous with overall performance. In a stable environment budgetary control allows for the management of complexity entailed by wider decentralization.

Decentralization versus centralization

A stable environment makes it easier to delegate as controls are easier to carry out. The link between decentralization and the type of environment is then brought into question. For Burns and Stalker (1966), a stable environment requires a mechanistic and relatively centralized structure. For Lawrence and Lorsch (1967), a stable environment entails little differentiation and thus little delegation. Similarly, for Thompson (1967), the turmoil of the environment requires decentralization. However, the cases we have studied negate this relation. On the contrary, a stable economic background seems to encourage decentralization, the extent of the latter varying as between different companies. EDF, for example, appears to have been more centralized than Total. This is easy to understand if we consider that a manager is more willing to give up a part of his/her responsibility if he/she has the means easily to control the way delegation is used. Knowing the conditions in which his/her subordinates will work makes control easier. This point shows that authority is not delegated only if there is a great deal of environmental uncertainty. The relation seems to be more complex. The environment's complexity and the size of the company – which also increases complexity – are no doubt variables at play.

This idea is underlined by Desreumaux (1992) in his report on the work of Huber *et al.*: 'the widespread belief that decentralization is needed in cases of unsettled environment and/or of the large company is not as well-grounded as generally thought' (Desreumaux, 1992: 225). Indeed, our study shows that a stable environment paves the way to easy decentralization because, in this environment, we have at hand the tool which is able to integrate the various components of the organization, i.e. the budget.

Controlling diversification

The visibility given to companies by the stability and predictability of markets enables them to extend their operations to new activities as well as increasing their existing ones. In so doing, top executives become snowed under by the huge quantity of information. This extra work does not stem from a complexity heightened by the turmoil of the environment, but from the actual fact that the span of control has widened appreciably. Delegation of authority is then undertaken to relieve executive managers. The reluctance entailed is overcome thanks to the predictability of markets. The latter makes it possible to forecast a certain level of activity and thus generate a result against which the efforts of any subordinate can be assessed. This reduces the information asymmetry between agents and provides the means for delegating more widely. Companies involved in increasingly capitalistic processes are looking for a guaranteed profitability. Indeed, it is vital to link delegation to a stricter performance control. Once quantities and prices are more or less secure, maximum profit has to be achieved from the activity. This is what accounts for the development of budgetary control.

According to Chapman (1997), organizations have a choice between planning when uncertainty is low and flexibility when it is not. When uncertainty grows, the top of the hierarchy is flooded with information because exceptions then become numerous. The different means of co-ordination, such as rules, programmes, procedures and hierarchy, are no longer satisfactory. However, in the case of the companies we have studied, uncertainty in our meaning of the term was low yet head offices were indeed overwhelmed with information. The complexity of the activity, especially the diversity of markets under consideration, seems to be the reason behind this phenomenon. This increased complexity was made possible by low market uncertainty, which widened the relevant field of activities a manager could control. Budgetary control developed to run this complexity. However, resource allocation in the budgetary process is potentially flawed due to organizational slack, since it rests on the hypothesis that a manager knows the needs of subordinates, which is not always the case. If environmental uncertainty is low, information asymmetry between the person made subject to the budget and his/her boss is mastered better and the organizational slack is lower. In these conditions a budget is not an expensive means by which to manage complexity. Uncertainty is an important factor since a low level of it enables better control of decentralization but is not a direct cause of budgeting.

Conclusion

Managers try to reduce uncertainty through specific mechanisms, such as the formation of monopolies, through the negotiation of inter-company agreements, decentralization or via exceptionally favourable circumstances (e.g. high growth) which result in the environment facing top management becoming more predictable. The latter know either the targets operational staff have to reach or those they set out to reach. Monopolies, agreements and high growth provide means to master a market more fully and to initiate optimization programmes.

The problem facing these companies is to make sure that all possible means are implemented to maximize profit. It becomes more difficult to achieve this aim when the market environment becomes too unsettled, hence making forecasting increasingly difficult. This echoes the conclusions of Mintzberg (1994) regarding the problems of strategic planning, which, he pointed out, is relevant only as long as the future is a logical sequel to the past. Thus, if uncertainty is low, and if companies succeeded in reducing it, then the budget is a fully relevant management tool.

In a predictable market, budgetary planning enables the isolation of production from outside turmoil and thus the optimization of production flows. It also extends internal predictability and simplifies resource-allocation mechanisms. By so doing, budgetary control as a tool in a stable environment gives a company the means to delegate more widely and thus to curb the complexity facing the agent.

Notes

1 For a fuller development of the argument presented in this section, see Berland (1998b). Further details, both of the companies and the sources used can be found in Berland (1999).
2 According to economic theory, a monopoly represents a situation in which a firm is protected from the uncertainty caused by the competitive system in a specific sector.
3 This view is somewhat conjectural, the archival evidence not allowing a definitive conclusion.
4 The idea is also used by Merchant (1984).

References

Berland, N. (1998a) 'The availability of information and the accumulation of experience as motors for the diffusion of budgetary control: the French experience from the 1920s to the 1960s', *Accounting, Business and Financial History*, 8(3): 303–29.
Berland, N. (1998b) 'Le contrôle budgétaire, outil d'un environnement routinier: un point de vue historique', *Entreprises et Histoire*, 20(December): 67–82.
Berland, N. (1999) 'L'histoire du contrôle budgétaire en France: les fonctions du contrôle budgétaire, influences de l'idéologie, de l'environnement et du management stratégique', thèse de docteur en sciences de gestion, Université Pais IX – Dauphine.
Braudel, F. and **Labrousse, E.** (1979–1980) *Histoire économique et sociale de la France – Tome IV 1–2/ 1880–1950*, Paris: PUF.
Bunce, P., Fraser, R. and **Woodcock, L.** (1995) 'Advanced budgeting: a journey to advanced management systems', *Management Accounting Research*, 6: 253–65.
Burns, T. and **Stalker, G.M.** (1966) *The Management of Innovation*, London: Tavistock.
Carré, J.J., Dubois, P. and **Malinvaud, E.** (1972) *La croissance française*, Paris: Editions du Seuil.
Chandler, A., Jr (1977) *La Main Visible des Managers: Une Analyse Historique*, Paris: Economica.
Chapman, C.S. (1997) 'Reflections on a contingent view of accounting', *Accounting, Organizations and Society*, 22(2): 189–205.
Cyert, R.M. and **March, J.G.** (1963) *A Behavioral Theory of the Firm*, Englewood Cliffs, NJ: Prentice Hall.
Desreumaux, A. (1992) *Structures d'entreprise*, Paris: Vuibert.
Duncan, R.B. (1972) 'Characteristics of organizational environments and perceived environmental uncertainty', *Administrative Science Quarterly*, September: 313–27.
Dyas, G.P. and **Thanheiser, H.T.** (1976) *The Emerging European Entreprise*, London: Macmillan.
Emery, F.E. and **Trist, E.L.** (1963) 'The causal texture of organizational environment', *Human Relations*, 18(August): 20–6.
Govindarajan, V. (1984) 'Appropriateness of accounting data in performance evaluation: an empirical examination of environmental uncertainty as an intervening variable', *Accounting, Organizations and Society*, 9(2): 125–35.
Hayes, D.C. (1977) 'The contingency theory of managerial accounting', *Accounting Review*, January: 22–39.
Hopper, T. and **Armstrong, P.** (1991) 'Cost accounting, controlling labour and the rise of conglomerates', *Accounting, Organizations and Society*, 16(5/6): 405–38.

Hopwood, A. (1974) *Accounting and Human Behaviour*, Englewood Cliffs, NJ: Prentice Hall.
Johnson, T.H. and **Kaplan, R.S.** (1987) *Relevance Lost*, Boston, MA: Harvard Business School Press.
Kalika, M. (1988) *Structures d'entreprises: réalités, déterminants, performances*, Paris: Economica.
Kaplan, R.S. (1984) 'The evolution of management accounting', *The Accounting Review*, 59(3): 390–418.
Lawrence, P. and **Lorsch, J.** (1967) *Adapter les structures de l'entreprises*, Paris: Les Editions d'Organisation.
McArthur, J.H. and **Scott, B.R.** (1970) *L'industrie française face aux plans: Harvard ausculte la France*, Paris: Editions d'Organisations.
Merchant, K.A. (1984) 'Influences on departmental budgeting: an empirical examination of a contingency model', *Accounting, Organizations and Society*, 9(3/4): 291–307.
Mévellec, P. (1994) 'Coûts à base d'activité: un succès construit sur un malentendu', *Revue Française de Gestion*, January–February.
Mintzberg, H. (1982) *Structure et dynamique des organisations*, Paris: Les Editions d'Organisation.
Mintzberg, H. (1994) *Grandeur et décadence de la planification stratégique*, Paris: Dunod.
Peters, T. and **Waterman, R.H.** (1982) *In Search of Excellence*, London: HarperCollins Business.
Rojot, J. and **Bergmann, A.** (1989) *Comportement et organisation*, Paris: Vuibert.
Thompson, J. (1967) *Organizations in Action*, New York: McGraw-Hill.
Weick, K.E. (1969) *The Social Psychology of Organizing*, Reading, MA: Addison-Wesley.

This chapter originally appeared in *Accounting, Business & Financial History*, 11:1, March 2001, pp. 59-77.

Berliet, the obstructed manager: too clever, too soon?

Henri Zimnovitch

Abstract

Marius Berliet, a pioneer of the car industry, was one of the first to introduce Taylorism in France. He wanted to implement standard costing techniques in his company at the very same time they were conceived in the USA, around the time of the First World War. Given that this technique was to become popular in France only during the 1950s, this article seeks to understand the reasons which prevented it from being applied at Berliet's company forty years earlier. One obvious explanation is the burden of the cost accounting methods which prevailed in France until 1950. The paper also considers the hypothesis of a lack of interest, and skill by those who could have promoted this new technique, especially managers and engineers.

Introduction

Works on cost accounting which were published in France prior to the 1920s paint a picture of a discourse which remained untouched by the innovations which had occurred in the USA since the end of the nineteenth century, particularly standard costing (Zimnovitch, 1997a: 26–72). Was the quest by the French accounting profession to become a recognized institution (achieved in the 1940s) a factor in the resistance to the introduction of new techniques for calculating cost prices? The case of Saint-Gobain enabled us to examine the 'quarantine' period (i.e. 1920–60) that this technique had to undergo before becoming widespread in the 1950s (Zimnovitch, 1997b). Nevertheless, there is the issue of the extent to which this glassmaking group can be used as an exemplar in terms of accounting innovation for the first half of the twentieth century. In this age-old firm, it is possible that tradition carried much weight, the company thus maintaining, to the detriment of ideas which appeared during the second period of industrialization, a system of cost calculation passed down from the First Industrial Revolution. Furthermore, the fact that the company operated in a cartelized sector may have contributed to the lack of interest in the new calculating techniques for costing that appeared at the beginning of the century.

In an attempt to address some of these questions and, in particular, France's reluctance to embrace the new methods for calculating cost prices which were promoted widely for half a century from 1880, this paper examines the case of the car and truck manufacturer, Berliet. This company's birth corresponds almost to that of the Second Industrial Revolution and occurred at a time when there was fierce competition in the car industry so that those involved had to innovate constantly in order to maintain their position in a sector in which conditions suited the application of Taylorism. In this regard, Marius Berliet was indisputably considered a pioneer, even before the First World War broke out. The industrialist from Lyon has provided us with food for thought on the way in which American methods for costing, which emerged in the USA before 1925 and remained largely unchanged until the 1980s, were accepted in France.

The first twenty-five years of the Berliet company, from 1894 to 1919, were a triumph worthy of an American success story. This period of the company's development is examined in the first part of this paper. Here we find evidence that Berliet himself wished to move from a strictly accounting and financial approach to the measurement of cost price to one which made use of pre-determined standards. The second part of the paper deals with the experiences of the business following the First World War. Following the cessation of hostilities, the firm experienced major difficulties, which forced its owner to go before the commercial court in 1921. Although he narrowly avoided bankruptcy, Berliet nevertheless lost control, at least temporarily, of the business that he had founded. Attention will be focused on how cost prices contributed to this crisis and the changes which were made between 1919 and 1923 to the method of cost calculation.

From the success of the car industry to the failure of costing: 1894–1919

In 1893, Marius Berliet embarked upon designing his first vehicle. When the First World War ended, Berliet was one of Europe's largest car manufacturers and his Vénissieux factory, then under construction, would enable him to become one of the world's largest, equalling the giant Ford: the ultimate symbol of success in his eyes and those of his contemporaries.

In 1917, Marius Berliet determined to use standards costs, some thirty years ahead of the time when specialists would recommend their use. In 1919, however, it was obvious that the Berliet company did not even have a sufficiently advanced accounting infrastructure available to enable it to calculate cost prices. Indeed, the industrialist's attitude to cost calculation appears to have been somewhat casual. The situation, however, was not simply one of a success story for the car industry but a failure for costing. In what follows, we shall go beyond this simple contradiction, and, via an analysis of the facts, endeavour, first, to understand the development between 1894 and 1914 (initially by Berliet, and then in his company) of the method of costing according to a product's life cycle. Second, we shall attempt to assess the influence that the Great War exerted on this method of calculation.

A calculation of cost prices in phase with the life cycle: 1895–1914

The take-off phase: 1894–1904

After the short-lived success of the first car, built in 1894, Marius Berliet received his first order for a car and delivered it in March 1897. The customer tested it, drove sixty kilometres without any incident, but gave it up, considering that the engine was too complicated. In 'compensation he paid [Marius] ten thousand Francs, a sum which hardly covered the expenses incurred for this work' (Muron, 1995: 23).[1]

Nevertheless it did not take long for costing to become one of Marius Berliet's concerns; as the notes scribbled in a notebook prove, a vehicle was priced by approximately multiplying its cost by two, a method referred to as the 'somersault' (Saint-Loup, 1962: 52). Although this was a very crude method of calculation, in the start-up period for the product it was not without its effectiveness, and the business was able to expand. In 1904 Berliet, 'a small provincial industrialist' as he liked to call himself, was at the head of a medium-sized company which employed two hundred people. Ten years later the company had more than three thousand salaried employees.

The growth period: 1905–14

1905 marked a turning point for the Lyon-based company. For, in that year, a large locomotive manufacturer in the USA, the American Locomotive Corporation, decided to purchase from Berliet a licence to manufacture one of his models, considered among all the existing models at that time to be the most appropriate for satisfying the USA market. The choice made by this company was decisive, enabling Berliet to expand after a successful launch phase and providing him with the means to purchase premises on the Champs-Elysées. This shop-window for Berliet's products fitted well with the reputation for quality that vehicles sold under the Berliet brand name had developed. The firm exhibited a concern to supervise quality up to the point where the owner took possession and, from 1905, carried out tests in its factory in order to guarantee its product's reliability.

The expansion of the Monplaisir factory to 10,000 square metres followed in 1908. 'But this new manufacturing system required research and strict supervision of cost prices. Marius Berliet [thus] called upon Pierre Thibaudon, secretary at Lazare Wolf and manager of the Cottet bank' (Muron, 1995: 45), whom a friend had recommended to him. It is unquestionable that the need for a system of costing was felt and Muron has claimed that, as of 1910, 'each work station [was] subject to a detailed examination separating overheads, depreciation costs, renewal of equipment and purchases' (1995: 45),[2] using a technique utilized by the Société Française des Câbles Electriques, but it has not proved possible to check the accuracy of this claim.

The precise nature of the costing system at this time is unclear. Saint-Loup has claimed that Berliet had perfected a 'routing order' system, so that 'the sheet follow[ed] the unfinished part, from its departure from the raw materials factory to its outlet at the workshop . . . thus with an extremely precise operating check for the period and with all the means for serious costing' (1962: 105). But doubt can be cast on this if we accept the following quote from a stores memorandum of 1913 which highlights the weaknesses encountered in the follow up of stores purchases and their allocation to the cost price:[3]

> There are raw material difficulties that need to be solved. They would be solved quickly if accounting accepted making colleagues out of those who only deal with statistics on the fringe of true accounting.
>
> We are keen enough on doing efficient work in order to request that the question be examined. We shall see that although not using the same methods, we have the means for controlling and balancing accounts daily which do not give way at all to the most rigorously exact accounting. We furthermore have proof that our method is the quickest and as clear as the former system.

It is therefore questionable how seriously the company took cost calculation on the eve of the First World War, but things were clearly about to change.

Influence of the war on the calculation of cost prices: 1914–18

A market dominated by tenders

When hostilities began, the military authorities already had confidence in Berliet since they had been able to judge the robustness of his trucks in several fields of operation for some ten years. At the height of the hostilities he manufactured up to fifty per day at the Monplaisir factory.

The manufacture of artillery shells and, from 1917, tanks was added to the manufacture of trucks. Without forgetting the know-how of Berliet's salesman to the Ministry of Armament, Mr Perrin, the choice of the Lyonnais industrialist to satisfy the demands that Louis Renault was unable to fulfil alone bears testimony to the fact that the qualities of Berliet were recognized by both his powerful customer (the army) and his main rival (Renault). But on what basis were the supplies, required by the army in ever-increasing numbers, negotiated? As of 1915 the British government equipped itself with departments whose responsibility was the calculation of cost prices for purchased products (Loft, 1988). This was not the case in France. Indeed, it was not until the end of July 1916 that a special tax on war profits tried to correct the excesses which had occurred as a result of the powerful position occupied by suppliers when it came to negotiations over prices in respect of the needs of the army.

If, in France, the different ministers in charge of armaments and re-supply (Albert Thomas and Etienne Clémentel) did not carry as much weight as they would have wished as to the prices of deals made, they did on the other hand exert very firm pressure so that industrialists who benefited from the contracts were organized rationally, in order to reduce their costs and increase their productivity and, in consequence, their productive capacity in the event of a labour shortage.

Rationalization and the concept of costing

This pressure from the authorities added to the worries of Marius Berliet who, at the end of 1915, took on a young assistant manager, Edward Banks. British by nationality, he spoke perfect French and had gained experience in the American company, Westinghouse, which had applied the Taylor system. He, in turn, attempted to introduce this experience into the Monplaisir factory in 1916 with the support of his employer whom he admired deeply, for such was the legend of Berliet even abroad.[4]

Calculating cost prices did not escape the efforts undertaken to rationalize the company's operations. There was a lot to be done, according to Banks who, possibly somewhat mischievously, wrote, at the end of 1916: 'no-one ever took the trouble to analyse our expenses in such a way as to keep a firm hand on the running of the factory' (Muron, 1995: 105).

Marius Berliet began to organize meetings to discuss Taylor's methods, and during one of these meetings both the diagnosis of and the prescription for the problem of calculating cost prices in order to control performance were dealt with exceptionally clearly, especially if we take into account the fact that it took place in 1917. In the minutes of that meeting it is noted that 'most of the methods for costing were invented by accountants in order to benefit mostly financiers',[5] but it is subsequently noted 'that the main accounting function [should be] to constantly inform the shop foreman whether he is manufacturing or not at the lowest possible cost, which did not occur with 99% of ordinary bookkeeping where the information did not arrive or arrived far too late for it to be of any use'. Having exposed the current system's faults and its reasons, the minute took on a prescriptive tone in favour of a more rational allocation. Although no names were mentioned, the prescription clearly drew inspiration from the ideas developed by Gantt in 1915: 'overheads chargeable to a given production should be in the same proportion to the overheads of a factory running at full production as the production in question is to the production made when the factory runs at full output.'

The reasoning was extended to direct overheads, resulting in a perfect expression of the functions that standard costing can fulfil, as stated in the following lines:

> Cost prices themselves have no value. They only have a value when compared and this comparison only acquires its full benefit when the cost price is compared with a standard, the determination of which is the engineer's main

> function. It is the accountant's job to keep the foreman informed of the way he has reconciled the standard and informing him of the differences.

After making this statement, Berliet closed the meeting by inviting 'Mr. Thibaudon & Mr. Segard to introduce a similar organization into the factory.'

What was the outcome of this attempt to develop a new form of costing? A partial answer to this question is contained in a note written in April 1919, i.e. two years later, in which can be found the following passages:

> Does cost accounting, such as it exists today, correspond to today's needs? The answer is clearly not.
>
> . . . Cost accounting is more or less unorganized: everything needs to be changed or created. . . . There is only one outline of what this especially important [costing] department should be. In order to carry out the work the staff is restricted to one single employee and an assistant.
>
> On taking over this department, we found several thousand job order forms in arrears, not completed: some with an hourly rate (but not stating the hourly price); others with time bonuses; most with piece bonuses without any indication of the value of the time spent.
>
> They were sold haphazardly for any old price. Two sets of the same tools gave differences in price, double and even more.
>
> Several surveys have enabled us to check that the value of the tools deducted from the different departments had errors of 200, 300% and more!

These few lines, from a memorandum stretching to fifteen pages, provide just a brief overview of the arguments presented by the author, Mr Gros-Burdet, with regard to the carelessness in calculating cost prices. Faults included an absence of material accountancy, no follow up of labour and equipment, and the rough pricing of overheads. This report preceded a whole series of other descriptions which lead us to believe that there was a significant difference between what had been considered desirable in 1917 and what existed in practice two years later.

Had the use of standards, which was evoked in 1917, been introduced, however, since they were normally used for management purposes, not price setting, the issue of the use costing as an aid to setting prices would still have been neglected. This was a negligence for which Marius Berliet was to pay dearly after presenting his 15 HP model, nicknamed 'The Silver Star', at the Paris Motor Show in October 1919.

From the failure of cars to the implementation of cost accounting: 1919–23

The failure of the 15 HP, however, is not the only factor which explains the difficulties that the Lyonnais manufacturer encountered after the Armistice. First, we shall examine the causes which led Berliet to lose, in 1921, control over the management of the company that he had created; we shall then examine the efforts made simultaneously to introduce a system of cost accounting, which became fully operational only in 1922.[6]

The causes of the compromise settlement of 26 April 1921

The crisis with which Berliet was confronted after the signing of the Armistice can be divided into three elements. Underlying it was a depression which extended beyond both individual and national boundaries. Second, the attempt to implement a strategic investment decision, planned a decade earlier, failed in circumstances which would have been beyond any manufacturer. Finally, there was the calamitous launch of the 15 HP, mentioned above, and for which Marius Berliet carried the responsibility. We shall now examine each of these factors in greater detail.

The post-war depression

In the aftermath of the First World War there occurred an imbalance between productive capacity and demand in the USA, resulting in excess capacity. Although demand existed in Europe, this could not be satisfied due to the shortage of dollars and, unlike in 1947, there was no attempt to provide help through the equivalent of Marshall Aid. The *dollar gap* was partly responsible for the monetary crisis which shook France for the first time at the end of the war in 1919. In the context of an international crisis, France's economic activity was heavily disrupted: the general index of industrial production in 1919 dropped to a level representing only 57 per cent of the level of output experienced in 1913. In some sectors of industry, production fell to an even greater extent and it can be imagined that Berliet, who during the war had converted his car factory to enable the manufacture of shells, found himself in an even worse situation. The truck department was no better off; not only had the Army's orders stopped, but the Army itself became an unfair competitor, which sold surplus equipment and spare parts at reduced prices. To this situation were added American surpluses.

Car manufacturers were able to resist the crisis thanks to the profits made during previous years. Furthermore they had still to pay the tax on war profits, which, in the case of Berliet, continued to be nothing more than a threat and affected the company only at the margin. It was Berliet alone, however, who set himself the task of backward integration, modelling his approach on US producers, in particular Ford: 'when a third of the factory [at Vénisseux] had been completed in 1918 it was already larger than Detroit's Ford factories' (Moutet, 1992: 131).[7]

An untimely investment

In 1919 the mechanical engineering industry's output index was at a level of 58 (1913 = 100), in line with the general index, but that for the metallurgical industry was only 29. Nevertheless, prior to this point in time, the idea of owning one's own steelworks had been a very attractive proposition: no longer would Berliet have to depend on external suppliers of variable quality. Indeed, such an addition would complete the Vénissieux site where Marius Berliet desired rationality, an economy of movement and 'automation' to prevail.

In order to achieve this objective, the Lyonnais industrialist opted for what he thought was the best equipment, namely that manufactured in Pittsburgh. In 1916 he ordered a 'ready-to-go' (or 'turnkey') factory from Carnegie at a price of sixteen million Gold-Francs. Alas, the contract was worded in dollars and, following a fall in the value of the Franc, more than 37 million Francs had to be paid out. This represented a pure loss since, when the steelworks was finally completed in 1920, the price of steel had plummeted. If the technical problems with the plant, which were never really solved, are also taken into account, the whole affair can be considered a fiasco.

Although the outcome ultimately proved unfavourable, the project did not lack industrial intuition at the time, before the First World War, when the initial decision had been taken. If we bear in mind that, in France before 1919, the idea of devaluation was simply unthinkable, and that in 1917 Berliet, which had by then become a joint-stock company, returned a profit of almost seven million Francs (slightly more than in 1916), investing in a steelworks was not a mad idea.

The calamitous launch of the 'Silver Star'

Blinded by the success of Henry Ford's Model-T in the USA, Berliet, whom his biographer Saint-Loup has referred to as inflexible, chose to copy the formula by focusing his manufacture of private cars on a single model, the 15 HP. Drawing inspiration from the experiences of the American Locomotive Corporation (ALC) which, in 1905, rather than designing its own model, and thereby losing precious time, had bought from him the licence for his model, Berliet determined to adopt the same strategy, choosing Dodge as his source. However, whereas ALC had carried out a series of tests prior to making their final choice, it may be questioned whether the master from Vénissieux exercised similar precautions. Otherwise, how can the setbacks subsequently encountered be explained? Due to a lack of works comparable to those found in the USA, which were capable of producing high-quality steel, the vehicles were constantly subject to technical faults, which undoubtedly tarnished Berliet's long-term image, at least in the individual car market.

In October 1919, when the model was presented at the Paris show, the price of 7,500 Francs proved attractive to customers, with 9,000 orders being taken. However, the 'cost price, as far as it can be estimated, using services which seemed to be dormant in the euphoria of victory, came roughly to 11,500 F' (Saint-Loup, 1962: 146). Additional orders were also taken. Admittedly not all of these orders were honoured, some customers preferring to withdraw, having been warned about the vehicle's mediocre performance. Nevertheless such withdrawals were small and it is not absurd to suggest a level of loss attributable to the launch of the Silver Star equivalent to that resulting from the steel-making adventure. Furthermore, as we have seen, the deficit was not only purely financial, the launch also having a detrimental impact upon the image of the company's brand name with car owners.

If not all of the lessons to be learnt from these various setbacks were immediately exploitable, one lesson to be learnt from the calamitous launch of the 15 HP which could be applied very quickly was in respect of the need for the introduction of a costing department. We shall see that even before the compromise settlement was made on 26 April 1921,[8] measures in this direction had been taken. The new management, which was implemented in June 1921, continued down this path, which resulted in the nomination, a year later, of Mr Pradel as manager of the completely new costing department.

Efforts to introduce a costing department

When Marius Berliet reflected on the causes which led him to turn to the commercial court, among the faults committed he recognized 'the mistake in having believed the affirmations of the engineer who had bought the equipment and set up the factory for 100 cars per day to be able to deliver the finished car for 7,500 Francs [and having followed a] sales policy without worrying about cost prices'.[9]

As early as 1920, Berliet began to take action, having become aware that the system for calculating bonuses had covered up problems encountered in the manufacture of the 15 HP,[10] and also recognizing the damage caused by sale prices based on fantasy estimates.[11] Two years were needed for his efforts to pay off, with a costing department that was capable of producing regular information. However, the solution was to calculate accurate cost prices using double-entry bookkeeping methods, the method of *prix de revient comptable*, not the development of standard costing.

Efforts that paid off

In 1922 Mr Pradel became the first manager of the costing department.

> By enforcing decisions taken by the board of directors at its meeting of June 20, the management committee has decided to entrust Mr. Pradel with the task of organizing and supervising cost accounting capable of providing the management committee with cost factors and all the statistical documents on the running of the business. In order to accomplish his job, Mr. Pradel was able to draw on all the factors of general accounting and the special accounting of the different departments.[12]

The task had two facets: on the one hand, 'organizing and supervising cost accounting' and on the other hand supplying 'all the statistical documents on the running of the business'.

We have seen that cost accounting in 1919 was deficient. At a meeting held on 11 September 1920, M. Berliet marked out the line for the future: 'it is not a question of creating minutely detailed bookkeeping to the very last centime, but simply reporting on the factory's general running.' In order to do this, he asked 'for the storekeepers to immediately cost the follow up sheets and send them stamped at the same time as the goods.'[13] With regard to overheads these were 'obtained by multiplying the price of labour by a coefficient given by the central accounting department. At present for manufacturing this is 400% of productive labour and for machinery 200%.'

The follow-up of direct salaries from production bonuses and their integration into costing had already begun some fifteen years earlier. They were subject to careful consideration between 1921 and 1923, in order to study the improvements which could be made and to ensure their due recording by the cost accounting system.[14] This study was carried out in the light of different systems (Taylor, Gantt, and so on) which were known during this period. Likewise, the introduction of cost accounting took into consideration the ideas of many writers on costing (Berran and Fuzet, Bertrand Thompson, Fejès, etc.) whom we believe to have influenced those who were in charge of implementing cost accounting at Berliet at the end of the 1920s.

Unfortunately no special journals or ledgers which would enable us to see with certainty when the system was used have survived. Nevertheless it can be suggested, with a large degree of probability, that it was not perfected before Mr Pradel took up his post in June 1922, as the comments contained in a memorandum from April 1922 witness:

> In order to enable us to encourage our costing organisation further, two things are needed:
>
> No order should be enforced by the Lyon workshop without having been recorded beforehand by the Costing Department.
>
> No material should be delivered to a workshop without the knowledge of the Costing Department which must be able to see from the order which account is to be debited.
>
> This may seem obvious. However we have had until now to make do with information collected both correctly and incorrectly from workshops in order to know what they have been doing.[15]

The information that Mr Pradel's department was in a position to supply, from 1922, enables us to be sure that there was finally cost accounting which complied with the rules of double-entry bookkeeping.

This information was notably used for drafting estimates, such as that reproduced in Table 1. It can be seen that the cost of materials came from accounting data, labour costs were estimated, while overheads were estimated as different percentages on labour and materials, that on labour accounting for the major share. In addition 35 per cent was added to cover commercial expenses.

The system implemented in 1922 had the merit of working although, in order to achieve this, many difficulties had to be overcome.

Missed opportunities

Despite incomplete information, it has been possible to make some comments regarding the nature of the costing system used by Berliet before the First World War, though it is difficult to be certain exactly what was being done. For the post-First World War period, however, we have a greater knowledge of events,

Table 1 Example of an estimate in 1923: provisional costing of the new car known as 6 H

Name	*Average price for first 500*	*Average price, 500–1,500*
Materials (net)	4,722	4,722
Overheads on materials (10% on finished parts purchased)	262	262
Overheads on materials (20% on parts to be machined)	421	421
Labour	1,140	865
Overheads on labour (200%)	2,280	1,730
Special machinery	400	280
TOTAL	9,225	8,280
Sales overheads 35%	3,229	2,898
Chassis cost price (sales costs included)	**12,454**	**11,178**

Source: FAMB Berliet OST documents cost accounting, costing.

and it seems clear that, despite Marius Berliet's wish, standard costing was not introduced.

Although Berliet, in April 1917, had instructed that an accounting system based on standard costing be implemented, all the evidence points to the conclusion that nothing was actually done at that time. Admittedly, theoretical prices were set and led to unsystematic reconciliations with the work carried out, but this work was carried on outside the accounting system. We can see this from the following passage contained in a memorandum written in 1922:[16]

> The use of a uniform but fictitious price list would certainly simplify the bookkeeping of the materials account. With such a list we would have a very exact assessment of the situation and the output of each department given separately, but it would be impossible to list these results in the general accounting, since the figures given for purchases and sales for each department would not comply with the company's true purchases and sales. It is therefore necessary to cost . . . the prices of materials as exactly as possible.

There are many indicators which suggest, to the regret of the managers, that a system of accounting based on standards did not operate at Berliet before 1960. Nevertheless, this period is instructive with regard to the dissuasive effect that calculating real cost prices could exert on all other approaches, in particular that aiming to introduce pre-determined and fictitious standards.

We have seen the solution that prevailed at Berliet in the 1920s for charging overheads in the calculation of cost prices for vehicles, namely by applying a coefficient on labour (see Table 1 above). It is clear, however, that the Berliet departments had knowledge of the fact that a less basic approach was being used elsewhere Thus, a Renault company memorandum, studied by Berliet's departments, explained that: 'With modern machines overheads can reach up to eight times the value of labour costs. It is therefore dangerous to use labour costs as a basis . . . there are grounds for determining for each workshop or for each large group of similar machines all the following hourly expense'.[17] The method laid out, that of imputation rationelle, was based on a method of allocating overheads to each cost centre on a rational basis, somewhat akin to the scientific machine rate advocated by Alexander Hamilton Church. It is not known why Berliet neglected this path.

It seems clear that there was an absence of accounting based on standards and, instead, a system of charging overheads mainly on the basis of labour costs seems certain. It is more difficult to be certain about the existence of an accounting system based on 'theoretical prices', which, from the 1920s, enabled a department's profitability to be highlighted. A memorandum dated 6 December 1920[18] explains how the company should be divided into separate departments (ten for manufacturing and two for machinery) each subject to a separate account which was to be debited with labour costs, but not materials, and credited with production at a fixed rate.

In a similar manner, another memorandum from 1922 indicates that it had been decided that the forge and foundry would be considered as outside suppliers billing at a pre-established price, similar to competitors':[19]

> and not their real cost price. This method enables [both]:
>
> The losses or profits of the Forges and Foundries to be determined;
>
> The cost prices of company products to be calculated much more precisely by knowing in which department either the losses or profits are located.

Further, four months later, the board of directors decided that the workshops would be:[20]

> organized autonomously, and [that] production would be used in the most profitable way possible in the company's interest, and even, if necessary, working for third parties. But it is obvious that all the accounting and other measures will be taken in order for the real performance of the different units to be clearly established.

This stance taken by the board was reaffirmed on 20 June 1922 during the implementation of a costing department. We can thus read in the minutes: 'all the accounting and other measures will be taken according to the management committee's decisions for the real performance of the different units to be clearly established.' Such insistence makes this implementation suspect. If the same decision was taken again, was it because previous decisions had had no effect?

A phrase recorded in the minutes of the Board meeting on 20 June 1922 illustrates the problem that different methods of cost calculation could have in respect of power relationships within the organization: 'Each of the acting managing directors will set his own cost price and will submit it to the management committee for approval.' It would seem that an explanation for the different views as to methods of cost calculation lies in the struggle for power within the company which took place between Marius Berliet and the other members of the management which he had to endure until 1929, at which time he regained full control of the company. Saint-Loup sheds new light by describing a scene which supposedly took place in 1922 in the following terms:

> Pariset [administrator] has come to see Monnier [forge department manager] and said to him:
>
> Mr Berliet is no longer of any importance, now it's Gois [another administrator] who's in charge,
>
> Gois asked the forge master for accounts which he did not have.
>
> Create them. You'll set cost prices as though you were not part of the factory. Then, we will place orders with you 10% below the lowest price that we could obtain outside. Go on!
>
> Whether he liked it or not, Monnier created his accounts. Then Marius Berliet, whom the new master confined to two workshops, escaped and, re-appearing in the forges, he immediately noticed these large strange ledgers.
>
> What's that, Monnier?
>
> Bookkeeping for Mr Gois.
>
> The boss gave out a shriek of anger and with large pencil strokes crossing out the pages already covered in figures. Gois came back the next day and demanded that the accounting work begin again. Marius, once again, destroyed it. Caught between the devil and the deep blue sea which he no longer controlled, the forge master resigned.
>
> (Saint-Loup, 1962: 169)

Leaving aside the psychological aspects, if we restrict ourselves to the facts, we can see that the decision to introduce departmental accounting in order to monitor and assess the performance of departments was again taken in 1950, then in 1960. In fact, everything leads us to thinks that it was only from 1960 that such a procedure worked.

Conclusion

'Methods generally accepted for calculating cost prices are currently in a state of development as primitive as manufacturing methods were before Frederick W. Taylor launched the idea of scientific administration' (Harrison, 1918: 274). This phrase was highlighted in the most surprising document which is kept at the Marius Berliet Foundation at 39 avenue Esquirol, i.e. where the industrialist lived from 1913 until he was imprisoned at Montluc fort, when Lyon was liberated in 1944. This voluminous typescript, which was part of Marius Berliet's personal library, is nothing less than a translation into French of all the articles on standard costing that Harrison had published between 1918 and 1919 in a series of issues of the journal *Industrial Management*.

This quality translation, the only one which is known to exist, was for the exclusive use of the Lyonnais manufacturer and the many annotations show that he read it attentively. He thus highlighted the idea according to which 'if cost prices are not presented comparatively to any standard, they are not of much use in so far as a means of increasing a factory's output' (Harrison, 1918: 280). Although aware of this, Berliet failed to implement standard costing, thwarted by a conservatism in accounting which meant that the method of calculating cost prices conformed to the techniques of cost accounting born during the preceding century. But should we see this failure as a case of Marius Berliet being too clever too soon? Was he an obstructed manager who was unable to apply what he considered to be relevant calculation methods due to the actions of an accounting profession which, in order to advance its sectional claims, focused on accounting methods of cost calculation and eschewed ideas of standard costing?

While there may be much truth in this argument, it should nevertheless be remembered that Berliet himself exhibited a number of failings when it came to the issue of costing. First, he neglected its accounting side, which became apparent during the post-war era when he failed to apply, during the launch of the 15 HP 'Silver Star', the first rule of cost pricing: 'If we want to be able to conduct business with maximum security and profits, it is essential, before beginning work, to make an intelligent estimate of what the cost price will be' (Harrison, 1918: 279). Berliet himself had read this passage and underlined it, but nevertheless failed to follow its advice.

The failure, in France before 1925, to find examples of methods for calculating cost prices outside those proposed by accountants poses an important question as to the role and involvement of engineers in cost calculation. This is an issue which would form an interesting subject for further research.

Acknowledgement

I am grateful to Russell Craig for his comments on an earlier version of this paper.

Notes

1 The point is confirmed by Laferrère (1960), though it is possible that Muron is simply quoting from that source.

2 Laferrère writes: 'in order to enable purchasers to benefit from the savings afforded by the new production system, an attentive supervision of cost prices needed to be organized at Montplaisir. Mr. Paul Thibaudon's action [taken in 1908] was decisive: he applied the method used by Lazare Wolf in the administration of the Société Française des Câbles Electriques, i.e. a very advanced break-down of cost prices, the main elements of which were discussed at Board meetings. Thus, this obstacle, which so many craftsmen who become industrialists encounter, was, at least provisionally, overcome: the exact assessment of overheads, depreciation costs and equipment renewal costs, and their incorporation in cost prices' (1960: 370).

3 The Marius Berliet Fund Association (FAMB). File: organization of cost prices, Mr Gros-Burdet, 1913–25. Note dated 17 May 1913, J. Serrell.

4 Documents of E. Banks, sent to the author on 6 December 1995 by Mr Paul Berliet.

5 FAMB Documents Berliet OST Internal factory organization. eighteenth meeting, 17 April 1917. The following quotations are also taken from the minutes of this meeting.

When reading these minutes one is struck by the almost religious fervour with which Taylor's texts were studied and commented on by Berliet and his partners.

6 Much of the information relating to the investment in the steel works and on the launch of the 15 HP is taken from Declas (1977).

7 On the question of the consolidation of manufacturing, see Fridenson (1972: 131–40).

8 According to the Law of 2 July 1919, compromise settlements were authorized by which a large number of companies which were strangled by the post-war situation could reach an agreement with creditors and thus avoid bankruptcy. The benefits of this procedure had to be approved by the commercial court whose decision was accompanied by recommendations as to the organization of a company's management. In the case of the Berliet company, it was forced to adopt a management structure in which its founder no longer had full control, but rather took the position of managing director.

9 Typescript by Marius Berliet dated 1922, copy supplied by his son, Paul.

10 Saint-Loup quotes the following conversation: 'explain to me, asked Berliet, why we don't produce more than fifteen units while there are very satisfactory productivity bonus payments. . . . the workshops put a brake on the rate once every two months, he was told, constituting stocks of parts during the slack month in order to produce at maximum rate and receive the premium the following month' (1962: 147). We should remember that in 1919 the company, which had three thousand employees before the war, now employed three times as many.

11 According to Saint-Loup (1962: 153), Mr Damour, administrator of Gaz de Lyon, who had joined Berliet's board of directors in 1906, declared at a board meeting: 'your sales departments fix sale prices without taking into account cost prices of which they are not even aware' (Saint-Loup, 1962: 153). This reprimand supposedly took place in 1920, but there is no record in the company's minutes, thereby throwing doubt on the validity of Saint-Loup's statement.

12 FAMB Management committee documents, 27 June 1922. After the compromise settlement, a management committee was implemented. The Foundation kept the minutes of these meetings, together with those of the board of directors; it is therefore possible to compare the decisions of the two authorities, as in the case of the implementation of the costing department which was determined on 20 June 1922.

13 FAMB File: costing organization Mr Gros-Burdet, 1913–25.

14 FAMB Berliet OST-Staff/Pay 1921/3.

15 FAMB Berliet OST-Organization routing order.

16 FAMB File: organization of costing Mr Gros-Burdet, 1913–25. Note dated 24 January 1922.

17 FAMB File: organization of costing Mr Gros-Burdet, 1913–25. The memorandum is dated 28 January 1921 and marked, in the handwriting of R. Causse, as being for the attention of Mr Gros-Burdet. To find a Renault memorandum in the Berliet records is not a matter of particular surprise, given the extent to which the different manufacturers monitored each other's actions. It should, however, be noted that Berliet had to pay a fine of 10,000 Francs in 1926 following a claim filed by André Citroën for activities amounting to industrial espionage dating back to 1922. In the case of the Renault memorandum on overheads, however, it is possible that this was made public by Renault; General Delavallée, for example, assessed it in his manual specifying that 'this memorandum was the point of departure for the post-war revision of cost accounting in [artillery manufacturing companies]' (1898: 51) – we are grateful to Yannick Lemarchand for drawing our attention to this fact.

18 FAMB File: organization of cost prices Mr Gros-Burdet, 1913–25. Memorandum dated 6 December 1920.

19 FAMB File: organization of cost prices Mr Gros-Burdet, 1913–25. Memorandum dated 24 January 1922.

20 FAMB Minutes of the Board of Directors, 28 April 1922.

References

Primary sources

Archives Berliet, Amis de la Fondation Automobile Marius Berliet (FAMB), 39 avenue Esquirol, Lyon 69003.

Secondary sources

Declas, G. (1977) 'Recherches sur les usines Berliet 1914–1949', unpublished master's dissertation, University of Paris I.

Delavallée, General (1898) *Administration et comptabilité*, Ecole supérieure technique d'artillerie.

Fridenson, P. (1972) *Histoire des usines Renault: Naissance de la grande entreprise 1898–1939*, Paris: Seuil.

Harrison, G.C. (1918–19) 'Cost accounting to aid productions', *Industrial Management*, October–July.

Laferrère, M. (1960) *Lyon ville industrielle*, Paris: PUF.

Loft, A. (1988) *Understanding Accounting in its Social and Historical Context*, New York: Garland.

Moutet, A. (1992) 'La rationalisation industrielle dans l'économie française au XXème siècle: étude sur les rapports entre changements d'organisation technique et problèmes sociaux (1900–1939)', thèse d'Etat. Université Paris X.

Muron, L. (1995) *Marius Berliet*, Lyon: LUGD.

Saint-Loup (pseudonym) (1962) *Marius Berliet l'inflexible*, Paris: Les Presses de la Cité.

Zimnovitch, H. (1997a) 'Les calculs du prix de revient dans la seconde industrialisation en France', thèse en Sciences de Gestion. Université de Poitiers.

Zimnovitch, H. (1997b) 'The development of standard costing at Saint-Gobain, 1920–1960: forty years of quarantine?', *Accounting, Business and Financial History*, 7(3): 345–65.

This chapter originally appeared in *Accounting, Business & Financial History*, 11:1, March 2001, pp. 43-58.

Index

Page numbers in *Italics* represent tables.
Page numbers in **Bold** represent figures.